Teaching in America

This book has been awarded Harvard University Press's annual prize for an outstanding publication about education and society, established in 1995 by the Virginia and Warren Stone Fund.

Nel Noddings - Prof. of
Philosophy & educ.
@ Stanford.

TEACHING IN AMERICA

The Slow Revolution

Gerald Grant and Christine E. Murray

Harvard University Press
Cambridge, Massachusetts
London, England

Third printing, 2002

First Harvard University Press paperback edition, 2002

Library of Congress Cataloging-in-Publication Data

Grant, Gerald.
    Teaching in America : the slow revolution / Gerald Grant and
Christine E. Murray.
        p. cm.
    Includes bibliographical references and index.
    ISBN 0-674-86961-3 (cloth)
    ISBN 0-674-00798-0 (pbk.)
    1. Teachers—United States.   2. Teachers—United States—Case
studies.   3. Teaching—United States.   4. Professions—United
States.   I. Murray, Christine E.   II. Title.
LB1775.2.G73   1999
371.1'00973—dc21   98-38232

To Those Who Taught Us
Especially Judith Dunn Grant, David Riesman,
and James Sipe Fleming

Contents

1

Two Professions?

The central thesis of this book grew out of a paradox. In the course of our research we have watched hundreds of teachers at work in grade schools and graduate schools. One of us is married to a fourth-grade teacher, the other to a professor of political science. During our research and at the dinner table, conversation often turned to the problems and challenges of teaching. We talked as equals, teachers and professors, about common problems, as if we were members of the same profession. The fundamental acts of teaching and the central questions all teachers confront are essentially the same. But professors and precollege teachers are not seen as members of the same profession. Why should that be?

The work is essentially the same, but the conditions, status, and pay of one profession are vastly different from those of the other. The work is institutionalized in different ways. Yes, professors have more training, and do more research. The fact that professors are mostly men and schoolteachers are mostly women is also a large part of the answer. Professors took charge of their teaching and research in an early-twentieth-century revolution that stripped college presidents of their powers to determine the curriculum and fire the faculty at will. The American Association of University Professors established the rights of tenure and academic freedom that gave the faculty essential control of the educational process at the college level. Schoolteachers remained locked in a hierarchical system in which they were treated as hirelings whose work was mandated by a male administrative elite. As schools were urbanized and centralized in the course of the twentieth century, teachers' work lives grew more regulated. They followed detailed curriculum outlines and adjusted the teaching day to change subject matter when administrators rang the bells. Although teachers often complied only symbolically once the classroom door was closed since the supervisers couldn't watch everybody all the time, they were treated as functionaries, not as professionals capable of independent judgment.[1]

We use the term "slow revolution" to describe the gradual accretion of efforts by schoolteachers to take charge of their practice. At the end of the book we discuss whether this second academic revolution will culminate early in the twenty-first century, granting teachers the kind of autonomy that professors achieved early in this century. And if so, will this be a good thing for students and American society? We raise the possibility not only that the second revolution may falter but that there could be a reversal of the first academic revolution as professors in a "mature industry" are brought under new management and cost-cuttting controls. But we also see that the elements are at hand for a major transformation of the teaching profession.

In order to understand that transformation we should be clear about what constitutes the essential acts of teaching. Too many of the educational reform efforts of the late twentieth century have focused on organizational and management reforms. Teachers and the actual stuff of teaching have frequently been ignored. Certainly the factory model of schooling—processing students as if they were widgets on an assembly line—needs to change, but "restructuring" and "break-the-mold" organizational reforms have largely failed precisely because teachers themselves have too often played only a small role in their design. The ultimate test of any educational reform, including the reform of the teaching profession itself, must be whether it enhances or obstructs the essential acts of teaching, and thereby fires the imagination, deepens the competence, and touches the hearts and minds of children.

Note that we do not say the ultimate test should be whether reform raises students' achievement scores. We have plenty of evidence that scores can be raised by the worst sort of teaching for tests—often poorly constructed tests that do not adequately assess reasoning skills. However, evaluation is one of the essential acts of teaching, and although we applaud efforts to develop new forms of testing that assess a wider range of students' competence, we try in Chapter 2 to assess America's teachers by the results of the tests we have. Close examination of national and international assessments of student achievement shows that America's teachers are doing better than the popular media would have us believe, but are far from achieving what we should hope and expect. While our examination of the data reveals significant progress, it also points up the continuing need for major reforms of teaching, reforms that are more successful in engaging students and turning them into active learners and problem-solvers.

Much of the talk of educational reform is hortatory and facile. It dispenses prescriptions to presumably ailing teachers who have hardly been observed. Before we talk of reform we should examine what it is that teachers really do. In Chapters 3 and 4 we analyze the essential acts of teaching and the fundamental questions that all teachers must answer. We enter classrooms in cities and suburbs, kindergartens and colleges, to show teachers struggling to master their craft. They are engaged in the acts of motivating, questioning, and assessing students' moral and intellectual growth. They are reflecting on their own growth as well, and confronting fundamental questions about how to strike a balance between expertise and nurturance, and whether to teach to transmit a culture or to reform it.

We must understand both the form and substance of these things before we attempt re-forms. Most educational reforms have been mandated from the top and most of them haven't worked. We believe a second academic revolution is necessary because good teaching cannot be mandated or prescribed in a manual. Teachers need the proper authority and autonomy to nurture and assess good teaching. Students will not learn to be creative analysts and problem-solvers if they are taught by teachers who are not trusted to analyze and work out solutions to the problems of their own practice. To win support for more autonomy, however, many teachers need better preparation in professional schools of education and more thoughtful mentoring in their first years on the job. Internships are just as important for teachers as for medical doctors. Neither the craft of healing nor that of teaching can be learned at the highest levels without such forms of induction into the profession. Teachers also need more substantial, intellectually challenging opportunities for professional growth throughout their careers, like those architects and professors now enjoy, such as sabbaticals and opportunities for research and learning new techniques.

We examine a large range of experiments—not all of them successful —to establish new forms of socialization in the profession. In a suburban grade school we call Crestview, excellent results were achieved by a committee of teachers and parents who were empowered to design the school. Together they created a lively curriculum that made liberal use of computer technology; developed schoolwide commitments to new forms of instruction; hired the principal and teachers; and developed extensive partnerships with the community. At the end of seven years, teachers continue to collaborate across grade levels to foster student learning; joint teacher-parent governance of the school is unusually effective, and student achievement is above average.

Outcomes were more mixed in Rochester, New York, which was one of the first urban school systems to provide internships for all new teachers and to pay experienced teachers up to $70,000 for qualifying for new roles as lead teachers. We have looked closely at its experiment since its inception in 1987. The Rochester story dramatically illustrates the struggle of teachers who are trying to take charge of their practice. The teacher-reformers were sued by the administrators' union, which charged that the teachers were usurping administrators' powers, and attacked by the rearguard within their own union who did not believe teachers should take responsibility for rooting out incompetence. Adam Urbanski, the president of the Rochester Teachers Association, engineered the breakthrough contract in 1987 with Peter McWalters, then the superintendent of Rochester schools. The two were pictured arm-in-arm in all the major newspapers. By 1997, three superintendents later, members of a task force appointed by the mayor of Rochester and the County Executive had issued a report saying they would accept "no more excuses" for the failure of the schools, and the new superintendent threatened to have Urbanski arrested for pushing a security guard at a School Board meeting. Yes, the graph of student achievement scores was flat. But school budgets had been cut while more of the city's students fell below the poverty line. The teachers were scapegoated as they have been elsewhere, but our research shows that the Rochester mentoring program is a major improvement, and that teachers took significant steps to address the issues of teachers' quality and incompetence.

As we argue in Chapter 9, the second revolution will not be successful unless teachers convince the public that they have the will and capacity to make judgments about who is fit to teach and who should be dismissed for incompetence. Teachers must show that they have standards by which their peers can be judged as better or worse, and by which some teachers can be promoted to higher-level responsibilities for mentoring, curriculum development, and school-site management. Success will also depend on whether teachers develop an equivalent to the bar exam for lawyers—an examination of fitness to practice that will be seen as fair by teachers and as rigorous by the public.

Any understanding of how such examinations came about draws on the theory of the professions. This is not a book aimed primarily at theorists, but it is grounded in sociological explanations of the rise of all professions. In America, the dominant theoretical position, established by Talcott Parsons and Robert Merton, became known as the structural-functionalist school.[2] The functionalists took a benign view of the way stratification occurs and structures are shaped to carry out the necessary functions of any society. For them the rise of the professions was a necessary way of structuring the asymmetry of expertise between the professional and the client, and of using meritocratic means to select those most fitted to carry out the tasks of the profession. Those who applied the functionalist paradigm in a simple-minded way got into rating games, missing the complex logic of the functionalist analysis and its arguments about the way different institutions, including the professions, get differentiated and structured in modern society. That view was often popularized in checklists to be used to decide which occupations qualified as professions and which fell short. But the core of functionalist theory is about how trust gets established so that society has faith that different functions will be consistently carried out in various institutions. Society is naturally going to be more demanding about the performance of some functions (saving lives or deciding how property claims will be litigated, for example) than others (repairing shoes). A rational society will therefore stratify and select more rigorously for some pursuits than for others.

The functionalist explanation has been attacked by a variety of debunkers, including neo-Marxist and other conflict theorists who discount claims to specialized knowledge as mystifications or worse. Writing of medical education, for example, Randall Collins argues: "We can dismiss, I think, the proposal that this elite education is particularly laden with technical expertise . . . We know this because the actual technical skills are learned in medical practice; the content of medical schooling is largely background material in the sciences that have little bearing on actual performance. Scores in medical school bear no relation to professional success."[3]

In other words, inflated knowledge claims served to bamboozle the public, and to justify an elite that established a profitable monopoly over practice. Paul Starr presents a more complex view in *The Transformation of American Medicine*, describing the way that doctors shrewdly capitalized on scientific developments at the same time as they improved the quality of medical school training and exercised political muscle to stake new professional claims.[4]

Feminist critiques have raised our consciousness about how our conceptions of the professions are reflections of social structure in a patriarchy. Patriarchies have established professions as work that is hierarchically organized, controlled by men, based on a life and work style possible only for the "family-free man" who can give nearly total attention to his career. The feminist critique, as presented by Sari Knopp Biklen and others, asserts that women's work like teaching and nursing is devalued economically and structurally, although it may be overvalued in symbolic terms as motherly, caring, loving work that pays holistic attention to people, in contrast to the male-dominated occupational work that most values the abstract and distances the experts from the clients they supposedly serve.[5]

Finally, the ecological or jurisdictional argument has been advanced by Andrew Abbott in a brilliant book, *The System of the Professions*. Abbott's focus is on the competition among different occupational groups to establish the right to perform certain tasks or to engage in certain practices. His analysis is particularly ingenious in showing the way in which an occupation or professional group lays claim to a jurisdiction. He sees occupations/professions in continual competition for territory or jurisdictions, explains how they compete to fill a "vacancy," and how the structures of professions may advantage or disadvantage them in that competition. He shows that professions solve the problems of the division of labor in different ways—some by dividing the client groups, some by sharing control, some through advising, others through internal differentiation, as in the engineering profession. His book has the virtue of showing the shifting fate of professions in the context of complex factors that shape those fates in ways that cannot easily be predicted. In the ecological view, "Professions are diverse lots of winners and losers: Some never found a niche in the system at all." Hydrologists, Abbott explains, lost out to foresters; and solicitors in England lost out to the barristers, who appear in court and relegate to solicitors the mundane tasks of drawing up wills and property-management transfers. Abbott's fundamental question is: How do societies structure expertise? And the answer he gives is that they set up rules for competition over jurisdictions.[6]

Each of these theories speaks to the role that knowledge claims play in justifying a profession. And all of them are at least partly true. What the public believes about the knowledge base of a profession does affect the power, status, and economic rewards of its practitioners. The high-status professions actually make very different claims about the connections between knowledge and practice. Both medicine and engineering claim a highly codified, specific knowledge base, Randall Collins to the contrary. Architecture and law, however, base their claims on teaching a way to think about the problems of practice that are not grounded in particular subject matters. Each of these professions, as Mary Kennedy points out in an intriguing essay, has a minority viewpoint that argues the other side. There have been experiments, such as those at Western Reserve University Medical School, that have moved medical education toward more healing with less emphasis on the hard sciences, but these have not lasted long.[7]

Each of these professions has succeeded in cloaking its work in perceptions of great expertise, presumably won at the cost of long and hard study. Each of them has elaborated a saga of endless effort and frighteningly difficult examinations preparing practitioners to work through the night in emergency surgery or to turn over every book in the law library to find the precedent that will win the day in court.

The public has been less willing to believe any comparable saga about teachers. There are no compelling images of students in education burning the midnight oil to master difficult theories or to figure out a prescription for a vexing educational problem. Thus we see the recent development by the National Board for Professional Teacher Standards of a rigorous assessment of teachers' expertise as critical to the evolution of the teaching profession. It is no accident that, like doctors, teachers who pass this advanced test will be board certified.

Even though we agree with the neo-Marxists that the claims to knowledge by doctors and lawyers are inflated, we disagree with their contention that there are only weak relationships of the formal course of study to levels of excellent practice, and reject the assertion by some on the left that professions are little more than monopolies of greed and power. Despite evidence of abuses of that power by doctors, lawyers, and teachers, we see the formation of the professions not only as vital to ensuring high levels of practice but as a critical ingredient of the moral glue that binds together the society.

We agree with the feminists, however, that the high-status professions have neglected the moral aspects of practice and exaggerated the technical side. We can also learn from the ecological perspective how education, like all other occupations, competes for jurisdiction and how society structures expertise in that domain. The growth of voucher plans and wider school choice will intensify competition and threaten the quasi-monopoly now held by public school teachers.

In the end, however, it is not knowledge alone, or even knowledge principally, that determines the status or course of a profession. Even if there were an enormous technological breakthrough in education, the status of the teaching profession would still be affected by the sheer number of practitioners, the custodial aspects of the teacher's job that are not shared by other professions, and the perception that no agonistic struggle is involved in becoming a teacher.

Our research is both sociological and historical, and we hope it makes a small contribution to revising popular perceptions of the sweat and joy involved in, as well as the high intelligence required for, excellent teaching. The slow revolution has its roots in the formation of the teaching profession in the late nineteenth century. The school system in place today was largely invented then by the newly established educational administrators, who applied the principles of scientific management in order to build a massive educational enterprise. They were white Protestant males who assumed the leadership with religious fervor in the belief that only universal schooling could produce good citizens and effective workers for the maturing republic. Like the professors who gradually took control of the colleges, they had graduate training that certified them as the experts, while the teacher-workers with minimal training were expected to follow the manuals. Although partriarchal gender relations were undeniably a critical aspect of the story of the teaching profession—female teachers were paid far less than male teachers before World War II, and for many decades had been required to resign if they married—we do not want to caricature the complex history of its development by attending to only one theme. In fact, despite serious flaws, it was an enormously successful system, unlike anything the world had ever seen.

We attempt to explain the evolution of the teaching profession in all its human complexity from its nineteenth-century origins to the present through the biographies of two teachers. The first of these draws on the diary and papers of Florence Thayer, a white woman who was born in 1874. She attended one of the nation's first normal schools for teacher training, established in 1867 in Brockport, New York, and eventually taught in Rochester. The second portrays the life of a black teacher, Andrena Anthony, who began her teaching career in the tumultuous 1960s, struggled to refine her craft in the midst of multiple social revolutions, and eventually became a mentor teacher in a large high school in Syracuse in the 1990s.

The essential acts of teaching, we believe, are the same for a kindergarten teacher like Vivian Gussin Paley as for a Harvard professor like Howard Gardner. This book includes voices of teachers we know and admire as well as those we have come to know vicariously through their own accounts of the teacher's craft. The book is both an appreciation of those teachers and an argument for reducing the gulf between those in the schools and those in the colleges. One of our fundamental aims is to write for those who feel a call to teaching and who want to know what teachers really do and what they hold sacred. We hope this book will inspire those considering the vocation of teaching and that all teachers who read it, especially those who have let us into their lives and classrooms, will say our account is true to their profession.

2

Assessing America's Teachers and Schools

Although there's a recognizable genre of the teacher-as-a-hero, stretching from Mr. Chips to Jaime Escalante in the recent film *Stand and Deliver*, the literature is dominated by images of teachers as beseiged, living lives that are pinched and mean, drab and doltish. Teachers are seen as at the mercy of their slovenly pupils, who are unmotivated to learn, if not abusive and threatening. Teachers are beaten down in a bureaucracy that scolds them for going up the down staircase. At the end of the day they are filled with guilt because they have failed to meet the legitimate needs of many of their pupils. They are overloaded with expectations by a society that has shrunk from more radical reforms and salved its conscience by directing teachers to achieve equality in the institution of the school, which is seen as the universal solvent of the ills of a democratic society. Aging teachers are portrayed as tired from working second jobs and having made too many compromises during the school day. Even the school is seen as a shopping mall where teacher-clerks sell their wares too cheaply and are reluctant to make demands on fickle customers. Teachers have been buffeted by the winds of social revolution. Weary and confused, they survey a radically altered educational landscape in which they are no longer sure of their place or of their authority. They are the victims of intrusive parents and educational reformers who announce a new fad every week.[1]

All of these images are, at least to some degree, accurate. Yet teachers at the end of the twentieth century—and there will be more than three million of them by the year 2000—are happier and more satisfied than they have been in decades. They are better trained and doing a better job than most people believe. The profile of the teaching profession has undergone dramatic changes, and we believe these changes will accelerate in the next decade as major teacher turnover occurs. In this chapter we will look at a wide range of survey data and qualitative studies to assess these changes. We will attempt to answer the questions: Who chooses to teach? How qualified are teachers? What do they know and believe? How satisfied are they? And—perhaps most important and difficult to judge—how effective are America's teachers?

Who Teaches?

America's schoolteachers are overwhelmingly female and white. Well into the twentieth century, women were required to resign if they married or had a child. Now three-fourths of all teachers are married (nearly a third to another teacher) and have children. Teaching is a lifetime career, and the average age of a teacher is forty-three.[2] The fate of teaching is closely bound to the status of women. Seventy-two percent of all teachers, including those in private schools, are women. Even the high school faculties, once mostly male, are now predominantly female; 53 percent of the teachers are women, compared with 23 percent in Japan and 35 percent in France. The difference is more striking if one looks at the teaching of advanced mathematics. Only a quarter of those teachers are female in a survey of fourteen countries, but in the United States 48 percent of high school teachers of advanced mathematics are female.[3]

Teachers of both genders choose teaching for the intrinsic satisfactions and joy of the work. They feel whole and connected and engaged in meaningful work in a way that many in modern society do not. The leading reasons teachers say they chose the profession are that they like to work with children (66 percent), that they like the inherent meaning and value of the job (38 percent), and that they are interested in a specific subject-matter field (36 percent). Only one in five cited long summer vacations, while 17 percent said job security was a principal reason. Other surveys show that most teachers (87 percent) find their greatest satisfaction in reaching students and knowing that they have learned.[4]

Teachers of color are underrepresented in America's schools. While 32 percent of all pupils in kindergarten through grade 12 are African

American, Hispanic, Asian, or Native American, only 13 percent of their teachers are. In the last decade, there has been a slight increase—about 1 percent—in teachers of color. But recent data on new entrants to the teaching profession indicate that these proportions are unlikely to change significantly, although there will be some increase in the percentage of Hispanic teachers and a slight decline in the number of African Americans.[5]

The social-class origins of teachers have moved upward. Once they were predominantly from working-class and farm families, but now a majority of all teachers report that their fathers were professionals, semiprofessionals, managers, or self-employed. The family income of teachers themselves has increased significantly. In 1996, when the mean household income of all families was nearly $40,000, the mean for all public school teachers' families was $63,171. In 1998 in Rochester or Syracuse, two married public school teachers in their late forties with master's degrees could have a family income in excess of $100,000. Although the average salary for public school teachers in 1996 ranged from $31,000 in the Southeast to $43,000 in the Northeast, the salaries earned by the most experienced teachers in affluent suburban school districts (and a few cities) exceeded $70,000 for a ten-month school year.[6] Compared with teachers in twenty-five other nations, American teachers are well paid. The pay scale is higher than that in all the countries surveyed except Austria and the United Kingdom. But the somewhat lower status of teachers in the United States is reflected in the relationship of teachers' salaries to national wealth. On average, the countries surveyed pay teachers about twice their per capita Gross Domestic Product. The United States ranks low, paying teachers on average only one and a half times the GDP per capita, whereas the United Kingdom pays teachers more than twice the GDP and Portugal nearly four times as much. However, recent Gallup polls show some upward change in the American public's evaluation of teaching as a career: two-thirds of parents said they would like to see a child of theirs become a teacher and 73 percent of all respondents said they would encourage "the brightest person you know" to become a teacher.[7]

Teachers' Qualifications

As Albert Shanker, the honest and often acerbic president of the American Federation of Teachers was fond of saying, when you have three million of anything you get a lot of average. There are ten times as many teachers in America as doctors, and the higher pay of doctors and other high-status professionals attracts many talented students. The brightest students in high school are more likely to say they intend to be a doctor or scientist or lawyer than to be a teacher. Nonetheless, most popular accounts of teachers' qualifications underestimate the talent flow into teaching for two reasons.

First, they usually draw on comparisons of Scholastic Achievement Test scores of high school students who say they will become teachers. This estimation leaves out many students who decide later that they wish to be teachers. Many graduates of teacher education programs never teach, and many graduates in other fields later decide they wish to teach. In the mid-1990s, a survey of those who had been out of college for one year showed that a quarter of the education majors were no longer considering teaching. But a third of those who had majored in the humanities and 20 percent of those who majored in mathematics or the sciences said they were now considering careers in teaching. Many of these noneducation majors do their teacher training and certification in master's degree programs.[8]

Second, until the last decade we had no good studies that compared the actual college grades of students preparing for teaching with the grades of other college students. Two major surveys show that those preparing to enter teaching have slightly higher grade point averages than do non-education students. The average grade point average for all students in the latest survey was 3.17. The equivalent figure for those enrolled in teacher preparation programs was 3.31.[9]

The master's degree is now required for permanent certification of ~~not~~ *IL* teachers in most states, and 56 percent of public school teachers now hold the master's degree (up from 27 percent in 1971). Fewer teachers are left to sink or swim in their first years of teaching. The percentage of teachers who have the benefit of some induction or mentoring program in their first year of teaching has tripled in the past twenty years, and 48 percent of those entering teaching now report the benefit of such training, although this may include relatively short orientation programs.[10]

Contrary to popular belief, teachers take most of their courses in the liberal arts and subject-matter disciplines. Those preparing to teach at the elementary level take the most education courses, about one-third of their undergraduate total. High school teachers take less than a quarter of their courses in education, although there is great variance among the states: Wisconsin requires prospective high school teachers to take a full college major in the subject to be taught plus courses in teaching methods, curriculum planning, and human development, and also to do eighteen weeks of supervised student teaching; a Louisiana teacher could be licensed with neither a major nor a minor in the field to be taught and only six weeks of supervised teaching. About 90 percent of all public school teachers have probationary or permanent certification in their main teaching field. However, many teachers are also assigned to teach in another subject or field, and 41 percent have no certification in that second area. Thus about a quarter of all students are taught a course in mathematics by teachers who do not have even a minor in mathematics. These teachers are certified but assigned by principals to cover a class out of their field, often because budget restrictions prevent the hiring of an additional teacher certified in that subject.[11]

In addition to certification, usually a matter of a teacher having completed an approved course of study that includes supervised teacher training experience, teachers are required to pass written competency tests in about a third of the states. Most of these are tests of basic mathematic and verbal skills, and are not considered to be rigorous. States set different qualifying scores for the most widely used test, the National Teacher Exam. Candidates for the NTE biology test, which is scored from 250 to 990, will pass in Ohio with a score of 480, while Pennsylvania sets the bar at 580 and Connecticut at 730. Recently however, as we mentioned earlier, a rigorous examination considered to be on a par with those given to architects, lawyers, and other professionals has been developed by the National Board for Professional Teaching Standards. Now in the final stages of development, it has been adopted in twenty-three states and sixty-one school districts, and promises to become a widespread standard that will transform the assessments of teachers' qualifications in the United States.[12] It introduces major distinctions about levels of teaching expertise. Board certified teachers would be more qualified than others to take on such responsibilities as mentoring and curriculum development. This test confirms what teachers have long known: that teachers differ greatly in knowledge, skill, and expertise. Research on novice and expert teachers shows that expert teachers have a much broader repertoire of teaching and diagnostic skills. A study of nine hundred Texas school districts found that teachers' expertise—as measured by experience, scores achieved on a licensing examination, and degrees earned—accounted for 40 percent of the variance in pupil achievement.[13] And as we show in our discussion of a high school teacher in Chapter 6, teachers vary significantly in the amount of continued training they undergo and graduate work they complete beyond the requirements of initial certification. Continued on-the-job training has been increasing for all teachers, however. About a third now report that they have had more than thirty hours of training in the last two years.[14]

Teachers' Beliefs and Satisfactions

The percentage of teachers who said they would certainly or probably choose to become teachers again dropped markedly in the 1970s and 1980s to a low of 46 percent, but rose to 65 percent by the 1990s. And teachers under thirty, who will constitute the core of the profession in the early twenty-first century, were the most satisfied; nearly 70 percent of them would choose teaching again. When asked what most hindered their work, "incompetent and uncooperative administrators" was the top choice checked in 1991 (by 16 percent of all public school teachers), although only 11 percent targeted administrators in 1996, perhaps reflecting more shared governance. Heavy work load and lack of materials and resources were the next most cited (15 and 12 percent). Most teachers in the 1990s said they looked forward to going to work. Only 8 percent would change their job if they could. Their views of student abilities were positive, with only 11 percent saying students were incapable of learning the material taught.[15]

Surveys give evidence of what we have called the slow revolution—although it is still affecting only a minority—with 30 to 40 percent of all teachers perceiving themselves as having a great deal of influence over decisions about how they teach. That leaves 54 percent who say they are "told in detail what to teach at given times and what material must be covered." And teachers feel they have less influence than administrators on schoolwide disciplinary policy or key decisions such as teacher hiring. There were signficant differences between public and private schools, with teachers in the private schools feeling they had more say over school policy and reporting higher agreement with principals. Half of all private school teachers but only one-third of those in public schools felt that teachers and principals in their schools agreed on disciplinary policy, for example.[16] The evidence of the slow revolution is most clear in a 1993 report prepared for the Ford Foundation. It showed that only 41 percent of teachers feel that they had a voice in school decision-making that "has had a major impact on their school." But even so, teachers who did have a voice made a major difference in the practices adopted in their schools. Compared with teachers who did not have such input in their schools, teachers with a voice in decision-making were twice as likely to have structured time for meeting with colleagues, to observe colleagues teaching and provide feedback to them, to work in teams rather than always teaching solo, and to have more time to plan instruction. Teachers in such schools were more satisfied, more willing to counsel students in home visits, and more likely to rate the quality of education as excellent than were teachers in schools where they reported they had little voice in decision-making.[17]

Teachers' Effectiveness

Laments over the poor performance of America's schools have been a staple of mass media coverage long before the *Nation at Risk* report was issued in 1983. But appraisals have had more political clout since the development of sophisticated international testing that compares the United States with other nations and links educational performance with economic productivity. Scrutiny has also intensified with the unprecedented development of specific national goals, such as "By the year 2000, United States students will be first in the world in mathematics and science achievement." Progress—or lack thereof—toward these goals, established in 1990 by President George Bush and the nation's governors (including Governor Bill Clinton of Arkansas), is reported annually.[18]

It is now clear that the United States will not lead the world in mathematics in 2000, one of the goals announced. And all children will not have access to high-quality preschool programs, which was the first of the eight goals eventually agreed upon. Some critics have bashed the goals—arguing that it was foolish to set such a ten-year goal in mathematics because even if all desired reforms in education were immediately adopted and funded, students who entered kindergarten in 1990 would not be out of high school by the year 2000. Others have bashed the schools or the teachers, saying that they have been reluctant to change long-established practices and need to meet deadlines for achieving high standards. Parents who refuse to set limits on television viewing or oversee the completion of homework have also come in for a share of the blame.

Most of the media attention, however, has focused on the schools, often distorting complex data, as in a *Newsweek* story which gave U.S. schools "An 'F' in World Competition." The big news to come out of a 1996 meeting of governors and business leaders was a report that the Nynex communications company had to test 60,000 applicants to fill 3,000 jobs. From the other side, defenders of the schools have exaggerated the positive results (by claiming that the rankings separate countries by only a few points, or that student samples were unfairly drawn) and charged the critics with manufacturing a crisis in order to push their own ideologies of reform.[19]

Our reading of the data gives a mixed picture. In brief, the international performance of American children varies greatly by subject and grade level. It is generally high in reading, average in geography and science, and low in math. The international comparisons have gotten most of the media play, but they do not tell us as much as more recent national testing designed to assess practical reasoning and performance skills. Below, we shall look in more detail at these results, and analyze them in relation to teachers' practices and the implications for educational reform. By any reading, the assessments reveal major shortcomings in American schools and establish a strong warrant for both school and social reform. Unfortunately, Americans have too often expected the schools to do it all, as if we could teach ourselves out of poverty or racism. But before we return to some of these issues, let us look at the test results in recent decades. We are aware of the limitations of the kind of standardized, norm-referenced tests we report here. Such tests measure only a small amount of what students can do. The Yale Professor Robert Sternberg, author of *Successful Intelligence*, argues that although these tests identify children with good memories and high abstract-analytical abilities, they predict only about 10 percent of the variation among people in real-world measures of success. As we have said, we applaud the movement toward new forms of assessment that attempt to capture more of what we want schools to do in producing thoughtful, caring, students with a broad range of skills and qualities of mind. Teachers are only one influence on children's learning, and they should not be held *solely* acccountable for test scores. Nonetheless, we believe it is naive to dismiss the standardized national and international norm-referenced tests. They do measure real and important skills that schools should teach.[20]

Reading

America may be a couch potato culture, but a high proportion of the teenagers have a book in their hands even when the television is on. American fourteen-year-olds report a higher reading frequency than their counterparts in most nations, and their reading achievement is above average. The United States ranked seventh of nineteen nations in an assessment of overall reading comprehension of fourteen-year-olds. Finland was first and France second, but in terms of statistical significance the American score was comparable to that of second-place France. The United States ranked ahead of Germany, Canada, Norway, Spain, and Belgium. The mean for Finland was 545, the U.S. mean was 514, and last-place Belgium had a mean of 446. Among nine-year-olds the U.S. achievement was second only to that of Finland, which shows that American primary school teachers are among the best in the world, although the gain in proficiency from fifth to ninth grade is not as great as in Finland.[21]

The results in reading support the view of those who have argued that the much-ballyhooed drop in scores on the Scholastic Achievement Test (SAT) taken by college applicants in the United States is misleading, largely (though not entirely) reflecting a broader demographic pool of those taking the test rather any decrease in real abilities. The SAT was originally a "prep school" test normed on a population that was 90 percent white, 60 percent male, and 40 percent private school students. Currently the SAT test-takers are 30 percent minority and 52 percent female, with higher proportions from public schools and low-income families. The meaninglessness of a major drop in SAT scores is also confirmed by analysis of the results of the National Assessment of Educational Progress results over the past twenty-five years. As we will explain later, the broad national samples included in those tests show reading and writing scores have been roughly level for twenty-five years, although they sagged in the late 1970s.[22]

Science

A rigorous international test given in 1995 showed that American fourth- and eighth-graders scored above average in science, while falling near the bottom by twelfth grade. The fourth-graders, with a mean score of 565, were bested only by those in Korea (597) and Japan (574) among the twenty-six nations tested at that level. The international fourth-grade average was 524, with Kuwait at the bottom with 401. By eighth grade, the Americans at 534 were only slightly above the average of 531 for forty-one nations tested. Singapore led with 607, the Japanese mean was 571, and Hungary's was 550. Among those scoring below the United States were New Zealand with 525, France with 498, and Cyprus with 463. The differences were more significant than those in a 1991 study, which showed that scores among nations were more closely clustered. In the later study, 37 points on the scale was estimated to represent about a year's growth in science achievement. On average, Japanese eighth-graders were about a year (40 points) ahead of their counterparts in the United States, and the American youngsters were two-thirds of a year ahead of those in France.

The analysis of twelfth-grade results, which was not published until 1998, showed that Americans had dropped well below the average of 500 for the twenty-one nations tested in general knowledge of science. Sweden was at the top with 559 and South Africa at the bottom with 349. The United States students, with a score of 480, were clustered below the mean with France (487), Russia (481), and Hungary (471). The most embarrassing showing for the United States came in physics, where American students hit rock bottom with a score of 423. Only those students who had taken advanced coursework in physics were tested. The mean for the sixteen nations tested was 501. Norway led with 581, followed by Sweden with 573 and Russia with 545.[23]

Geography and History

In geography there was much less of a spread. American youngsters have often been criticized for their supposedly sketchy knowledge of geography, but they scored about average in the international comparison. Although reinstating geography as a separate course more often has been proposed, analysis of students who had had such a course showed that they did no better than others. There are no international comparisons of understanding of history. The last major national assessment, in 1994, was not reassuring, however. While 61 percent of the eighth-graders had achieved a basic level of understanding of history, only 43 percent of the high school seniors demonstrated that level of understanding.[24]

If teachers are to blame for this state of affairs, then so are college professors. A 1996 Roper poll of college seniors showed that less than half knew how many U.S. senators there are; only a quarter could identify Nazi Germany's two main allies in World War II; and less than one in ten could trace "government of the people, by the people, for the people" to Abraham Lincoln's Gettysburg Address.[25]

Mathematics

Perhaps because mathematics is believed to be the most international "language" and lends itself to more precise scoring than do other disciplines, international comparisons have received the most attention from both scholars and the media. As with science, the third international math study in 1995 showed American fourth-graders performing significantly above average. The international average for the twenty-six nations tested was 529 and the U.S. score was 545. However, U.S. eighth-graders did not do as well in math as in science; math scores dropped into the bottom third of scores from all nations. Countries that the United States had surpassed in science and reading, such as Canada and France, outscored America in math. Asian nations were clustered near the top, with Singapore at 643 and Japan at 605, followed by Belgium and the Czech Republic, with the Russians near the median at 535. The United States scored 500 and Iran was at the bottom at 428. These are highly significant differences. To put it another way, the average U.S. eighth-grader scored in the same range as the bottom quarter of Asian students.

By twelfth grade, American scores in general knowledge of mathematics had plummeted, as they had in science. The United States scored among the lowest of twenty-one nations tested with a score of 461; the international average was 500. The Netherlands was highest with 560, and only Cyprus with 446 and South Africa with 356 were lower than the United States. Comparisons of American students who had taken advanced mathematics courses were similarly dismal. They achieved an average score of 442, compared with the international mean of 501. France led with 557 and only Austria at 436 scored lower than the United States.

This disappointing news was partially offset by a major mathematics reform movement initiated in the early 1980s that has begun to show some improvement in U.S. scores. Although the improvements on the

National Assessment of Educational Progress were small, they were statistically significant. Average scores rose for all children at ages nine, thirteen, and seventeen in the years from 1982 to 1992.[26]

This good news was, however, overshadowed by generally poor results on national assessments incorporating new standards for mathematics achievement that required students to do more practical problem-solving and to explain their reasoning. The National Assessments of Educational Progress (NAEP) instituted in 1992 adopted the standards developed by the National Council of Teachers of Mathematics. These assessments showed that students' problem-solving skills were extremely weak and that significant achievement gaps existed for African American and Hispanic students. With respect to problem-solving skills, most American students performed at or below the minimal level set by the new standards. Less than 10 percent achieved the highest level of "in-depth performance." Generally, students' ability to give adequate explanations of their reasoning process was limited. Only 22 percent of fourth-graders and 59 percent of eighth-graders were able to solve this problem about earning money for a class trip: "If Jill earns $2.00 each day on Mondays, Tuesdays, and Wednesdays, and $3.00 each day on Thursdays, Fridays, and Saturdays, how many weeks will it take her to earn $45.00?"

Another question on the 1990s test reflects more traditional testing: "There are 50 hamburgers to serve 38 children. If each child is to have at least one hamburger, at most how many children can have more than one?" Four choices are listed: 6, 26, 38, and the correct answer, 12. The hamburger problem, a one-step subtraction problem, allows a child to guess in a multiple-choice format (on average a fourth will get it right even if the guessing is purely random). Two-thirds of the fourth-graders and 92 percent of the eighth-graders picked the right answer. The new standard is illustrated in the question about Jill's class trip. Jill's problem was not presented in a multiple-choice format; children had to write the correct answer in the blank, and it required several steps to arrive at. As noted, only a fifth of the fourth-graders got it right and less than three-fifths of the eighth-graders could figure it out.

Discussion of the problem "Treena's budget" further informs our analysis of the reasons for the poor math performance of U.S. pupils. This problem involves whole-number computations, budgeting, and comparison of possible outcomes. All students had a calculator available to them during the test. Here is the problem as presented to eighth-graders:

This question requires you to show your work and explain your reasoning. You may use drawings, words, and numbers in your explanation. Your answer should be clear enough so that another person could read it and understand your thinking. It is important that you show *all* your work.

Treena won a 7-day scholarship worth $1000 to the Pro Shot Basketball Camp. Round-trip travel expenses to the camp are $335 by air or $125 by train. At the camp she must choose between a week of individual instruction at $60 per day or a week of group instruction at $40 per day. Treena's food and other expenses are fixed at $45 per day. If she does not plan to spend any money other than the scholarship, what are *all* choices of travel and instruction plans she could afford to make?

The problem required no unusual creativity or novel work for an eighth-grader beyond conceiving different combinations of expenditures Treena might choose. But most students could not achieve a 3 (partial understanding) on the 5-point NAEP scoring classifications. The scale ranges from 0 (no response), to 1 (incorrect, "I don't know," or irrelevant), to 2 (minimal understanding, poor reasoning, incomplete and serious flaws), to 3 (partial understanding, some serious flaws), to 4 (satisfactory, an acceptable approach, generally well developed but with minor weaknesses), to 5 (complete understanding, correct and fully developed). Under this scoring, which has been criticized by some as too severe, a student could get the "right" answer but receive only three of five points because the reasoning was flawed or poorly explained. In accord with the new standards, the grading gives considerable weight to reasoning and to communicating one's thought processes.

About three-fifths of the eighth-graders either left their papers blank or gave a wrong or irrelevant response such as: "Add everything other than scholarship and you will get 230." The other two-fifths got it partly or completely right, although only 4 percent were considered to demonstrate full or extended reasoning. A student who answered at that level wrote, "1) take air, group, food. 2) train, group, food. 3) train, individual, food," and showed that each of these three possible options cost less than $1000.[27]

These new standards set by the National Council of Teachers of Mathematics are far from trivial. They represent a huge shift from an emphasis on shopkeeper's arithmetic to an emphasis on reasoning and communicating. The new national assessments incorporating these standards are more demanding than the international tests of mathematics. And although the performance of American children has been heavily criticized in the media, we have no good measures of how well their parents or grandparents would have done on these tests as fourth-graders. One cross-generational study of high school performance in history and literature showed that contemporary students scored about as well as their forebears. Moreover, as we have noted, most of the attention has focused on math scores, while the superior international performance of American pupils in reading and their respectable showing in science through grade eight have been less noticed. Even in math, performance on the National Assessments of Educational Progress, has shown some improvement over the last decade.[28]

That being said, what might explain Americans' below-average results in international comparisons of mathematics achievement in grades eight and twelve? Some argue that the explanations have little to do with what happens in school. They point to cultural differences and technical problems of sampling on international tests. There have been some serious criticisms of the way samples have been selected in some Asian nations to produce more elite groups of test-takers. Moreover, it is believed that these students are pressed to do well to uphold national honor, while American pupils have no incentive to do well on these tests and their teachers place no emphasis on preparing them for international tests. But the weight of scholary opinion lies on the side of fair sampling, and why would American students do so well on the reading tests if they put no effort into them?[29] American children would do better if they watched less television and did more homework, others believe. Yet the world has become more "Americanized," and differences in television watching are not as marked as they were a generation ago. Students in Scotland, Hungary, and Israel report watching more television than those in the United States (the Hungarians and Israelis still do more homework, but Scottish pupils do less).[30]

Cultural differences cannot be ruled out, however. Japanese students are socialized from their earliest years to work cooperatively in groups. They may spend a whole morning in fourth grade working in small groups on the problem of estimating the volume of water in bottles of different dimensions, then explaining their solutions to the others. Mathematics reasoning is more visible in Japanese society. Japanese television news programs have more graphs and charts than appear on American screens, and economic data are discussed in more mathematical detail. Inequality of family incomes is far less pronounced in Japan than in the United States. The United States has the highest rates of child poverty and single-parent families among industrialized countries. Bruce J. Biddle argues that mathematics achievement for a typical "advantaged" American school—one with high per-pupil funding and low student poverty—would rank above all the European countries and below only Japan.[31] Fewer children in Japan come to school suffering from malnutrition or inadequate health care. And they enter classrooms with more cultural respect for the role of the teacher. Starting teacher salaries rank among the top 10 percent of all government salaries in Japan.

Cultural factors aside, what do we see if we look more closely at the curriculum and teachers' practices inside schools?

The alarm sounded by the *Nation at Risk* report was heard in state legislatures across the nation and resulted in raising the high school graduation requirements in most states. In the decade following the issuance of the report, the percentage of students completing a core academic curriculum recommended by the National Commission on Education Excellence tripled, from 13 to 40 percent. This core curriculum included four years of English, three years of social studies, science, and mathematics, and two years of a foreign language, which was most frequently Spanish. Females were as likely as males to take the core curriculum, although males took more science and were more likely to take calculus while females took more courses in foreign languages and visual and performing arts. The United States was one of only three nations that displayed no gender gap in math on international tests, although on average boys did better than girls in science. There were some differences by racial and ethnic group: Asian students took more math; black and Hispanic students were less likely to take the core curriculum, but the percentage of both groups who studied geometry doubled from 30 to 60 percent in one decade. Greater rigor in course work was also shown by a threefold increase in registration for Advanced Placement tests, with students from all racial and ethnic backgrounds sharing in this growth.[32]

American students are taking more courses and their teachers are working long hours—an average work week of forty-nine hours when grading papers, preparing lessons, advising school clubs, and other after-school teaching duties are counted. Contrary to the image of teachers scurrying for the parking lot at 2:30 P.M., teachers in the United States lead the world in hours of instruction per year. In the primary grades, American teachers spend 1,093 hours per year in classroom instruction. The Netherlands is second with 1,000 per year, France spends 944, and Sweden, 624. In the United States, eighth-grade teachers instruct 1,042 hours, whereas those in the United Kingdom teach 669 hours in a year. Similarly at the senior high level, the international average is 745 teaching hours but the United States average is 1,019.[33] This comforts some taxpayers but it may be poor educational practice. It means American teachers spend more time in front of the class but, compared with teachers in England or Japan, much less time in study, preparation of lessons, responding to a student who drops in with a problem, or collaborating with their colleagues. More instructional time does not necessarily translate into more effective teaching. Rather, it reflects the factory model of schooling, with teachers seen as at work only after they have punched the time card and are working at the production line.

Our teachers don't believe this.

In a careful study of social studies teaching in highly regarded suburban high schools, Linda McNeil found that teachers believed there was no reward or incentive for encouraging depth of understanding. The emphasis was on the efficient production of credentials and on moving all students smoothly through the system. The one exception in her sample was a school headed by a principal who had been an outstanding teacher and gave teachers the time and resources and encouragement to develop challenging and engaging approaches.[34]

Recent analyses of the poor math performance of U.S. students blame it in part on an "'incremental' assembly line philosophy" that "encourages breaking complex learning down into simpler learning tasks." A faith in mass production and batch processing combined with programmed instruction has chopped the U.S. curriculum into too many bits and pieces. "Our curricula, textbooks and teaching all are a mile wide and an inch deep," a Michigan State University study concluded.[35]

The U.S. curriculum covers too many topics too superficially. American eighth-grade science texts are two to four times longer than other countries' books, and cover thirty to forty major topics compared with the ten to 15 covered in other nations. Algebra is begun in the fifth grade in Japan, and children deepen their concepts over several years. In the United States, it typically is delayed until the ninth grade, and calculus is not studied until college. Contrary to the complaints of many critics, American children get too much of the "basics" in the sense that math teaching is very repetitive—students divide longer numbers in the fifth grade than they did in fourth—rather than engaging students in more analytical depth. What is studied and whether it is studied in depth matters greatly. Analyses of the international results link them to the patterns of instruction within each country. It is important to note that no country scores well in all the subtopics in mathematics or science. For example, Singapore's fourth-graders had higher average math scores than their American counterparts, but the Americans out-scored them in the geometry of shapes and positions. Eighth-graders in the United States, who earned above-average scores overall on the science exam, scored second from the bottom on the subtopic of physi-cal changes but second from the top in questions about life cycles and genetics.

Scholarly evidence is mounting to show that America's children are disadvantaged by pervasive tracking and ability grouping that begins as early as fourth grade, which may be the most significant factor in the decline in overall achievement as they move into middle school and high school. None of the nations that bested the United States in mathematics separates its students into tracks as early or as heavily as do schools in America. The American belief that tracking is most efficient and increases the achievement for average students as well as for those in the high-tracked courses simply is not supported by the international comparisons. The high-scoring nations, such as the Czech Republic, France, Hong Kong, Japan, and Korea, offer the same mathematics course to all eighth-graders, whereas 75 percent of Ameri-can eighth-graders are in schools with two or three separate math tracks. Moreover, those countries require students to take advanced courses, and begin rigorous algebra, geometry, physics, and chemistry by the eighth grade. In the United States, not only are these delayed until high school, but many students do not study them at all. About 40 percent of American high school graduates have taken no advanced algebra, 45 percent have had no chemistry, 75 percent no physics, and 80 percent no advanced math other than algebra. American students who are tracked into the lower math classes in middle school can seldom make up in high school. Even those students who are prepared for advanced classes in math and science often opt out of them to take less demanding courses. Whereas only 20 percent of Americans take algebra in the eighth grade, all Japanese eighth-graders do. Math teaching for most American eighth-graders is dominated by "show and tell" methods and encourages rote learning, whereas Japanese teachers place more emphasis on hands-on Socratic methods and problem-solving in small groups. An analysis of videotapes comparing 131 Japanese and American classrooms revealed that American children spent twice as much time doing routine procedures as did the Japanese, and less than a tenth of the time inventing and analyzing problems.[36]

The new standards of the National Council of Teachers of Mathematics were adopted to change passive classrooms characterized by heavy emphasis on drill and memorization. They push teachers to spend more time working with manipulatives—blocks, egg cartons, rulers, and beads—and to engage in activities that will help children visualize mathematical problems. They require students to question procedures and results, discuss alternative approaches, and compare their reasons for solutions to problems. There has been some significant change, but progress has been slow.[37] Depending on grade level, from 61 to 84 percent of U.S. pupils say "learning mathematics is mostly memorizing." Although three-fourths of eighth-graders report that they participate in discussions about solutions to math problems at least once a week, only a fifth are asked to write a few sentences about how they solved a problem during the week. Even though U.S. students are the most tested children in the world—more than half having a written test every week—they are seldom asked to explain problems to peers or to present exhibits or portfolios (only 20 percent say this happens at least monthly). The traditional written tests usually present the same problems students have solved in class rather than giving students new problems that they must think through using the principles they have learned. Only 11 percent of seniors say they encountered problems on tests that they had not worked on previously, and more than half say they slogged through traditional worksheets weekly. This may explain the high percentage of papers left blank in the national assessments that present new problems, such as Treena's problem. There is little use of manipulatives such as measuring devices or geometric shapes in math classes, and three-fourths of high school students say they rarely use computers in math courses. Although 93 percent of eighth-grade teachers say they feel well prepared to teach mathematics, just 55 percent feel similarly prepared to use computers.[38]

Safe, Decent Schools

When parents and the general public are asked, "What do you think are the biggest problems with which the public schools in this community must deal?" curriculum and test scores do not rank at the top of the list. Since 1970, Gallup polls have shown that the public is most concerned about the lack of good discipline, the sale and use of drugs in schools, and the financing of schools. One person in four spontaneously mentions discipline as a major problem. Until 1977, only 4 to 7 percent mentioned poor curriculum. But when the category was changed after 1978 to link curriculum with concern about standards of student achievement, it was cited by 8 to 15 percent. In the 1994 Gallup Poll, violence was tied with discipline as the number-one problem in the eyes of the public.[39] This finding was affirmed in polls by The Public Agenda, which found that 58 percent of white parents with children in public shools considered drugs and violence serious problems in the schools in their area, and 80 percent of African American parents cited them as serious problems in schools in their area. In focus group interviews with parents, The Public Agenda found that parents often link low academic performance with poor discipline: "It seems axiomatic to people that schools should be safe, orderly and conducive to teaching and learning . . . For most Americans, three images sum up their sense that the public schools are failing: metal detectors in high schools, students outside smoking during school hours, and supermarket checkout clerks who can't make change."[40]

Both Gallup and Public Agenda pollsters note that they are dealing with public perceptions strongly influenced by the mass media. The media attention given to a small minority of shocking problems of school violence undoubtedly skews public opinion. A third to half of the public sees weapons, drug use, and drinking in school as problems that occur frequently or fairly often, whereas roughly half as many teachers do.[41] Yet interviews with parents with children in public schools reveal that many have reports from their own children of weapons in schools, drug use (although it has been declining in the last decade while abuse of alcohol has increased), and toilets harboring people who may attack students as they enter. Public and teacher estimates are closer on behavior that disrupts classes (57 percent of teachers and 60 percent of the public citing it as occurring fairly or frequently often), disobeying and talking back to teachers (45 percent of teachers, 56 percent of parents), stealing (32 and 38 percent), cheating (45 and 46 percent). The president of the American Federation of Teachers felt the evidence on violence was serious enough by the mid-1990s to warn that parents will abandon public schools unless basic safety can be assured for all children and sterner measures are adopted to deal with disruptive pupils.[42]

Parents do not hold teachers solely accountable for discipline problems. They cite lack of discipline in the home as a primary cause and believe the courts are too lenient in treating violent and weapons-bearing students. More than 40 percent say the "courts have made administrators so cautious that they don't deal severely with student misbehavior." But 42 percent also believe that teachers are not properly trained to deal with discipline problems, and nearly a third say misbehavior results in part from a "failure on the part of teachers to make classroom work more interesting." When asked what schools should teach, 89 percent of those polled by The Public Agenda answered that schools should put most emphasis on teaching "honesty and the importance of telling the truth." Yet the Gallup Poll notes that 54 percent of the public cites "lack of respect for law and authority throughout society" as reason for poor discipline and cheating, acknowledging that the moral reach of teachers is limited.[43]

Finally, no fair assessment of the effectiveness of America's teachers and their schools in recent decades can fail to point out that teachers taught in the midst of overlapping social revolutions. The years when achievement scores began to drop were also the years in which the schools were the major sites of social change. It was primarily in the schools that racial attitudes were changed, that gender barriers fell, and disabled children were given the opportunities they deserved. Teachers taught while National Guardsmen patrolled the halls and crowds jeered at black children who got off buses at formerly all-white schools; they taught as severely disabled children were integrated into their classrooms by the thousands. Achievement scores in mathematics, science, and reading on the best national comparison—the National Assessments of Educational Progress—began to fall in the early 1970s, reaching a low point in the early 1980s when these social revolutions were peaking, and generally returned to or slightly exceeded the 1970 levels by 1996. In science, for example, the average score for thirteen-year-olds was 255 when the test was first given in 1970, dropped to a low of 247 in 1977, and was 256 in 1996. At the same time as these averages rose to "prerevolutionary" levels, significant reductions in the gaps between white and black students were achieved. The average white-black gap in the mean score achieved by thirteen-year-olds was reduced from 46 to 29 points in mathematics, from 49 to 40 in science, and from 39 to 31 points in reading.[44]

3

The Essential Acts of Teaching

Teaching and learning are both largely mysteries. We are often at a loss to explain how we caught on to something, how we finally hit the tennis ball with a beautiful spin after dozens of hours of patient demonstration. Or why it took so long to see how the parts of a new toy fit together, or to understand a paragraph by Noam Chomsky. We finally "got it." The penny drops. Aha!

Similarly, the teacher wonders why Jaime got it with an explanation that went nowhere with Kristen. What, she thinks, did I do right this time? Teachers vary greatly in the repertoire of skills they employ to make learning happen, and beginning teachers are often puzzled about what to do to help the penny drop. As they gain experience they realize teaching is more art and craft than science, and that it involves trying first this piece of the puzzle and then another, learning from mistakes, and overcoming embarrassments. Yet it is not all mystery. There are many things that can be taught and learned by practitioners of any craft. Although there will always be an element of the sacred and the intuitive in the practice of teaching, for it shapes the heart as much as it does the mind, the craft of teaching can be analyzed in terms of its essential acts.

In this chapter we discuss what teachers do, drawing on observations of teachers at every level of the educational system in hundreds of classrooms. An oddity of contemporary scholarly discourse is that teaching is seldom thought of in this way. Researchers who study teaching in the public schools rarely talk with those who do research in colleges and universities. The unstated assumption is that teachers and professors are engaged in entirely different professions. Although, as we have noted, schoolteaching and professing have been institutionalized differently, in their acts as teachers, those teaching the fourth grade and those teaching university graduate students are members of the same profession doing essentially the same thing. What are these essential acts they perform in common as teachers?

They are not such things as patrolling hallways, writing attendance reports, attending faculty meetings, or collecting money for a field trip. These are often necessary to the smooth running of schools, and may consume many of a teacher's work hours, but they are not the essential acts of teaching. A teacher can do all of those things without ever doing anything that would count as teaching. Our discussion focuses on what happens in the teacher's encounter with students that enables learning to take place. Although planning is critically important to the success of teaching, we will not say much about how to make a lesson plan. Nor will we dwell on techniques of organizing and delivering a good lecture. Rather, we will attempt to get inside the minds and hearts of teachers to illustrate what they are doing when they are doing the real stuff of teaching. These essential acts are knowing their students, engaging them in learning, acting as models of a good life, assessing students' moral and intellectual growth, and reflecting on the arts of teaching that enable that growth.[1]

Knowing the Students

All teachers must know their stuff, the subject that they teach. Teachers of biology must know the difference between RNA and DNA, between a zygote and a gamete. They should know the forms of inquiry and competing explanatory frameworks for interpreting biological data. English teachers should know a wide range of texts from Shakespeare to Toni Morrison and be aware of different critical traditions from New Criticism to semiotics. Only a house of straw can be built on a foundation of sand. We applaud the increased emphasis on subject-matter preparation for teacher licensing in most states, although too many students still suffer from teachers who lack a deep grasp of their subjects or who are not committed to lifelong renewal of their knowledge. But it is knowing in another sense, knowing students, that we turn to now.

A poor cellist is unlikely to be a good teacher of the instrument but even a great player will need to attend carefully to each pupil: to observe the placement of fingers, to listen scrupulously to the sounds produced, to know the kinds of errors this pupil is inclined to make, and later to see into the the soul of the disciple to understand what will move her or him to the highest levels of interpretation. The pianist Theodor Leschetizky used to remonstrate passionately when a student did not hear a particular note:

> "That must not be told you twice. You must *hear* it! If a stranger heard you play that way he would say that you were a very talented person, but you had a bad teacher. It isn't your [lack of] strength at all, it is your ear! Why the bass so loud?" he says, coming over to my piano. "Never cover up the top when it has anything to say. Yes, that one note one calls bad, really bad," he says. I try again.
>
> "Stop!" he calls. "Wait! You do not have to catch any trains, have you, or *have* you perhaps?" he said, going back to his piano. "I haven't any to catch, and here I sit waiting to hear a plain A flat played with tone."[2]

Listening with care seems self-evident in the case of teaching the piano, yet it is an often overlooked aspect of most good teaching (although a student of the brilliant architectural historian Vincent Scully at Yale wrote that Scully taught him and many others to *see* while only rarely listening to them).[3] But most teachers do not have the charisma of Vincent Scully, and they need the help of someone like Kiyo Morimoto. When student protests at Harvard escalated in the late 1960s and complaints about undergraduate teaching multiplied, Kiyo Morimoto of Harvard's Bureau of Study Counsel hit upon a stunningly simple way to improve the work of the graduate assistants, called teaching fellows there, who taught the discussion sections in large courses. Morimoto had these assistants, who included Gerald Grant, listen to tapes of each other's discussion groups. What most of us sheepishly learned was that we were so filled up with new knowledge that we had organized into incredibly complex lesson plans that we hardly heard what the poor sophomore had just said. We were busy imparting the Truth, and we rushed forward in slavish devotion to our outlines, often impervious to profound questions or comments students across the seminar table had raised. What we "taught" them was to sit passively and then withdraw. Yet we were peeved to be greeted by silence when we did occasionally stop our headlong rush and ask for questions.

Our irritation was soon followed by panic and we hastily plunged back into our outlines or, worse, dismissed the class early, for we did not have the courage to bear the silence. We were terrified by the emptiness and the ticking clock. We did not know that one must also teach by silence, as a Benedictine monk once taught.[4] The teacher needs not only to listen for what has not been said, often out of fear of ridicule, but also to encourage the reflection that produces the most thought-provoking questions.

The heart of the educational process at St. John's College in Annapolis, Maryland, is the twice-weekly seminar in which all the students struggle with the original texts of the same great books from Euclid to Freud. Although St. John's is a highly selective college, most of the students who enroll have never experienced anything like a St. John's seminar, which is typically led by two tutors who know the books intimately. The young tutor is usually paired with an old hand, and what the pairing enables him or her to do is to listen: "Listen for the grain of truth and follow the question where it leads," as the renowned dean and tutor Jacob Klein taught. Every word of Klein's admonition should be memorized by those who wish to teach, but none is more important than "listen." Listen for the grain of truth, let the nervous sophomore's chaff fall to the floor, then tease out the question, follow *it* where *it* leads and pay no mind to your lesson plan. Listen for the real life that unfolds in the moment before you.

David Riesman often started his famous lectures on American character and social structure with a question a student had posed to him on the way out of the lecture hall at the last meeting of the course. What the student learned was how carefully Riesman listened to the student's question, not only its original formulation but what the student said in response to Riesman's answer and what the student was able to teach Riesman because he listened so carefully, sometimes inviting the student to continue the discussion at lunch. Even though hundreds of students enrolled in his course, most of them felt Riesman responded conscientiously to any opportunity they gave him to know them.

Riesman's counterpart in kindergarten is Vivian Gussin Paley. She often left a tape recorder running in her Chicago classroom, especially when she drew the children together to help her think about an important question, such as whether they should adopt the rule "You can't say you can't play." At home the evening of this discussion she replayed the tape and listened to exchanges stimulated by a shy girl, Clara, who had been crying:

> "Cynthia and Lisa builded a house for their puppies and I said can I play and they said no because I don't have a puppy only I have a kitty." This is the longest sentence she has spoken in school to date. There is more to come. "They said I'm not their friend." Clara hugs her tattered kitty and sniffs back tears.
>
> "We said if she brings a Pound Puppy she can play," Lisa explains.
> Nelson frowns. "Ben wouldn't let me play."
> "Un-uh, it was Charlie not me," Ben argues. "He was the boss."
> "Me neither they wouldn't let me play," Angelo mutters. "Nobody that worries me like that I don't care about."
> [Later, when the suggested rule is brought up again, Lisa responds:]
> "But then what's the whole point of playing?"

Later, on a plane to Arizona, Paley plays the tape again, admitting what experience has taught her: "The replay of children's voices often helps clarify a problem for me. I cannot hear everything the first time around." She may inquire next what Ben meant by "boss" and what the rules are for being a "boss," or write a story that includes some of the children's spontaneous dialogue.[5]

Paley's tapes were a form of record keeping that enabled her to see her children more clearly. Teachers need to ground their observations in many dimensions of a child's life, writes William Ayers, in order to overcome our prejudices and "the wacky idea that children are puny, inadequate adults." Teachers must be part detective and part researcher, sifting the clues children leave, collecting data, testing hypotheses and "looking unblinkingly at the way children really are . . . in order to fill out and make credible the story of their growth and development."[6]

Patricia Carini of the Prospect School in Bennington, Vermont, raised this kind of observation to a high art. When Gerald Grant visited the school in the 1960s, she explained that every teacher participates in the staff reviews, where an hour or more is spent pondering what the teachers have learned about a single child. The goal is to see the whole child as fully as possible in order to enrich the school experience of that child and to help the child's teachers answer the question: Given what I now know, how do I best teach this child? The experience of analyzing even one child in this way can change forever the way a teacher looks at any child. Carini went on to write about her method. Editing out the real names, she included excerpts of the reports that Prospect teachers had distilled from the staff reviews:

> Sid is a tall long-limbed nine-year-old with an insistent voice and noticeably awkward movements . . . His tendency to spread out, oblivious of both body and belongings, frequently irritated his fellow students. He bumped into them, jarred them with loud noises, or disturbed their work. His lack of self-awareness put people off. Although he slowly gained a place among the other children, it took considerable mediating on the part of his teacher for him to gain acceptance from the group. Sid's responses were often puzzling. His initial reaction to the conflict his behavior projected was often panic and denial . . . Yet his face would light up with wonder when an idea caught his interest. His full attention was captured by anything mysterious, a problem requiring analysis, or connections to be found among an array of elements.

The report goes on to discuss Sid's love of drawing, cooking, and constructing mazes and his facility at improvisation, as well as his careless reading, and to suggest ways of building on his strengths that would help to remedy his weaknesses. The Prospect process underscores the need for multiple insights and observations as a way of knowing that enables good teaching.[7]

Jessica Siegel got to know her pupils by getting them to write their own stories. Siegel was an extraordinary teacher of English in the 1980s at Seward Park High School on the Lower East Side of New York, where throngs of immigrant children arrived each September and stood outside the principal's office waiting to be registered. They had names like Sean Singh and Pura Cruz, Chun-On Cheng and Anton Vidokle. Jessica Siegel first saw their names on Delaney Cards, small slips of paper produced by the bureaucracy. But knowing their names was not enough. She could not teach names, only persons. She learned something about them on the first day, when she asked for a paragraph about what they thought a good class should be and what they expected of Ms. Siegel. But it was the next assignment that she most relished. Entering class on the second day, they saw the assignment written in four-inch high letters on the blackboard: "Journal Topic: Who Am I? Describe Yourself." Some of her colleagues thought Siegel was inviting disappointment and heartache. These students' lives were filled with tragedies, and those colleagues didn't think it would help to know too many excuses for poor performance in the classroom. But for her it was required in order to accomplish other acts of teaching that were to follow: knowing enough to know how to spark the students' interest, to motivate them, to pick out the character in a novel with whom they would deeply identify and want to write about. Let's turn next to these matters of motivation.[8]

Engaging and Motivating

Most accounts of great teachers say little or nothing about the critically important act of motivating the student, of engaging her or him in learning. Those who teach master classes—whether in the violin or theoretical physics—can choose their students from many eager supplicants. The pupils' intense desire to learn, second only to demonstrated promise, is the primary basis of their selection. The master teacher is unlikely to hear, "Get out of my face, old man, you ain't got nothing to teach me." Or to hear what some public school teachers are likely to hear if they look at a student too sharply: "Don't you even think of touching me, or I'll have you arrested."

If the teacher's duties once were wrongly held to be only carrying buckets of knowledge into the classroom, today it is often just as unfairly believed that it is all her fault if the students refuse to drink. Too little emphasis may be placed upon the responsibility of parents, the students themselves, and other interested parties for setting expectations in a school. In the best schools, everyone strives to keep even the recalcitrant student engaged, while in the worst the hidden curriculum of selecting and sorting may push students out rather than invite them in.[9] And a skeptic might question the central or universal importance of motivation. Many premed students have little intrinsic motivation to learn biochemistry or molecular biology, a faculty colleague in medicine reminds us. "A lot of motivation comes from the sequence of learning, which is nonnegotiable, nonarbitrary, and which, if not completed, closes down professional options. Science and math are like that. So are certain courses in law school or business school. One doesn't have to be fascinated by each subject in the prescribed curriculum; one just needs to accept that wiser heads have prescribed the course as 'good for you at this stage', and get the job done."[10]

Yet the individual teacher's art is perhaps nowhere more evident than in her or his ability to motivate and engage students in learning. Even our medical school colleague wanted us to know that "I still try very hard to make biochemistry come alive for anti-intellectual medical students." Such an effort should not be described as cajoling. But it does involve questioning, appreciating, inventing, providing experiences, and guiding—occasionally even goading.

A good question engages us and puts the mind into gear with nearly irresistible force. Ask a group of fourth-graders: When did you last see the moon and what did it look like? Can you predict when you will next see it and what it will look like then? Under the guidance of a good teacher, they will soon be engaged in lively discussion about different answers to the first question and they will generate different "theories" about how to answer the second. Within an hour they will be asking why they see the moon in vastly different places in the sky from early evening to early morning, and why it changes its shape. They will respond eagerly to the teacher's suggestion that they keep a moon-watching notebook by their bedside for the next month. In class their theories will grow more complicated as they compare drawings and notations they have made in their notebooks. They will need to develop reasons to explain the data they have collected, and they will discover that some of their data cannot be explained by the reasons they give, and that other students have different explanations. Their theories will change as the data get more complicated, and they will weigh the power of competing explanations for what they have glimpsed of the moon's movements. They will have new knowledge of a very important kind: not just about the moon, but what it means to know anything.[11]

Visitors to Japanese classrooms have noted that teachers there are more apt than American teachers to engage students in puzzles. A primary school teacher may come into class in the morning carrying a tray bearing half a dozen bottles of different shapes and sizes. She will divide the class into groups of three or four students each and ask them to rank order the bottles from those that will hold the least amount of water to those that will hold the most. The groups are not allowed to fill the bottles but must estimate the volume through observation only. They may spend most of the morning on the task. Then each group will come up to place the bottles in the order it has ranked them, and explain why. The teacher does not correct "wrong" answers but attempts to draw out the reasoning that led the group to that conclusion. Those who have studied the superior mathematics achievement of Japanese students believe that it can be traced in part to this style of teaching, especially the attention paid to the patterns of reasoning and the emphasis on informal peer tutoring in small groups.[12]

Good teachers also encourage students to formulate their own questions. Beginning a unit on Asian history, they may say, "Let's all take five minutes to write three things we really want to know about China." *Experientialist* Questions that connect reflection with personal experience are usually powerful. Students at Paul Robeson High School in Chicago spent weeks pondering their responses to the question, "Is the Civil War really over?"[13] Raymond Coppinger, a biologist at Hampshire College, began a memorable seminar by challenging students to figure out what questions they would need to ask to explain: "How do we get the shit out of Amherst with least damage to the environment?"

Questions that launch both students and teacher on a genuine search are the most compelling. Students in a multiracial high school in Syracuse wrote engrossing essays after reading an account of life at St. Paul's, an elite prep school in New England. They were asked to write a letter to a St. Paul's student about to move to Syracuse who wanted to know how life at their high school would be different from life at St. Paul's.

A teacher in Winchester, New Hampshire, built a semester's work in seventh-grade science around the children's curiosity about whether the streams in their town were becoming more polluted, and what the causes of that pollution might be. By the year's end the students had collected and analyzed samples of water from many locations and presented a report to the town board.

Like that seventh-grade teacher in Winchester, in our best graduate seminars we have posed questions to which we have no settled answers. In one we explored the problems of human assessment, beginning with readings about the evaluation of persons to be selected for spying assignments in World War II and ending with an examination of the validity of efforts to judge student work submitted in portfolios or in other nontraditional forms. A research project connected with this seminar involved visits to a dozen colleges that were developing so-called competence-based curriculums. Each researcher made independent visits to the college and wrote up notes that were shared with the other researchers. They were supposed to read those notes before they came as a team to do further research at a given site. At dinner the night before beginning our team visit to one of the sites, we interrogated the researcher responsible for that site about questions we had about her notes. This exploration of the significance of what was reported in the notes, or missing links, or doubtful interpretations became known as the Question Box. This was an extraordinary learning experience for all of us, and it motivated us to do better interviews the next day.[14]

The Question Box was an accidental invention that we were glad to seize upon and develop. Happy indeed is the teacher who has a gift for invention. The originators of the Outward Bound experiment certainly had such a gift. What a brilliant idea to teach a course on how to survive in the woods, and then put a teenager on a remote island with only rudimentary supplies to enable her to forage alone for three days! Part of the genius of such invention lies in its refusal to be wordy. The teaching skill lies in the invention of an experience that will do most of the teaching. Extended explanations are unnecessary, although considerable time may be spent afterward in reflecting upon and "unpacking" the experience. It may be a simple role-playing exercise: One student takes the part of a teacher who has been fired. Others assume roles as lawyers or parents in support of her reinstatement or as school board members that will judge her case. Students remember these occasions. They are vivid learning experiences that required them to think on their feet, to put knowledge into action, to exercise a variety of skills in logic, persuasion, and the use of evidence. And the feedback is powerful and immediate.

Thoughtfully planned experiences can also shape character. The anthropologist Thomas Rohlen describes this kind of pedagogical invention in his discussion of training methods used by a Japanese bank that wanted to encourage cooperation among its employees. The trainees spent two weeks at a special facility in a provincial city. They were told the training period would end with a twenty-five-mile endurance walk, and had participated in other climbing and hiking activities in preparation for the event. All were eager to try it when the day arrived:

> The program was simple enough. We were to walk the first nine miles together in a single body. The second nine miles were to be covered with each squad walking as a unit. The last seven miles were to be

walked alone without conversation. All 25 miles were accomplished by going around and around a large public park in the city. Each lap was appoximately one mile, so in total we were to go around the park 25 times. There were a number of rules established by the instructors. We were forbidden to drink water, soda pop, or take any other refreshment. During the second stage each squad was to stay together for the entire nine miles and competition between squads was not encouraged. Finally, we were strictly forbidden from talking with anyone else when walking alone in the last stage. The training staff also walked the 25 miles but they went in the opposite direction, thus passing each of us each lap. Some dozen or so young men from the bank, recent graduates of previous training programs, were stationed along our route and instructed to offer us cold drinks, which we, of course, had to refuse. This was the program, and there was no emphasis at all placed on one person finishing ahead of another. We were told to take as much time as needed as long as we completed the entire 25 miles. We began around 7:30 A.M. and generally finished around 2 P.M. There was no time limit placed on us.[15]

Rohlen reflects at length on the profound lessons embedded in this experience. Time passed quickly in the first nine miles when the participants enjoyed easy fellowship, laughing and talking. Despite the injunction not to compete, once the squads were formed group members put pressure on the slow walkers to speed up and lap other squads. By the end of those nine miles the effect of the pace on the fast walkers, who had become overheated and near prostration in the noonday sun, was obvious. The last seven miles walking silently alone forced all the participants to summon the courage and persistence to keep going despite their thirst and blisters on their feet. They reflected on the loss of group security and the negative effects of bullying slower walkers to increase their pace. Even the least reflective among them had seven miles of silence during which they could not escape their own thoughts. Rohlen was sure that most pondered the same lesson he did: that the real competition takes place within the individual. All were exhausted at the end, but the joy and exhilaration at having persisted and endured was evident the next day.

Teaching by experiencing can also be a disaster. The experiment Rohlen described would certainly be inappropriate for children. We recall witnessing an outing at Johnston College that struck us as macabre and ill-conceived. After the class read poems on death, the professor led the students up a hill in the moonlight to a spot where the students dug a grave. They then took turns lying in it while others shoveled small amounts of dirt upon them. The college, an experimental unit of California's University of Redlands, has since closed.

But we should not end a discussion of invention without mentioning Shirley Brice Heath's experiment in teaching future teachers. Actually her work at Stanford illustrates both the acts of observing and of motivating at several levels. Through television cameras in the classroom, the student-teachers observed a class of sixth-graders in a nearby school. They discussed the general dynamics of the sixth-grade class, and each of them also observed one student in particular over a period of six weeks. Then the college students began visiting the grade school on a regular basis to work with the child they had observed with the aim of preparing that child to be an effective tutor of a poor reader in second grade. The student teachers discussed possible "lesson plans" with the sixth-graders. Then the sixth-graders wrote in their journals what they planned to do in the first tutoring session. The next day each spent half an hour tutoring a second-grader. The sixth-graders then returned to their homerooms to write their reflections on how the tutoring went and what they would do in the next session. The student teachers read the journal entries and helped them think more about what was working well.

This experiment worked on many levels. Second-graders became better readers because they were motivated to perform well in one-on-one sessions with an older student they had come to trust and respect. Sixth-graders were motivated to write as a means of reflecting on and understanding the progress they were making. And what they wrote was not just an assignment for a grade but a means of real communication with someone who could provide them with useful feedback and answers to questions that had arisen in their work as tutors. The university teachers-in-training were motivated by the challenge of coaching and learning how to employ peer-tutoring techniques that would increase their skills as teachers in their own classrooms.

Modeling

Teachers in the classroom can never escape the role. They often teach most vividly what they least suspect they have transmitted. Both intellectually and morally, teachers model good and bad ways of being in the world. There is no morally neutral classroom. Who could ever forget Miss Firenzi, a fourth-grade teacher who punished the boys with what she called the camp-style position. We called it Firenzi's torture. After two warnings for misbehavior, she handed you two hard peas, which you placed on the floor about six inches apart. You then kneeled on these two peas, holding your arms and palms outstretched, while she stacked three or four volumes of the encyclopedia across your wrists and lower arms. If your arms drooped, she rapped your palms with the edge of a ruler while ridiculing your weakness.

Teachers also exhibit their lack of virtue in less gross ways, sometimes by doing nothing, as when they fail to "notice" a student in the hall using a racial slur or muttering that a girl is an "ugly fat bitch." They may be unaware that they call more frequently on boys than girls, or that they fail to challenge an inadequate response from an African-American student that they would not tolerate from others.

Teachers model caring by hearing and responding to the pain of others, and by creating a sense of security in their classrooms so that children will be unafraid to express their hurts—or to express their disagreement with the teacher. Unfortunately, too many of Miss Firenzi's descendants still populate America's classrooms. One survey of American children showed that only a third of them felt their teachers cared for them and less than one in ten would go to a teacher for advice.[16] More distressing, 7 percent of children who were poverty-stricken claimed that no adult really cared for them. But before we condemn the majority of teachers or assume there is some easy way to remedy the lack of caring, we should recall the wisdom of Nell Noddings, who reminds us that "there is no method . . . that will allow teachers to meet 150–200 new students every year and yet establish the atmosphere of caring" children deserve.[17]

One of the best reform ideas of the last two decades has been the effort promoted by Theodore Sizer of the Coalition of Essential Schools to create smaller schools with more coaching and personalized teaching. Sizer should be especially commended for showing how to organize high schools through block scheduling and interdisciplinary teaching so that teachers would have responsibility for only seventy-five or eighty students each day and hence be able to get to know them well—and to do this with only modest increases in cost.

We also have evidence from a small-scale study of mentorship that caring teachers are a critical lifeline for many students. Interviews with adolescents in a poor urban neighborhood revealed that teachers were mentioned often by teenagers as persons to whom they looked for guidance beyond subject-matter instruction. Thus while only a third may say on national surveys that they feel a teacher cares, for that third—millions of children—the teacher can provide a letter that gets them a summer job or be the person they seek when they are feeling deeply depressed.[18]

Schools should be communities of caring and inquiry, and one of the most essential acts of teaching is to exemplify the life of learning—to stand in a line linked to that ancient clerk at Oxford who spent all that he had on books and learning, "and gladly would he learn and gladly teach."[19]

Not to madly teach, with too much frothy enthusiasm, as Mortimer Adler once punned, but to take delight in sharing the fruits of one's own learning, and to be glad to discover one's own mistaken asumptions or inadequately understood data. Students sense not only the mental effort it takes to climb the high plateau on which all good teachers stand, but also the exhilaration of the view and the joy of freshened perspectives on landscapes never seen in this light before. The life of learning can be revealed in small ways as well: Ilustrations of differences in Japanese and American culture can be drawn from a film by Akira Kurosawa that the teacher saw last weekend. Copies of graphs and tables from yesterday's *New York Times* can be introduced that bear on a continuing classroom discussion of income inequality, especially an article that has led the teacher to revise his own views. In one case, three days after a student made a profound comment about Bigger Thomas's sense of guilt, the teacher returned to it, acknowledged the comment's lasting impact on her, how it led her to take Richard Wright's *Native Son* off the shelf yet again, then to ponder comments by other murderers in works by Dostoyevsky, Dreiser, Capote, and Mailer, relating the authors' treatment of motive and remorse to what the student had said, and finally to return to her students a pearl of thought without price yet without too much ado.

What this teacher models is caring for ideas. She is saying to the students: Your ideas and what you are saying about Bigger Thomas matters to me; I am here to learn, too. We are in dialogue, we are cutting through things together and opening them up in ways that can change my beliefs and my understandings as well. It is not only my interests and perspectives that shape our work together. You have minds and interests and questions that are a valid and essential part of the "currriculum of study" in this classroom. Our "curriculum" is not a preset plan imposed from above but a mutual creation of lively minds and feeling hearts. At her best, the teacher embodies a vision of what it means to be alive to the possibilities of growth of mind and feeling in such a way that students will want to actualize their own capacities. The best teachers inspire us because we are falling in love with what we want to become; we are awakening to our own latent capacities. Good schools save us from infatuation, however, because their faculties are diverse and exemplify a rich variety of kinds of growth and ways of being. They honor many talents and gifts and kinds of human creativity—the work of the skilled boatbuilder as much as the verses of the poet who praises him.

Judging and Evaluating

Is there a teacher alive who can honestly say he or she loves digging into that tall stack of exams or papers? Most teachers continue to dread the work, not least because of demands that they confer higher grades. In fact, grades for students have been steadily creeping upward. There are several explanations for the widespread grade inflation that has occurred in the last few decades, especially in American colleges and universities. Increased competition for students and insistence that faculty submit to student evaluation of all their courses led some professors to trade grades for praise (their hell will be to hear the everlasting derisive laughter of students who hold up a three-page paper, snorting, "Can you believe he gave me an A-plus for this?"). Another theory is that faculty feared charges of discrimination as their campuses grew more racially and ethnically diverse so that professors gave nearly everyone at least a B (their hell will be to have brain surgery by a student who should have been flunked). Most plausible, perhaps, is that as workloads and class sizes grew for faculty they skimmed through the hard work of grading and out of guilt over sloppy work, and lacking the evidence they would need to make careful discriminations of quality, pushed most papers toward the high end. Most admirable, however, are the growing numbers of teachers who see all writing as rewriting and give their students an opportunity to earn a better grade through revision. *parents don't agree.*

Formal grading is but one of the aspects of judgment and evaluation. The informal judgment involved in clarifying, coaching, advising, and deciding on an appropriate challenge for this boy or that girl is a constant of classroom life. Sarah Lightfoot captured this kind of assessment when she observed a ballet class of nine students under the eye of a rigorous taskmaster at St. Paul's School. The dance teacher, Mr. Sloan, had demonstrated a new step and was walking around the floor pausing to offer a word of criticism or support to individual students:

> Suddenly he claps and says "No." Music and motion stops. One dancer is singled out. "Maria, get your arms down . . . in the same rhythm open your arms and plié." Maria, a tall, angular Hispanic girl, tries the step again without embarrassment, as everyone turns silently towards her. An hour later, when the dancers are doing complicated, fast-moving combinations across the floor, the teacher singles out Michelle, a pretty, petite Black girl, whose steps have been tentative and constricted. "That's a good start, but take a chance, a risk . . . Go for it, Michelle," he bellows. It is a tough challenge as he makes her do it over and over again. She is awkward, unbalanced, and almost falls several times, but the dance master won't let her stop. As Michelle struggles to master this complicated step in front of her classmates some watch attentively, without laughter or judgment. Others practice on their own around the edges of the floor waiting for their turn. Everyone, including Mr. Sloan, exerts great energy and tries very hard. Imperfections are identified and worked on without embarrassment.[20]

This is the work of the good coach: noting small differences, pinpointing the need for improvement, demonstrating what he means, encouraging, raising the bar enough to be a challenge for each dancer without defeating the student's motivation. We have discussed this passage with many of our own students, and they rarely fail to express their admiration for Mr. Sloan. They long for more teachers like him, teachers who honestly judge them on *this* day's work, and provide carefully orchestrated feedback about how they can do better. Students at the bottom of the class may feel teachers are too likely to give up on them rather than figure out the specific small steps they should work on, as Mr. Sloan did with Michelle. Students at the top believe their reputation often deprives them of tough criticism they need, and carries over into subjects where they know their performance is not worth the A they are routinely given. Good coaching also includes advising some students against a career in dancing, or helping them see that they are more likely to make a creative contribution in history than in physics.

Students in Sloan's class were also learning as they watched him make judgments about their classmates. He made the grounds of his assessment clear. He taught them how to look and evaluate in a way that enabled them to independently become more skilled in making self-judgments. It's the wise grandmother who asks the child, "How do you think your sewing is going?" because she will see from the child's self-assessment how much the girl has learned about sewing even though she may not yet have the skill or muscle coordination to execute what she knows.

Sister Joel Read and her colleagues at Alverno College in Milwaukee saw the lack of development of powers of self-judgment as a lamentable defect of most forms of traditional liberal arts education. They sought to remedy it in two ways: first by expanding the kinds of competence that were evaluated at the college, and second by involving outside assessors and the students themselves in the work of evaluating competence. In the core skills of learning to think critically and communicate effectively, Alverno established six levels of competence that all students must meet.

In their first weeks at Alverno, students are required to stand in front of a camera and give a three-minute talk on any topic of their choosing. To pass this first level of communication skills, the student need not give a good talk but must show that she can recognize her own strengths and weaknesses. We watched from behind a one-way mirror one day as a slightly plump, nervous young woman came to review the videotape of her speech and make her assessment of it. Here is an excerpt from our notes:

> The speech that appeared on the screen was a terrible, almost incoherent performance. It was obviously painful for the student to look at it. In fact, she kept averting her eyes and occasionally slapping her forehead softly in disbelief at the image before her. I scribbled these assessments as I watched: "garbled speech, stumbled, voice too low, poor transition from point to point, exceedingly nervous, lost train of thought, little eye contact, little development of argument, false stops and starts, and ends with a slogan that makes no point."
>
> I also graded the sheet before me, giving her "no" on all six criteria. Joan [the student] began to fill in the rating form as the faculty assessor, a pleasant woman of about forty, sat patiently beside her. She did not hurry the student or express disapproval in any way. After Joan had completed the form, the assessor went over each point. The student

had given herself negative ratings on five of the six categories. The assessor had given her six "no's" as I had. Thus they had agreement on five, so she informed the girl that she had passed. "You don't have to do a smashing job," said the faculty assessor. "You must be able to look at [the tape] and make an objective critique, and you did."[21]

With that reassurance, Joan's teacher then went on to say it was obvious that the girl was frightened, and Joan nodded vigorously in assent. The teacher assured her that that was perfectly natural, that many students are frightened by the television equipment, and that she knew Joan could overcome her fears and learn to give a clear and stimulating speech. She pointed out ways in which Joan had been hesitant, had mumbled, and had not spoken clearly or crisply. She spoke about Joan's lack of voice projection and poor eye contact, although she complimented her on occasional lively facial expressions. She reminded Joan of the need for voice variety, asking her to think of changes of tone and gesture in family dinner table conversation. Then she turned to questions of organization of her talk, pointing out that Joan had never addressed the title question, "Should there be entrance requirements for college?" or taken a position on it. The conversation went on in this way for nearly twenty minutes, with the student gradually taking a more active part in the analysis. At the close, the faculty assessor suggested Joan work on some of her skills in the speech laboratory before attempting the next assessment.

The teaching that went on in this encounter was focused and powerful. It was enabled by careful attention to the criteria of judgment as well as sensitive response and coaching of this student's weaknesses. It was combined with the inventive process of videotaping, which engaged the student and helped her stand outside herself, develop a sense of detachment, and hold a mirror up to her own performance. Such student self-assessment at Alverno is a recurring feature of its program.

In later stages students who have completed certain competence levels often join faculty or outside assessors in judging peers who are attempting to attain those competencies. In one exercise, students take roles as union representatives, businesspeople, civil rights leaders, and politicians who are members of a state Democratic Party committee who must choose a nominee to succeed a United States senator who has just died in office. Sitting around a table, each argues for a different candidate, while faculty assessors, student peers, and external assessors from the Milwaukee community rate the students on their effectiveness in advancing their arguments, responding to others, and coming to a decision. In judging others, and in comparing the reasons that they give for their judgment with those of faculty and outside judges, students are learning to exercise their critical faculties in a profound way. Faculty are also doing fundamental teaching by organizing such encounters and by explaining to students the grounds of their own judgments.

As teachers gain wisdom about the ends of teaching and means of reaching those ends, the grounds of their judgment necessarily change. A recent study of the effects of the Apple Classrooms of Tomorrow experiment, which made the latest computer technology available to every child in a group of schools, showed that many classrooms were transformed as they became more student-centered. Students began to work more independently, to tutor each other, and to collaborate on problem-solving tasks. As students began to demonstrate these new learning outcomes, teachers had to rethink what it was they were evaluating. These new forms of learning could not be easily assessed by the old standardized tests that mostly measured basic recall, simple computation, and factual knowledge. Assessing the understanding of concepts and problem-solving skills is much more difficult, and calls for more imaginative forms of making judgments, such as those the Alverno teachers devised. Teachers' behavior in these schools changed radically as they deemphasized lecturing and began to move around the room coaching students in support of their projects. When traditional supervisors came to evaluate the teachers, they would sometimes stay for awhile and then say they would return on a day when they could observe the teacher "actually teaching."[22]

Most standardized testing in American schools breaks knowledge into small bits and pieces and asks students to pick the right bits in multiple-choice tests. The emphasis is on speed and recall and the application of formulas. We do more of this kind of testing than any nation on earth. Taking these tests seldom teaches anybody anything, although they have a limited value in sorting students on dimensions of intellectual quickness. They are only rarely used for diagnostic purposes. Imagine you have just finished a year of sixty-hour work weeks as a young architect. The head of the firm calls you in and says you received a grade of 587 on a scale where 800 was a perfect score. That's it, 587. You passed. Keep trying. See you next year. No feedback on why a few of your plans were stunning while others seemed poorly conceptualized, or on how effective you were in presentations to clients.

A frontal attack on this kind of assessment has been waged by those who joined the Coalition of Essential Schools organized by Theodore Sizer. Rich forms of assessment should drive the whole curriculum, Sizer believes. Schools in the Coalition are urged to ignore the standard forms of testing and the accrual of credit by hours of seat time spent in math or English classes. Instead, they devise "performances" and "exhibitions." In a downward spread of the Alverno reforms, high schools in the Coalition work at devising assessments that involve producing real products for feedback from real audiences. Students may participate in debates, fill portfolios with plans for a playground, research the history of their neighborhoods, publish a journal reflecting on their experiences as interns in a childcare center, work in teams to understand how the geography of Latin America affected patterns of settlement there, write autobiographies that end with their plans for life after high school. Faculty and students respond to the debates; architects write comments about the playground plans; local historians read the neighborhood histories; the director of the childcare center and teachers raise questions about the intern's journal; the team's work on Latin America is examined by a panel of faculty and students; post-graduation plans are assessed in light of the student's present work and course load.

This account is misleading, of course, because it makes it seem so easy. In fact, the devising of exhibitions and new "exit requirements" for high school has proved to be the most challenging of the nine principles that shape the Coalition's work. In visiting a dozen of these schools in 1988 and again in the mid-1990s, we found that progress was slow. The idea that teachers should first decide what they want their students to know and be able to do upon graduation, and then design courses that help them get there is a bit daunting for most, particularly when it is combined with the principle that all students should learn to use their minds well and that every student should demonstrate mastery in something. Good schools are good at helping students demonstrate what they are good at. The act of assessing ought to drive the skills and knowledge we want our students to develop. Do we want students to be able to synthesize divergent sources of data and craft a well-reasoned argument? Do we expect them to be able to answer questions in a public meeting and work cooperatively in a group? Should they know their rights as citizens and where the levers of political change are to be found in their own towns and cities? Then teach and assess in ways that expect demonstration of those capacities.

It is not easy to reach agreement on such matters, and most high school faculties have never had a serious and sustained dialogue about them. Nor, having reached agreements on desired outcomes, have they had the experience of comparing their judgments of student work in an open forum. Not many English departments have asked all faculty to separately grade the same half-dozen essays and then meet to discuss the results and reasons for the variation in grading. The divergence can be startling. Assessment, one of the most critical acts of teaching, has usually been done in private.

That kind of public "tuning" of assessment standards has become fairly common in Coalition schools. Teaching is also frequently combined with assessing, as when faculty comment on an exhibition of a student's work, whether that is an architectural model the student has constructed or a poem she has written. New forms of examination developed in Great Britain now encourage teachers to prompt students who are grasping for an answer, and if they still fail to come up with it, to stop and teach the appropriate skill then and there. Here's an excerpt from a teacher's manual for administration to fifteen-year-olds of an oral mathematics test on the ideas of perimeter, area, and circumference:

1. Ask the student: "What is the perimeter of a rectangle?" [Teacher writes student answer.]
2. Present sheet with rectangle ABCD. Ask: "Could you show me the perimeter of this rectangle?" [If necessary, teach.]
3. Ask, "How would you measure the perimeter of the rectangle?" [If necessary, prompt for full procedure. If necessary, teach.]

. . .

10. "Estimate the length of the circumference of this circle."
11. "What would you do to check your estimate?" [String is on the table. If no response, prompt for string.]

. . .

13. "Is there any other method?" [If student does not suggest using $C = pd$, prompt with, "Would it help to measure the diameter of the circle?"] [23]

The student's final score is calibrated on a scale divided into two categories, "unaided success" and "aided success," and further delineated according to the level of the student's performance within each category. But the point is that whatever the score, the student has also had an opportunity to learn from the assessment itself.

Reflecting and Renewing

Two of the most common criticisms of teachers are that they don't know their subject and that they know the "stuff," but they don't know how to teach it. Critics on the right dwell on the first point, shaking their fingers at the "educationists" who overprepare student teachers in methods courses of presumed low value at the expense of rigorous courses in the basic subject matter of the disciplines. Critics on the left have bemoaned forms of teaching that view children as little experts-in-the-making to be stuffed with prescribed subject matter regardless of their true interests.

The first criticism had less merit where the preparation of high school teachers was concerned. Since the end of World War II, most colleges and universities have required that future secondary school teachers have a major in the relevant discipline. Education courses counted for a quarter or less of their degree program. Of course, in times of teacher shortages or budget cutbacks, these requirements did not stop school boards in many districts from assigning football coaches to teach math classes.

Until recent decades, elementary school teachers commonly took half or more of their college credits in education departments. That is no longer true. In many states, a master's degree is now required for permanent certification even for grade school teaching. In New York and some other states, the master's degree must be in education or a discipline thought useful to elementary school teaching—history, English, or mathematics, for example. The education courses at the undergraduate level may constitute only a third of the certification program. Serious discussion is likely to focus on which mix of the basic disciplines is the best preparation for an elementary school career—how much history, child psychology, literature, sociology, science, or mathematics—as well as on the form of professional preparation in pedagogy.

A good teacher-preparation program—and there are many of them—begins a process of lifelong reflection on the arts of teaching. One of the most aggressive educational reform efforts in America today is aimed at the improvement of college and university teaching, because the old guard in colleges of arts and sciences has been forced to admit that knowing the subject is not enough. Although some of these professors were creative enough to figure out how to do something more than endless lecturing, the rank and file of tenured faculty often taught as they were taught in college classrooms—and they have stacks of lecture notes to prove it. Those professors who figured it out might have been fortunate enough as university students to have enjoyed good models of effective pedagogy. But certainly they spent many hours in the essential act of reflecting on the aims and methods of teaching, of ways to renew their own understanding of their subject and how to make it accessible and useful to their students. Those professors learned that good teaching enables a student to see the world differently (and perhaps act differently) because the student has come to share the meaning of knowledge that she never thought would touch her, was too difficult and beyond her reach, even repugnant.[24]

How do teachers create that shared understanding? Is it simply a matter of telling students what the teacher knows? Let us lay aside for the moment the complex question of how a teacher defines his or her subject. Recall the "exhibitions" discussed above and the kind of interdisciplinary teaching that would be required to prepare students to demonstrate their competence in those tasks. Let us take the clearer example of a university professor deeply knowledgeable about her discipline of sociology. She has read deeply in the primary works of theory and methods of sociology, is widely acquainted with the research published in sociology, has done significant research herself, and keeps up with new discoveries and controversies in the field. Sociology has a magisterial structure in her mind. She believes students at her university are impoverished if they graduate without the ability to see the frameworks of society through the eyes of Karl Marx, Emile Durkheim, Max Weber, Ruth Benedict, or Erving Goffmann, if they do not understand how we unwittingly perpetuate social structures that reproduce forms of sexism and ethnic hatred, or perceive the way social roles shape people's behavior.

Her understanding of her subject matter, then, gained over a lifetime of study and experience, was more than adequate. But her first years in the front of a classroom were anything but satisfying. She was at first puzzled, then depressed, and on some days was seized with terror as she entered the classroom. Reluctantly, for she was offered no aid, she sought help from a sympathetic colleague who had won awards for teaching excellence. Her understanding of how to teach, how to make sociology effective knowledge in the hands of her students, took years of reflection and learning from trial and error. Because she wanted to be a good teacher, she worked as hard at gaining pedagogical knowledge as she once had worked at gaining knowledge of her subject.

She would not have called it that, and like most traditionally trained Ph.Ds might even once have scoffed at the idea that "pedagogical knowledge" was worth serious pursuit. What is it, then, that she learned? Or is pedagogical knowledge just a lot of piffle?

First, she had to unlearn bad ways of teaching she had unconsciously adopted. She came to see that much of what she was doing was cramming, oppressively stuffing students with texts—an overload of information, facts, and concepts that the best students could sort out and adapt for their own interests but that most encountered as a confusing mess. She learned that good teaching involves helping students crack the code of her discipline and integrate it with other knowledge so that they can put it to their own uses. This required her to rethink the structure of sociological knowledge for the particular students she was teaching. Her job was to creatively reframe the insights of sociology into focal questions and concepts that they would perceive as relevant. She thought hard about how to make these concepts come alive in the minds of students, to pose problems to which they would have to apply these concepts, to work these into larger themes and connections and more sophisticated applications. She devised ways to get them to test their understandings of concepts against contrary views and to develop their own perspectives. She discovered how to empower them to use the methods of sociological analysis to find out useful things on their own. She had to learn how to organize students in cooperative teams, to employ a wider repertoire of teaching skills as coach and mentor, assessor and guide. She did not totally abandon lecturing, but saw lectures less as ways of parceling out information and more as small dramas in which a curtain is raised on an intriguing scene. The students are drawn into that scene, introduced to a few key characters who may be in conflict or a state of doubt. At the end of the lecture hour the conflict may not be resolved but the students will depart stimulated to write their own end to the scene, perhaps, or to try to connect what they have heard to the larger themes of what they are studying.

She could now look back with a smile at a course she taught when she was first appointed to the faculty. The department had been asked to develop the course at the request of the college of education, and none of the men wanted to take it on. She had been one of the first women appointed in sociology, and she had done some research on the role schooling played in social stratification. In planning the course, she had picked from her mental catalog of sociology all the works and research she thought would have a bearing on education and arranged them into a reading list that could be covered in a semester. She worked hard to explain, summarize, and give pertinent examples in lecture after lecture. Most students sat dutifully taking notes—it was a required course for them—and then regurgitated what they remembered on the midterm and final exams.

The course she now taught bore little relation to its precursor. The reading list was cut by two-thirds, and not all of that was by sociologists. She now taught the entire course as an inquiry into the nature of the teacher's intellectual and moral authority. She found that although sociologists had laid claim to the concept of authority, philosophers had written more tellingly about the nature of moral authority. She also found it necessary to read more widely in history to understand the origins of the exercise of professional authority in education and how that had changed over time in the United States as the nation urbanized and educational systems were centralized. The students were awakened on the first day to the realization that they had never thought very seriously about the grounds of their authority as intellectual and moral agents who would have responsibility for shaping the lives of children. The course unfolded as a series of questions about how they understood their own authority, how it had been shaped historically by the development of bureaucratic and legal systems, and how they would exercise their authority in various realms. They had to figure out when teaching veered toward indoctrinating, what was the difference between educating and merely socializing, and what constituted abuses of their authority. They were plunged into a series of controversies that they had to take positions on, and then they had to argue for their opinions in small group discussions. They took part in a mock trial of a teacher who had been fired by her school board for assigning a novel that sympathetically portrayed a lesbian relationship. They were organized in teams to develop a model curriculum for multicultural education and then present their report to a mock school board whose members were known to be divided on the issues of multicultural education. As part of their preparation for that task, they were required to interview students of different ethnic backgrounds on their own campus about their former school experiences and incorporate that research in their report to the school board.

Developing and refining this course was the work of applying pedagogical knowledge. It represents the continuing reflection and renewal of what works with this student or that seminar to make the subject come alive and have meaning for the student. This kind of reflection is perhaps the most essential act of teaching.

The examples we have drawn on here have mostly portrayed teachers working alone. In later chapters, especially Chapters 6–8, we will give more emphasis to teachers working collaboratively, observing each other teach, working in teams and reflecting together on the practice of teaching. The work of mentoring, curriculum planning, and peer review are at the heart of the latest phase of what we have called the slow revolution. No committee of administrative experts, no curriculum guide can do these things for teachers, although guides may be useful and experts may help. Teachers themselves are the true guardians of what we have called the essential acts of teaching. These are modeling a good life, knowing our students, engaging them in learning, assessing their moral and intellectual growth, and reflecting on the arts of teaching that enable that growth. These are the essential things that teachers and those who educate them should be most concerned about, and that the profession of teaching should most zealously protect and nurture.

4

Three Questions Every Teacher Must Answer

Every teacher must answer three fundamental questions. Some teachers may not be conscious of the questions or even aware that they have given an answer because it is written in the texts of their lives. Each question concerns a fundamental relationship that a teacher constructs and re-configures throughout his or her life. The first of these concerns the form of the relationship with the child: What balance do I strike between expertise and nurturance? The second concerns the teacher's relation-ships with colleagues and parents in the school community: What is my responsibility for shaping the ethos of the school? The answer to the third question determines the teacher's relationship with the society: Am I primarily a transmitter or a transformer of my society's values?

Together, the answers given tell us how a teacher understands and exercises her intellectual and moral authority. Some teachers will exer-cise their authority in ways that will justify descriptions of them as authoritarian, others in ways that could be called feckless. But most will fall in between those extremes. A variety of good patterns are possible and desirable. Each teacher elaborates a pattern in a quilt of action that is stitched together over a lifetime, although most teachers come to moments of insight that lead to major rearrangements of patterns or even to discarding the old ones altogether in a bold change of style.

Answers to the questions about the teacher's relationship to the wider school community and the society take shape more slowly, but the teacher cannot avoid giving some answer to the first question from the moment she sets foot in a classroom. The folklore of teaching furnishes her with prepared scripts such as "Don't smile until Christmas," or "Whatever you do, don't lose control." The folklore emphasizes the image of command, not nurture: Keep them busy. Better to be an ogre than to risk mockery.

Although no teaching can go on in pandemonium, and the establishment of good order is of undeniable importance, every teacher at every level must work out a comfortable balance between presenting herself as expert or as someone who cares and nurtures. And we emphasize that it is a problem of balance, that a teacher can be a caring expert, but most teachers struggle to achieve that balance and often do a complete turnabout before they find their comfort zone. Is my subject matter, the curriculum, my discipline of foremost importance? Or should I see myself first as nurturer, counselor, therapist, one who cares for souls? Can I teach only after I have established trust and a loving relationship, or does the love and respect flow from the teaching of difficult and important material that may not be learned without some pain or threat of punishment?

Not only is the balance between these poles likely to shift over the course of a teacher's career, but a novice teacher's view of what constitutes subject matter may undergo a major transformation. Suppose a political science major begins teaching high school social studies with the conviction that history is the study of dull factual information. He turns his social studies classes into political science courses where students mostly debate contemporary issues. But the aridity of these debates gradually convinces him of the need to immerse his students deeply in the history. He begins to take a few graduate courses and becomes a passionate student of history. Where he was once content to have his students study current political debates about how to achieve racial integration in the school, he now immerses them in slave narratives, the contrast between Thomas Jefferson's early and late writings about slavery, the slow and tortured steps Lincoln took toward emancipation, and accounts of John F. Kennedy's appeasement of segregationist committee chairmen on Capitol Hill. His beliefs about the core of his subject matter underwent major change.[1]

Nel Noddings, a philosopher of education at Stanford, has caused even experienced teachers with settled styles to rethink their beliefs about caring. She has become one of the most persuasive voices for restoring nurture to a place of primacy in teaching. She wants to recenter discussion on "the quality of relationships needed for the healthy intellectual, moral and emotional development of children." Noddings reminds us how vital these relationships of caring are—how often we find that those who evoke our admiration for having overcome great obstacles and deprivations had in childhood an adult or teacher "who cared enough to spend time with a child, express his or her beliefs in the child's capacities, and provide the emotional support necessary to maintain the child's growth and confidence."[2] Vivian Paley, whose work we discussed in Chapter 3, believes that teaching students the ins and outs of social relationships is just as important as teaching them the ins and outs of spelling and phonics. And Martin Buber made caring relationship the very heart of education—"Children need to know that someone will listen to them and care what happens to them."[3] Noddings goes on to argue that some children are not blessed with parents who can give emotional support or provide models of what it means to be educated. Hence the caring role of teachers is critical to their development. In order for students to see that education is valuable and can change their lives, teachers and their children should stay together, with mutual consent, for several years: "Time should be spent on the development of trust so that the advice, care, and instruction given by the teacher will be received by students with understanding and appreciation."[4]

Looping

Noddings's answer to the long-debated question "Do we put more emphasis on teaching the curriculum or on teaching the child?" places her clearly on the side of Rousseau and John Dewey. She objects to the programs advanced by Mortimer Adler and E. D. Hirsch to teach the same curriculum to all children.[5] We might place more emphasis on the value of transmission of a common curriculum than Noddings, but she makes a good point when she asks us to suppose that we are the parents of a large and heterogeneous family. One child is highly academic and finds the usual academic fare fascinating. That child would thrive in Adler's school. But her sister is very artistic, another sibling very mechanical, a third gifted with extraordinary athletic ability, a brother blessed with exceptional "people" talents. Should all have the same education? With Dewey, Noddings believes that the teacher should care primarily about the children's individual motivations and allow them to pursue topics and subjects that genuinely interest them: "A plan under which all children must study exactly the same subjects regardless of interest seems unquestionably to favor those who are either interested intrinsically or whose families make extrinsic interests so important that they override the natural interests of children."[6]

Experientalist

Georgia Heard remembers a moment when she reconceived what it meant to be a poet. In a tutorial with a teacher she admired, the appreciation and criticism of her poems was subtle and insightful. But the advice that lodged in her heart was his answer to her question about the goals she should set for herself as a poet: "He said, 'You must first create the kind of person who will write the poems you want to write' . . . He had helped give some insights into my own poems, but more important he had given me a sense of hope, of belonging, of reassurance that I was headed in the right direction, that what I've been trying to be and to write is all part of what a poet does." She never forgot this lesson in her own teaching. She saw more clearly that her own students needed the kind of nurture her mentor had given to her. Georgia Heard saw her job as connecting with the student, which requires deep listening and deep caring, to "find out what guided the writing of the poem . . . what is underneath . . . What does the rest of the poem look like? . . . What's not written?"[7]

Or consider Ms. Payton, who is a no-frills teacher who has been teaching science to seventh-graders for fifteen years. She has rules about the proper way to sit and correct paper disposal but also drives sixty miles to spend several hours scouting an amusement park for activities that would provide lessons in physics during a class field trip. She is dedicated to teaching science, but she believes teachers have a higher obligation to serve children than merely to purvey a fixed curriculum: "I think it's morally wrong to demand of someone that which they cannot accomplish. It is wrong to frustrate a student. It is wrong to put them down. It is wrong for them never to find success in your classroom all year long. I think that's morally wrong. Therefore I will change my curriculum, and keep changing my curriculum so that some of my students will find success . . . What's right for one kid may not be right for another kid. Besides the academics, I'm dealing with a real human being." In the essay "Skills and Other Dilemmas of a Progressive Black Educator," Lisa Delpit writes movingly about the way she came to see the need to change her child-centered style to place more emphasis on skills and traditional teaching if children in her classroom, many of them from deprived homes, were going to be successful. They needed a foundation in phonics and other basic skills that children from more privileged homes had learned in nursery schools or other settings.[8]

As we said in Chapter 3, these questions are essential questions for teachers at all levels. Jane Tompkins, a professor of English at Duke

University, was approaching fifty when she realized that her teaching was unbalanced. She had been a high achiever at Bryn Mawr and loved the intellectual intensity of that college, whose unofficial motto was "Only our failures marry." When she began to teach she read Dante in the original, and Virgil and Ariosto and Tasso, and German and French and Old English. "But my first published article, on Henry James's 'The Beast in the Jungle,' a story about a man whose ignorance of himself catches up with him in the end, set off an alarm." Years later she knew that the alarm was telling her that she was a terrified performer who had failed to recognize her need to connect with her students. She came to believe that education must be holistic, that students "must learn how to be with other people, how to love, how to take criticism, how to grieve, how to have fun, as well as how to add and subtract, multiply and divide." In her wonderful memoir, *A Life in School*, she recounts her struggle to make teaching a less fearful activity and the university a less intimidating place. She saw that many of her middle-aged colleagues were depressed because they were afraid to try something new. She initiated radical experimentation in her teaching "during which I lost the investment I once had in making sure students knew what I knew and what I thought, and [that] eventually passes into existential territory where all the moorings come loose."[9] Of course that kind of letting go of stored-up knowledge may not work in the same way for six-year-olds.

But Celia Oyler provides a fascinating account of a first-grade teacher's move into that existential territory when she begins to share authority with her students. It begins with small moves—letting a child decide in which order classmates line up for lunch—and then expands to choosing which books to read or classroom activities to engage in. It causes some "bumps" in the teacher's relations with her colleagues, who see the children's growing assertiveness as disruptive and encroaching on the teacher's expertise. But the teacher sees that the children's choice of authentic interests empowers them and develops genuine expertise of their own, as when they advise each other about books they would enjoy. As the classroom revolution continues, a child who has come to enjoy school asks the teacher at the end of the afternoon: "How come we haven't done any work today?" A Hispanic mother who had dreaded attending the same Chicago school as a child, said she was happy for her son Ricky. "The biggest difference I see between Ricky's education this year and mine when I went to school here is that he gets to learn about real things. When he comes home every day I ask him what he learned in school, and it's always about real things like plants and animals. When I was in school, we never read about real things, just like Dick and Jane. He talks about real ideas."[10]

We asked a teacher of high school English to reflect on the questions discussed in this chapter. Lorraine Bédy, a ninth-grade teacher, was eloquent on the struggle to achieve a balance between discipline and nurture: "I had already started to think about this myself and how things have changed for me, in this regard, over the course of my career. I believe that now I recognize that, by nature, I am a nurturer. It is very difficult for me in any capacity to be other than that—whether as friend, teacher, wife, mother, daughter. I believe that I have come to understand that for me, the nurturer is a tone I set, an attitude I project, a posture I develop, a voice tone I cultivate." Yet she is clear that she is not primarily a counselor, parent, or friend to her students. "I am first and foremost their teacher and I believe I would be doing them a grave injustice by shortchanging them in that role." Not much is easy in the life of a ninth-grader, whose parents may be divorcing or whose friend may be contemplating suicide. But she must fulfill her promise to teach her students well. However,

> I do believe that my preference for teaching writing as opposed to literature stems from the opportunity writing gives me to stay in touch with my students through their work, rather than through someone else's text, regardless of how provocative that text may be. This happens through both my commentary on their papers and the conferences we have—the many brief ones and occasional (rarely) longer ones. I don't bend much when it comes to writing. I don't see myself as easy, kindly, or generous. I believe that students are often afraid to try clearly expressing their ideas because it is time consuming, and it leaves them vulnerable to ideas and contradictions they need to work through.

Early in her career, when she was a radical teacher who often treated her students as equals, she listened at length to their stories and troubles. Her students thought she was "cool" and told her she was the first teacher they had had who truly listened. She sacrificed more of the curriculum than she is willing to do now: "I spent a lot of time working on and thinking about those problems that were beyond me to solve, taking energy from those that were within my power—the development of strengths within my curriculum and the development of attitudes toward learning that would help my students grow and prosper." Too much sympathy conveys the wrong message—that the business at hand is not really important and can be repeatedly set aside.

> It is the way I go about this business of teaching that is most important. Do I leave space either for conversation or journal writing that indicates that I acknowledge that we are all people with troubles and joys? Do I share some of my own frustrations of life outside of school? Do I hold them when they cry? Do I drop a note unobtrusively on the desk of a student who seems out of sorts? Yes, to all of these and more. I cannot stop being the person in order to be the teacher. But I cannot forget that my most important role is to teach my curriculum.[11]

Lorraine Bédy's questions are every teacher's questions. A teacher can never put them totally out of her mind in the classroom. But there is another kind of nurture and listening that goes on beyond the classroom door. Some teachers avoid it or pay it little heed. And that is the kind of listening that is part of a continuing dialogue with colleagues and parents. A teacher's willingness to engage in that dialogue is derived from the responsibility she feels for shaping the broader life of the school or college. Will I mentor novice teachers? Will I work with colleagues in chemistry and biology to develop a new approach to teaching science by posing fundamental questions about the degradation of the environment? Do I think it's a waste of my time to join a committee of parents and teachers who are concerned about the moral climate of the school?

All of these concerns are part of the second question every teacher must answer: What is my responsibility for shaping the ethos of the school, for developing the special intellectual and moral character of this community?

Teachers in primary and secondary schools have traditionally resisted activities that drew them away from the classroom. They defined the core of their work as exchange with students within the classroom. Although defeats by students might mar the day, there they felt most empowered. Parents, principals, and even other teachers who crossed the classroom threshold were seen as intruders who interrupted the flow and reduced the rewards teachers valued most. Dan Lortie's surveys of teachers a generation ago captured those sentiments well. He found teachers deprecated transactions across the classroom boundary. Walls were perceived as beneficial; they kept the intruders out. Teachers described a good day as "a day when you really have the children to yourself. At the end of the day you feel you've taught them something."[12]

Lortie's surveys, completed in the 1960s, accurately described the attitudes of recently unionized teachers who had won better pay and more job security but still felt that they worked at the bottom of the decision-making hierarchy. They wanted more voice and "more elbow room to practice their craft," Lortie wrote. But "they hold back from asking for full autonomy and official independence . . . These respondents do not suggest that teacher independence be formalized or that they be granted official discretion over resources. They do not challenge the basic order."[13] Hence they more zealously guarded the limited discretion they had behind the closed classroom door because they felt they had little power to countermand the wishes of most intruders. In recent decades teachers have challenged the basic order, and it has begun to crumble. Although the traditional attitudes persist (and partly with good reason, for teachers need to exercise reasonable control over the context of their work), teachers now are more willing to open the door to colleagues and parents with whom they share power over basic educational decisions. These people are no longer defined as intruders but as persons with whom they make decisions that influence the distribution of resources.

Lortie's 1960s surveys found that only a quarter of all teachers reported they had much contact with colleagues. Most teachers worked in isolation in their own classrooms, and nearly half reported virtually no contact in planning classes or jointly reviewing student work. Our research in nine schools found that in 1997 slightly more than half of the teachers had sustained contact with colleagues in planning, mentoring, and jointly managing schools. Although the degree of involvement varied greatly from school to school, this represents a major change in one generation.

As we discuss in more detail in Chapters 7 and 8, however, the walls have come down slowly, and sometimes go back up when teachers are frustrated by the petty pace and uncertain outcomes of the decision-making process. Even when they are discouraged about the costs in time and effort, however, few teachers would willingly return to the status quo ante.

Yet pushing the classroom door open is not easy. Exposing one's practice to inspection by colleagues has its risks. The young teacher may yearn for mentoring but fear that it will bring judgments of incompetence. She is rightly concerned about how mentors are chosen, and whether the exercise of more corporate responsibilities by senior colleagues will impose narrow definitions of teaching. More seasoned teachers who aspire to mentoring or curriculum-development roles desire genuine dialogue about the questions of teaching and learning but also fear exposing their ignorance. Real colleagueship involves learning together, interrogating each other about questions of practice, comparing approaches and results, visiting each other's classrooms, engaging in mutual criticism, and taking responsibility for getting better results. It opens the teacher to the pains of disagreements about aims. Do I really believe in inclusive classrooms, or do I think some disabled children are better off in separate educational settings? How do I team-teach a new course in history and literature with a colleague who is less committed than I am to student peer tutoring methods?[14]

Negotiating new norms with one's colleagues can produce strain, particularly as teachers take on more responsibility for the moral climate of the school as a whole. We sat in on a meeting of teachers at Hamilton High in upstate New York when they first began to work together in the 1980s on a school improvement team. The principal complained of the difficulty of managing a school where "I don't really know what I'm managing because we don't have any philosophy of what we're doing as a school." Teachers sat silently. He pressed them, noting that they couldn't even agree to enforce a simple policy about classroom tardiness. Teachers should be out in the hall, making sure students move along. Moreover, if teachers were in the hall between bells, "Bad things wouldn't happen." Some teachers confessed that they had slipped up, and agreed that they should support the policy. But others did not. One said that she didn't think that was her job. Teaching was her job; taking care of hall traffic was a job for corridor aides. Another said she saw the principal's point, but felt that standing out in the hall and screaming at kids to get them in the classroom was destructive of the kind of personal relationship she wanted to have with students inside the classroom. A teacher who had earlier expressed concern about the increase in "legitimate" reasons students could be excused from class (to have their senior photos taken or get on the team bus) asked whether anyone could believe it was important to get students in their seats on time if they could be excused two minutes later for such nonacademic functions. Over the course of several meetings this seemingly minor disciplinary issue opened a discussion that involved admitting and hearing the real differences between teachers. It was more time-consuming than letting the principal decide, but it concerned vital matters: Could corridor aides really substitute for faculty authority in essential matters? Should teachers put up more resistance to the erosion of class time by extracurricular activities?[15]

This is a small illustration of the way that teachers' empowerment reduces administrative discretion but may, with enlightened leadership by the principal, produce higher morale and better outcomes. At Hamilton and many schools, parents now sit with teachers on school-based management teams, and teachers interview job applicants and have a say in choosing who will become mentor teachers. Few such teams are as empowered as the school councils in Chicago, which have control over a significant share of the budget and the power to hire and fire principals. But most grapple with significant issues and policies. They put teachers in a more direct partnership with parents, who formerly interacted with teachers primarily in discussions about their child. That remains the primary focus for most parents, and it has its inevitable tensions, especially when the teacher makes negative judgments about a child's behavior or level of achievement, but alliances formed around schoolwide issues can help to restructure teacher-parent relationships.

Although "local control" of schools has always been emphasized in the United States, it is a misleading description of school governance. It does not mean that decisions are made at the school level. On the contrary, a study of the level of educational decision-making in fourteen countries showed that only Switzerland ranked lower than the United States in the degree of school autonomy. Most decisions, more than 70 percent, are made at the district or state level in the United States. Only 26 percent of the decisions concerning educational planning, personnel, organization of instruction, or use of resources are made primarily by the teachers, principal, and parents of a particular school. This compares with three-fourths of such decisions being made at the school level in Ireland and New Zealand, and about half of them at the school level in Sweden and Austria. Even France, thought to be one of the most centralized school systems in the world, allows its high schools to make 35 percent of the decisions. In the United States as abroad, private schools register the highest degree of school-level decision-making. In fact, private schools in the United States are the most autonomous in the world, with 95 percent of decisions made by teachers, principals, and parents. Clearly, one of the things private school parents are paying for is the right to chart their own course.[16]

Public school parents want more school autonomy. Polls show the United States ranked first among twelve countries surveyed when it came to the question of public support for freeing the school from the overlay of bureaucratic decision-making. Three out of five people in the United States thought it was "very important for decisions to be made by the schools themselves." Surprisingly, in light of some reports indicating rising concern about the role of public schools in moral education, only 34 percent of those polled in the United States felt that the home should have more responsibility than the school for "personal and social development." Two-thirds thought responsibility should be equally shared, but only 3 percent would give more responsibility to the school than to the home.[17]

Thus strong support exists among both parents and teachers for more school-level autonomy in the United States. That consensus is strongest on the issues of the school's exercising more responsibility for improving discipline, teaching the importance of honesty, and raising school achievement in the basic subjects. But it also extends to giving the local school more authority over the selection and promotion of teachers and more input into how the school budget is spent and how subjects are taught. Support for the slow revolution remains weak, however, because no single issue has captured the imagination of the public in a way that mobilizes forces for increased school-level autonomy. With the exception of the school councils in Chicago, most of the new school-based governance bodies are advisory and do not represent significant change in the formal powers of resource allocation or hiring of teachers and principals.

From the point of view of the teacher who is trying to decide how much effort to invest in schoolwide issues, rewards are uncertain. The classroom turf is hers; she can move the furniture at a moment's notice, whereas hours may be spent on a schoolwide committee talking about rearranging the pattern of seating in the cafeteria with no outcome. Yet our research found that major transformations of school climate were achieved when both teachers and parents felt they were empowered.

For teachers and parents alike, the most perilous area is dealing with moral issues that divide parents. In a 1994 poll by The Public Agenda, 95 percent of Americans said that schools should teach "respect for others regardless of their racial or ethnic background." When asked what teachers should do if they observe students on a playground teasing another about his race, 93 percent said that the teachers should break up the situation and explain why the behavior is wrong. Support dropped to 72 percent when the child was being teased because his parent was a homosexual. Just 61 percent believed it was "very appropriate" to teach "respect for people who are homosexual"; and the figure dropped to 32 percent when the public was asked whether high school classes should discuss "whether homosexuality is an acceptable lifestyle." Some Gallup polls have shown slight majorities approving abortion and the nature of sexual intercourse as topics for instruction at the high school level, but The Public Agenda poll found only 42 percent approving discussion of the "morality of abortion" and 32 percent allowing use of sexual-education textbooks with "detailed photographs of nude men and women showing their sexual organs."[18]

These divisions confront teachers with questions of conscience and with decisions about whether they wish to push for change or accept the status quo. As we put it earlier, "Do I only transmit or do I also attempt to transform the dominant values of my society?" The third question asks every teacher whether her role is simply to transmit culture, preserving and conserving the settled forms and beliefs of the community. Or does the teacher challenge and reshape the child's outlook about the received wisdom of his or her society? "Dare the school build a new social order?" George Counts asked teachers in the midst of the Great Depression.[19]

Lorraine Bédy has always encouraged her ninth-grade students to examine unpopular ideas, but since becoming a parent herself she has become more conscious of the fact that "my students are someone else's children." She now approaches her students with more awareness that their parents are looking over her shoulder, wanting their children to learn and grow into their images of healthy adults. She feels the pull from parents to be a transmitter and an inner push to be a transformer and critic. She keeps parents in mind when she selects videos or books. She has always shown Franco Zeffirelli's *Romeo and Juliet* without censoring the brief nude scene. "Now I find myself wondering, 'Does this scene make some of my students uncomfortable?' . . . I have still not censored the scene, but I do wonder about it from a much different perspective than before."

She is confident and knowledgeable about a wide range of texts. "This leaves me the opportunity to push and pull within my curriculum, to be alert for those questions and situations in which the strengths and limitations of our society are brought out for inspection." She emphasizes that the idea of "inspection" is important: "I am careful to say, 'As I see it . . . or Some believe . . . or How might someone else think about this?'" As the months go by, her students expect to be challenged if they have no opinion on important questions, and they learn it is not acceptable to make condemnations without reasons. "When my students throw out the word 'gay' as a slam, I ask them why. I try to make them struggle to answer with their words," not indoctrinate them with my way of thinking about homosexuality. "They need to hear what they have to say before they hear what I have to say. I especially hold back on those ideas which I believe come from experiences I know my student cannot have had." However, she does expect students to make imaginative leaps: "We write about the heroism of Odysseus and his approach toward those things which are strange to him. We contrast this to our lives . . . We look to see if Creon is played out in those public figures who control our lives today, and wonder if Antigone could not have made a better point in another way."[20]

Lorraine Bédy's own political views have evolved radically since her girlhood in a Catholic school. She is still struggling with the question Mary Mercer Krogness posed. If Socrates were to reappear, Krogness wrote, he would ask every teacher in America: "How firmly are you committed to finding fresh and inventive ways of making school a viable, stimulating, and safe place where all young people can feel free to learn—no matter what the risks to you personally?"[21] One of Bedy's colleagues, Karen Stearns, took risks that cost her her job for supporting her students in their investigations of homosexuality and racial bias in housing in their own working-class community. Stearns had started out teaching the "canonical literature" and had gradually come to understand teaching as a mentoring act. "I mean that I was interested in the power of the curriculum to transform students' lives—their college choices, their career plans, and their personal connections with living a literate life." She began to search for "those books that are life-transforming." She grew sympathetic to Michel Foucault's criticism of schools as part of the "regime of truth" and agreed with Henry

Giroux that teachers should be transformative intellectuals.[22] She became a "transformer and a critic with what for my time and place was
a 'revolutionary' project . . . to engage students in questioning the value
of their own educations in ways that threatened the status quo."[23]

Stearns might still be teaching if she had worked for Deborah Meier,
who transformed several public schools in Harlem. Meier aimed to
break the pattern of silencing that many schools impose. Why were the
self-confident voices she knew so well at home and on the playground
muted in the schools she taught in? Meier wondered: "I knew that
human beings are by nature generators of ideas, what I didn't understand was how it was that some children recognized the power of their
ideas while others became alienated from their own genius. How did
schools, in small and unconscious ways, silence these persistent playground intellectuals?" In reinventing first several elementary schools,
and then a public high school in Harlem, she wanted to know if schools,
organized differently, could "keep this nascent power alive, extend it,
and thus make a difference in what we grow up to be? The constraints
that poverty and racism impose on the lives of children might be real,
but could schools loosen rather than tighten them?" Her experience
with the New York City school bureaucracy had taught her change
would not be easy: "The task of creating environments where all kids
can experience the power of their ideas requires unsettling not only our
accepted organization of schooling and our unspoken and unacknowledged agreement about the purposes of schools. Taking this task seriously also means calling into question our definitions of intelligence and
the ways in which we judge each other." With the encouragement of
an innovative Harlem district superintendent, Meier went on to break
the mold into which schooling for the poor had been cast. As principal
for twenty years of the Central Park East Secondary School in East
Harlem, she saw 90 percent of her students graduate in a city where the
average high school graduation rate is 50 percent. And nine out of ten
of those graduates went on to college. They had experienced the power
of their ideas.[24]

Meier is a politically engaged educator who writes for the magazine
Dissent. She stands in the liberal reformist tradition of the philosopher
John Dewey, who parted with his Columbia colleague George Counts
over the issue of how transformist teachers should be. Counts, in *Dare
the School Build a New Social Order?* wanted teachers to dare, to become
active agents for political change.[25] This was too much for Dewey, who

felt that teachers should raise the critical consciousness of students but not present platforms of change, which would inevitably turn the schools into agents of indoctrination. These issues were widely debated in the 1930s and again in the cultural revolutions of the 1960s. However, like the nation as a whole, American teachers are not highly ideological. Gerald Grace wrote *Teachers, Ideology, and Control* about education in Great Britain, where teachers identify themselves much more specifically on the left-to-right political spectrum than would be the case in America, where the major parties are much more centrist. Nearly 10 percent of Grace's sample of "outstanding teachers" identified themselves as radicals or Marxists; in America it would be surprising if more than 1 percent so identified themselves. Surveys show that most teachers in the United States fall within the moderate liberal to conservative range of the political spectrum; 61 percent identify themselves as "conservative or tend to be conservative," 31 percent as leaning toward liberal, and 8 percent as liberal; 76 percent claim membership in a church, synagogue, or other religious group.[26]

More teachers in training are encountering a wider range of writers on the left today, however, a change reflecting the debates within most colleges and universities about deconstructing the canon and pushing a more feminist and multicultural agenda. In education, books that formerly were ignored have now become standard requirements in many courses, among them Paolo Freire's *Pedagogy of the Oppressed* and bell hooks's *Teaching to Transgress*, along with a wide range of feminist writings, such as Kathleen Weiler's *Women Teaching for Change*. This has produced counter-thrusts from the right, such as Dinesh D'Souza's *Illiberal Education*, and Thomas Sowell's *Inside American Education: The Decline, the Deception, the Dogmas*, along with more thoughtful reassessments like Nathan Glazer's *We Are All Multiculturalists Now.*[27]

The professoriate, like teachers in elementary and secondary schools, also struggles with the questions of transmitting and transforming. A Carnegie Foundation poll of 3,400 full-time faculty members found that a majority of those in liberal arts colleges believed that preserving the cultural heritage should be an important goal of undergraduate education, while faculty in research universities were least committed to this goal. Yet most faculty were not just preservationists; three-fourths of all professors agreed that institutions of higher education should be active in helping to solve social problems, with women in the social sciences most committed to that goal, and faculty in engineering and the physical sciences giving it a much lower priority. The division over the weight faculty should give to transformation grows much sharper over the issues of multiculturalism and race and gender studies, just as it does in high schools. More than a third of the faculty polled refused to take a position on these highly contested issues. A significant proportion of the professoriate strongly resisted transformationist aims: nearly one-fifth were opposed to changing the undergraduate curriculum to ensure more exposure to the works of African Americans, women, and a variety of ethnic groups. But two-thirds believed that the growing emphasis on multicultural studies would have a positive effect on the curriculum, even if all of them were not yet sure about the best means to use to attain that end.[28]

The poll data present in more neutral language what has been described as cultural wars on the campus or the university under siege. Faculty meetings have not been as heated since the days of protest over the Vietnam War. English faculty who believe that the highest responsibility they have is to teach the great works of literature glare across the aisle at postmodernist colleagues who think the traditionalists' views are hopelessly outdated. The postmodernists radically challenge claims to objective knowledge; they are interested in the deconstruction of texts, in their sociological and psychological origins and semantical schemes. Gerald Graff explains the gulf from a student's point of view in his book *Beyond the Culture Wars:*

> An undergraduate tells of an art history course in which the instructor observed one day, "As we now know, the idea that knowledge can be objective is a positivist myth that has been exploded by postmodern thought." It so happens the student is concurrently enrolled in a political science course in which the instructor speaks confidently about the objectivity of his discipline as if it had not been exploded at all. "What do you do?" the student is asked. "What else can I do," he says. "I trash objectivity in art history, and I presuppose it in political science."[29]

The point of the story, Graff goes on, is not that students have "become cynical relativists who care less about convictions than about grades and careers." Rather, we should be surprised that more students do not behave in this way since the "disjunction of the curriculum" encourages it. Graff's response to this dilemma is not to paper over the divisions but to recognize them by having positivists and postmodernists teach together so that students may enter these debates and come to deeper understandings as they sort out different claims about which kind of knowledge matters most. We agree, while recognizing that parties at war do not easily come to the peace table. After all, deep divisions and competing paradigms of thought have always existed within the university, just as the tensions of being a transmitter or a transformer exist within each teacher as well as between teachers. What we have called the first academic revolution was the overthrow of a traditional curriculum rooted in theology and the Greek and Latin classics by those trained in the modern physical and natural sciences. We should note that those classics have not disappeared, and even the study of theology survives in some distinguished universities, although it is usually cordoned off in divinity schools.

These issues may be debated with more passion on the campus, because the professoriate enjoys a form of academic freedom not given to teachers in precollege settings, and because of the corollary responsibility college faculty feel for the design of the curriculum. But as teachers in elementary and secondary schools become more empowered, their debates are likely to intensify. We believe this will be a good thing, that it will deepen and enlarge the intellectual capacities of teachers just as lively debate on these issues between college students and their professors broadens the students' ability to consider competing ideas. We recognize that some may regard this as too facile a solution—they perhaps rightly fear that the gulf between competing ideologies has grown too wide, and the views across the divide too hostile.

Teachers in a democratic society do have an obligation to transmit the civic culture that sustains a democratic form of life. All children must be aware of their rights of citizenship and understand how the levers of change work in the constitutional system as it has evolved in the United States. But teachers must also have the degree of autonomy necessary to criticize and help the next generation feel empowered to transform that culture. William Bigelow, who taught at Jefferson High School in Portland, Oregon, embraced the role of the transformative teacher and saw his classroom "as a center of equality and democracy—an ongoing, if small, critique of the repressive social relations of the larger society." When teaching a course in U.S. History with his colleague Linda Christensen, Bigelow had his students role-play the forced removal of the Cherokee from their homelands. Students took roles as Native Americans, plantation owners, bankers, and members of the Andrew Jackson administration to experience the reality of pushing the Cherokee hundreds of miles from their homes. Then the students wrote about times their own rights had been violated and how they felt about that. They sat in a circle to share their stories. Christensen and Bigelow wrote their own stories and joined in the development of a "collective text" that emerged from the group portrait. They went on to discuss violations of student rights in school, and how students might confront injustice, and to raise questions about whether schools in America are overresponsive to the needs of capitalism and fail to realize the ideal of equal educational opportunity.[30]

One would have to spend time in Bigelow's classroom to see whether he was a creative teacher or an indoctrinator. Was his teaching a thoughtful treatment of the blemished history of capitalism, or a harangue? The evidence from his own account is encouraging, and shows a teacher who was aware and concerned about such problems, who criticizes his own teaching for at times overemphasizing victimhood.

We agree with Amy Gutmann that democratic governments will not survive unless they perpetuate a common culture and that teachers must cultivate the capacity for critical reflection on that culture. Although many others properly influence the political culture of schools—parents, school boards, legislatures—teachers have a primary responsibility to engage students in a critique of their cultural inheritance and to help them evaluate competing claims about the form a good life should take. Teachers must have the necessary autonomy to carry out this vital task. If they do not have the freedom in their classrooms to criticize their society, including the prescribed curriculum, they cannot teach their students to be intellectually independent. Whether such criticism is responsible, or engenders forms of group-think and subtle indoctrination, is best judged by a teacher's peers.[31]

Critics of hallowed beliefs are seldom loved, and teachers who trespass on the conventional wisdom should not have to put their jobs at risk if they do so responsibly, but they may lose them nonetheless. Courts have generally protected the academic freedom of teachers to criticize American society and to introduce controversial positions when they are a logical part of the subject at hand. In Tinker v. Des Moines Independent School District, the Supreme Court ruled that neither teachers nor students "shed their constitutional rights to freedom of speech or expression at the schoolhouse gate," although the

Court drew the line at forms of expression or protest that interfered with the educational process. The Court also ordered the reinstatement of a teacher who had been fired for publishing a sarcastic letter in the local newspaper criticizing school officials for overspending on athletics and shortchanging education. Lower courts have split, however, on protecting the jobs of avowedly gay or lesbian teachers.[32]

Although the balance teachers strike between being transmitters and transformers may be the most difficult to achieve, working out a response to any of the three questions we have reviewed in this chapter is seldom easy. Most teachers will find that the answer they give at any moment is likely to undergo revision, and that their lives as teachers are a series of endless transformations, some of them quite wrenching. It is the price they gladly pay for growth.

5

The Modern Origins of the Profession: Florence's Story, 1890–1920

At the turn of the twentieth century, teaching was being transformed by educational leaders. The localized, idiosyncratic employment of teachers by citizen school boards became more structured with the implementation of state teacher-certification requirements, formal teacher-training programs, and supervision of teachers by formally educated principals and district administrators. The following portrait of Florence Thayer highlights three characteristics which shaped the nature of teaching at that time: who taught, the social expectations for young women, and teachers' preparation and licensure.[1]

It was September 1890 and seventeen-year-old Florence Thayer was excited. She was about to leave home on a thirty-six mile train trip to study teaching at the Brockport Normal and Training School. Her dream of becoming a certified teacher was coming true. All the previous year, as she had taught in a one-room school near her home in Lakeside, New York, she had thought about going to Brockport. Now, Florence could hardly believe her good fortune. Since she had been recommended by her school district's education commissioner, and had managed to pass the tests in spelling, reading, writing, geography, and arithmetic, she was able to attend Brockport without paying tuition. At the end of the year she would even get a refund for the cost of her train fare back and forth from home. New York state was trying to increase the number of well-trained teachers. Free tuition was an incentive to encourage prospective teachers to enroll in one of the eleven state-supported teacher-preparation programs. Although her family was not wealthy, Florence's father thought he could scrape together enough money to pay the sixty dollars each semester for room and board.[2]

Brockport Normal School, located just west of the growing city of Rochester, was chartered by New York state in 1867 to train teachers. The term "normal school," which was widely applied to the growing number of schools chartered to train teachers, had been adopted from the French counterpart, the "école normale." The Latin root word, "norma," means conforming to a rule or model. Thus the newly created normal schools intended to prepare students to do exemplary teaching.[3] Brockport offered three academic programs, the Elementary English program, a two-year diploma program for elementary school teachers; the Advanced English program, involving three years of study; and a four-year collegiate, Classical Degree program for those individuals aspiring to high school teaching, principalships, and other professions. The Classical Degree program was somewhat unusual for a normal school, owing its existence to the fact that Brockport was a private classical institute before receiving its charter as a normal school. The institute's survival had been precarious until it was chosen as the site of one of the state's first teacher-training schools. Three hundred and seventy students were enrolled at Brockport during the 1891–92 year. Few would actually graduate. In 1892, only twenty-five completed the Elementary English program; twelve earned the Advanced English diploma; and nineteen graduated with the Classical Degree.

Florence was enrolled in the Elementary English certificate program. After she graduated, she hoped to teach younger children, and not have to struggle with keeping order among boys and girls of all different ages, as she had in the rural one-room school. Upon her arrival at Brockport, Florence was greeted by Miss Rhoades, the Normal Hall preceptress, who also taught rhetoric and English literature. Miss Rhoades showed her to her room and introduced her to some of the other young women. Florence was eager to meet her classmates, most of whom were in their late teens and early twenties with backgrounds like her own. Unless they lived at home, the young women were required to board at the normal school. The young men boarded with families in the village.

As soon as she was settled, Florence and the other new female students were called to a meeting by Miss Rhoades. It was important, the students were told, that they understand and follow the rules of the normal school and that they act like young ladies at all times. Miss

Rhoades expected them to ask her permission to participate in any social activities. Young men were absolutely prohibited from entering the residence side of the normal school. Since they were living away from home, it was Miss Rhoades's responsibility to assure that the young ladies conducted themselves with decorum. In her eyes, the students' moral behavior was just as important as their academic studies. After all, how could young teachers be expected to shape the moral characters of their students if they themselves were not morally upright.[4]

Since a high school degree was not required to attend Brockport Normal School, Florence's first year of study was designed to assure that she had sufficient academic knowledge and skill to be able to teach at the elementary school level. She attended classes in arithmetic, grammar, physical and descriptive geometry, vocal music, spelling and impromptu composition, linear drawing, penmanship, botany, reading, physiology and zoology, composition and rhetoric. Much of Florence's class work involved doing recitations, reciting specific passages by memory.

It was not until her second year that Florence finally got to study what she had come to Brockort to learn—how to teach. In the fall term she had a full schedule of education courses: philosophy and history of education, school economy, civil government and school law, declamations, essays and select readings, and methods of giving object lessons and of teaching the subjects of the elementary courses. Florence thought the object lessons were the most interesting. Instead of just asking her students to memorize and recite their lessons, she could actually have them study an object from their own world. The class included lessons on objects, form, inventive drawing, size, color, place, weight, sounds, animals, plants, the human body, and moral instruction. Florence thought that it would be wonderful to engage her students in discovering the properties of familiar objects and to have them really think about their differences. She was also required to prepare and offer demonstration lessons to the rest of the class, for their critique. And she had to offer criticisms of her fellow students' lessons as well. Her teaching-methods professor placed great importance on the students' ability to critique each other's teaching.

All eighteen of the normal school teachers were college educated; fifteen were women and three were men. They took their charge of preparing professional teachers for the public schools of New York state very seriously. Professional teacher education was important because, as one faculty member wrote, "we find in this, highest of professions, persons with little aptitude, no love for the work, and without any special training for it, experimenting on the most susceptible and delicate material; while a similar attempt in other professions would subject the person to ridicule."[5] It was hoped that as more teachers graduated from the normal schools, the quality of teachers in New York would dramatically improve.

During her second year, Florence learned first hand just how serious Miss Rhoades was about assuring the correct moral behavior of her young ladies. One evening, Florence stayed too long talking with a gentleman visitor. At least, Miss Rhoades thought it was too long. She called Florence to her office the next morning. In a motherly way, Miss Rhoades adjured her to think of the customs of the best society, reminded her that she had to set an example for the younger girls, and asked her to promise that she would have no more late company. Florence, however, had her own opinion about the incident. She did not think she had done anything wrong and she told Miss Rhoades just that. Compared with practices at some normal schools, Miss Rhoades's reprimand was a modest punishment. In Ontario, Canada, any communication between male and female normal school students was prohibited, upon threat of expulsion. The architects of one normal school created separate entrances and corridors for each sex, and male and female students practiced their teaching in separate schools to assure that proper relations between the sexes were maintained.[6]

Despite Florence's minor rebellion, she was quite happy at Brockport. Her days were busy with classes and her evenings and weekends were filled with activities, like concerts, sleigh rides, and religious revival meetings. Sundays were generally spent at morning church service, often followed by Sunday School. The afternoons were devoted to writing letters home. Although she chafed a bit under the rules against fraternizing with young men, for the most part she embraced the social conventions of the time about the proper behavior for young ladies. Religion and the expectations of upright, moral Christian behavior were woven deeply into the fabric of her life.

Finally, it was time to actually teach! Florence would spend her last term teaching in the practice school, located in one wing of the normal school building. She would complete two practice teaching experiences, one in a lower grade and one in a higher grade. Both practice teaching experiences were supervised by a critic teacher who met with the students twice a week to review their progress. The practice of having student teachers offer "criticism lessons" for critique by their peers also continued.

Florence was nervous about student teaching, but after her first day, discovered that her anticipation was worse than the actual experience of teaching. She wrote in her diary, "Everything went off well and I found that dreading it was much worse than teaching." Florence completed her studies and graduated in June 1892. By the end of their two-year program, the graduates were viewed as well prepared to be teachers. Commenting on their preparation, the Brockport faculty wrote, "We can truthfully say that although inexperienced, they taught with as much power and success as most of the teachers of long experience whom we have observed in the common schools."[7] Normal school graduates were sought after, and Florence was hired to teach in the village of Fairport, ten miles east of the city of Rochester, for an annual salary of $320.

Who Taught?

Florence Thayer entered teaching at a time when the number of teachers was growing dramatically. Between 1870 and 1900, the number of teachers in the nation more than tripled, to 450,000. Teaching positions, especially at the elementary level, were increasingly filled by women. In 1870, two-thirds of all teachers were women; by 1900 the number of women teachers had increased to three-fourths of all teachers. This shift from men to women entering teaching was most apparent in urban areas of the Northeast.[8] By the beginning of the twentieth century the pattern of employment that characterized teaching as a female-dominated occupation was well established.

The historian Geraldine Joncich Clifford suggests there are multiple reasons to explain this shift. During the nineteenth century, as urbanization accelerated, the traditional pattern of family self-sufficiency declined, and work increasingly took place outside the home. Responsibility for child-rearing and, by extension, the education of children increasingly became women's responsibility. Catherine Beecher, a strong proponent of women becoming teachers, championed women's role as educators as early as the 1830s.[9]

At the same time, a declining birth rate, and new inventions that mechanized farming, freed girls from the family demands of helping with younger children and cooking meals for large numbers of farm laborers. This trend, in addition to the tendency for women to marry later, or even to consider remaining single, created an opportunity for young women to expand their horizons. Women activists were arguing that women could lead independent lives. Teaching was one of the few ways women could achieve greater control over their lives.

Teachers were needed in greater numbers partly because of the growing demand for universal public education. But the dramatic increase in immigration between 1880 and 1925 also meant more teachers were needed, particularly at the elementary level. This demand was largely met by paying women teachers lower salaries than men teachers.

Finally, school reformers were pressing for new teacher education requirements to improve the quality of public education. It is likely that as the formal preparation for teaching increased, the profession became less attractive to men. Men who did teach often held other jobs in addition to teaching. With increased demands for professional preparation, without any increase in salary, men found more lucrative opportunities elsewhere. Women took their place.

Teachers, both women and men, came generally from the middle-class and lower-middle-class families of businessmen, artisans, laborers, or farmers. Like Florence Thayer, most lived in rural areas. Only 5 percent of teachers were black at a time when 11 percent of the population was black. Black teachers were restricted to teaching African American children, usually in the most ill equipped and impoverished segregated southern schools. Generally, teachers were in their twenties and thirties, with the average age for women teachers being twenty-seven and the average age for men teachers being thirty-two. The range of ages varied widely, however, with rural schools hiring teachers as young as fifteen or sixteen.[10]

Most teachers did not remain in the classroom long. Men often used teaching as a platform from which to move to other work, either within education or in another profession. Women taught until they were married; many districts imposed hiring restrictions against married women. Single women often sought more attractive teaching positions in larger communities; for this reason urban teachers were often the most experienced.[11]

The relative status of teaching was very much determined by the eye of the beholder. The lower the status of the viewer, the higher the status of teaching.[12] For young women who needed employment, teaching was a desirable option among the choices available. Upper-class young women, who did not need to seek employment, perceived teachers as their social inferiors. But for African Americans, teaching was one of the few professions open to educated blacks, even though the impoverished conditions of most black schools resulted in their often being staffed by very poorly prepared teachers.[13] Despite the varied views of teachers' status, however, the tendency for teachers to be overwhelmingly young, white, and female meant that their position in both society and the schools would be colored by the prevailing attitudes about and the expectations for women.

The Social Expectations for Women

Miss Rhoades, the Brockport Normal Hall preceptress, was most vigilant. Her young ladies followed proper social conventions. Florence's experience mirrored the experiences of women at the time, often reflecting conflicting beliefs and expectations.

Acting as wife and mother was considered women's primary responsibility. Women were homemakers; the work of the world was done by men. The sociologist Lester F. Ward, in his book *Dynamic Sociology or Applied Social Science*, published in 1910, observed: "The theory of life for women is that every woman of marriageable age is actually married to a competent man to protect and support her; that her sole duty is to bear children, keep her husband's house, and be ornamented according to his tastes; that all labor, whether of production, exchange, distribution, politics, or war, is done by men, and women found engaged in any of these pursuits are deemed violators of the social code and their services and productions are discounted proportionally."[14] As homemakers, women were afforded the special, if limited, role of serving as the moral, spiritual, and emotional caregivers. Their place was not the world of work. This domestic ideology presumed women were to remain pure of spirit and to serve as models of proper decorum and behavior, finding their rewards in their children and in their homes. Young women were expected to marry and use their talents nurturing their families. Teaching was an acceptable interlude until marriage and offered one of the few acceptable alternatives for women who had to work either because they were single or because they were widows.

It was also widely believed that women were intellectually inferior to men, and consequently less capable of dealing with worldly affairs.[15] This view was offered well into the twentieth century by schoolmen as an explanation for the status of education and as means for bolstering a cry for more men to enter teaching, with higher salaries to attract them. Professor Henry E. Armstrong, a visiting British educator commissioned to study the status of American high schools in 1904 concluded, for example: "Those who have taught women students are one and all in agreement that, although close workers and most faithful and accurate observers, with the rarest exception, they are incapable of doing independent work. Throughout the entire period of existence woman has been man's slave; and if the theory of evolution be in any way correct, there is no reason to suppose, I imagine, that she will recover from the mental disabilities which this has entailed upon her within any period which we can regard as reasonable. Education can do little to modify her nature." Women by their very nature were believed to be less capable than men. It is no surprise that, with the exception of female elementary school principals, school managers and policy-makers were men.[16]

At the same time these beliefs prevailed about women, feminists were vocal in their efforts to change women's subordinate status. Upstate New York was the home of a number of activist leaders, including Elizabeth Cady Stanton and Susan B. Anthony, herself a former teacher. Early in her career as a social activist, Susan B. Anthony focused on the activities of the New York State Teachers Association. At the 1853 convention, held in Rochester, two-thirds of the five hundred teachers attending were women. The women teachers were allowed only to observe the proceedings. In a letter describing the event Anthony commented: "My heart was filled with grief and indignation thus to see the minority, simply because they were men, presuming that in them was vested all wisdom and knowledge; that they needed no aid, no counsel from the majority. And what was most humiliating of all was to look into the faces of those women and see that by far the larger proportion were perfectly satisfied with the position assigned to them."[17]

After two days of silent listening, the topic of discussion turned to why the profession of teaching was not as respected as that of lawyer, doctor, or minister. Susan B. Anthony determined it was time for her to speak. Her biographer, Ida Husted Harper, recounts what happened next:

A bombshell would not have created greater commotion. For the first time in all history a woman's voice was heard in a teachers' convention. Every neck was craned and a profound hush fell upon the assembly. Charles Davies LL.D., author of Davies' textbooks and professor of mathematics at West Point, presided. In full-dress costume with buff vest, blue coat and brass buttons, he was the Great Mogul. At length recovering from the shock of being thus addressed by a woman, he leaned forward and asked with satirical politeness, "What will the lady have?" "I wish to speak to the question under discussion," said Miss Anthony calmly, although her heart was beating a tatoo. Turning to the few rows of men in front of him, for the women occupied the back seats, he inquired, "What is the pleasure of the convention?" "I move she shall be heard," said one man; this was seconded by another, and thus was precipitated a debate which lasted half an hour . . . At last a vote was taken, men only voting, and it was carried in the affirmative by a small majority. Miss Anthony then said: "It seems to me you fail to comprehend the cause of the disrespect of which you complain. Do you not see that so long as society says woman has not brains enough to be a doctor, lawyer or minister, but has plenty to be a teacher, every man of you who condescend to teach, tacitly admits before all Israel and the sun that he has no more brains than a woman?" and sat down. She had intended to draw the conclusion that the only way to place teaching upon a level with other professions was either to admit woman to them or exclude her from teaching, but her trembling limbs would sustain her no longer. The convention soon adjourned for the day and, as Miss Anthony went out of the hall, many of the women drew away from her and said audibly: "Did you ever see such a disgraceful performance?" "I never was so ashamed of my sex." But a few of them gathered about her and said: "You have taught us our lesson and hereafter we propose to make ourselves heard."[18]

For the next ten years Susan B. Anthony attended the annual teachers' conventions and lobbied for the rights of women teachers to have a vote in association matters, to have a visible place on the program, to hold positions as officers and on committees, and to have equal pay for equal services. By 1862, these rights, except for equal pay, had been achieved, and she turned her attention to other efforts.

These victories were not sustained, however. The voices of tradition prevailed, and forty-five years later, following the state teachers' convention of 1898 in Rochester, Susan B. Anthony commented in a newspaper interview in the local paper:

I have fought some of the hardest battles of my life for women school teachers, and yet many of these of today know little of what was done for them in those early years. They appear to be lacking in spirit and content to occupy subordinate positions; they do not seem to have the ambition to sustain their rights. On the program of this convention not a woman's name appeared for the principal meetings. Not an address was made by a woman and not at one where I was present did I hear a woman's voice raised on any question. There were ten women to one man, and yet the men ran the convention to suit themselves and took the credit for whatever was or had been done. The women, to be sure, were on the programs and managed the meetings of the side shows, but that is all they did do.[19]

In education women activists' challenge to the predominant beliefs about women and their continued efforts to change the status of women led to struggles to have a voice in teacher association business, attempts to get women salaries comparable to those of male teachers, and efforts to improve teachers' job security and retirement benefits well into the twentieth century. Despite their efforts, women's choices remained limited and inequity within teaching persisted. In one of the few articles about teaching written by a woman teacher in the journal *Educational Review* between 1900 and 1910, the author commented that if teachers were asked, more than half would say that they did not like teaching but that it was the only way they had to earn money, and it involved less risk than most other occupations. Teaching was one of the few viable employment alternatives, and most women teachers accepted their roles without question. After all, teaching did offer women the opportunity to have a life outside the home, and for some, it served as a route to other public activity.[20]

Teacher Education and Licensure

Florence Thayer would have been viewed as a well-educated, highly prepared teacher. Since the 1830s, reformers had championed improving teachers' qualifications. The most ambitious proposals called for graduate-level programs after the completion of a liberal arts bachelor's degree. An educated teaching force was included as a critical component in the crusade to achieve universal public education. State-funded normal schools, teacher-training institutes sponsored by urban school districts, and extensive summer teacher institutes were all promoted as ways to meet this goal.[21]

Despite these multiple efforts, as late at 1910 more than a third of all teachers had not completed high school, and only 5 percent had more than a high school education.[22] By 1921 only fourteen states required a high school diploma to teach, and very few required any teacher training. By 1937, the number of states requiring more than a high school degree, usually one to four years of college, had risen to thirty-two.[23]

New York was one of the first states to create minimum requirements for teachers. The Education Law of 1895, "an act to encourage and to promote the professional training of teachers," attempted to create minimum education standards for teachers and also to incorporate a preexisting, complex system of certification by examination that included four different certification levels.[24] For most of the nineteenth century the teacher licensure process was certification by local district superintendents. Prospective teachers merely had to meet the requirements of this individual. In 1888, the New York State Superintendent of Public Instruction adopted a policy of uniform examinations for all local certificates. By 1894, the state was grading all exams, beginning the process of standardization. Successful candidates were required to score a minimum of 75 percent correct answers in each subject area.

Three different levels of certification, none of which had formal teacher education prerequisites, were available. The lowest, a level-three certificate requiring no prior teaching experience, was issued for one year; the level-two certificate, requiring ten weeks of teaching experience, was issued for three years; and the highest, or level-one certificate, requiring two years of experience, was issued for ten years. The lowest-level examination included questions on arithmetic, geography, grammar, orthography, penmanship, reading, English composition, physiology and hygiene, American history, and school law. The highest-level test had additional questions on methods and school economy, algebra, bookkeeping, civil government, current topics, drawing, elementary physics, and the history of education.[25]

In addition to the three local certificates, the State Department of Public Instruction had the authority to issue a permanent Life State Certificate. This certification also had no formal professional education requirements and could be obtained by teachers who had two years of teaching experience and successfully passed the life certificate exam. Dr. Charles R. Skinner, Superintendent of Public Instruction for New York State from 1895 to 1904, urged teachers to study for the Life State Certificate for their professional development, but the number of teachers who pursued that certification was low.[26] Teachers with level-one certificates could renew their certification without further examination as long as they had taught for at least five years. New teachers could receive a training class certificate, also renewable, by completing a one-year training program offered by most of the urban school districts. Or, like Florence, they could receive normal school certificates after two years of study, and these certificates were also renewable. Certification based on completion of a bachelor's degree was permanent. Apparently, teachers were not convinced the life certificate added much further professional recognition.

Beyond these state certification requirements, individual districts retained the authority to create additional requirements for teachers. The Rochester City School District extended its teacher-training school curriculum from one year to two in 1900, thereby requiring all applicants to have at least two years of teacher training. For high school teachers, graduation from an approved college was required for appointment.[27]

These new requirements led to a substantial increase in the number of formally educated teachers in Rochester, from 33 percent in 1901 to 71 percent in 1910. The greatest increases were for teachers with normal school diplomas, from 10 percent to 25 percent, and for teachers with training class certificates, from 17 percent to 39 percent. The increase in college graduates was slight, from 5 percent to 7 percent.[28]

Compared with requirements for other occupations for which New York state was granting licenses at the turn of the century, the requirements for teaching were far more flexible. Statewide standards for physicians, dentists, and lawyers, for example, were much more specific. To practice medicine one had to hold a degree of bachelor of medicine or doctor of medicine. To practice dentistry required a three-year dental degree or the doctor of medicine degree and two years of dental training. Preparation for law involved either three years of law school or a high school diploma followed by a clerkship in the office of a practicing attorney of the Supreme Court of New York.[29] Although the state wanted higher standards for teachers, the history of local certification and the increasing demand for teachers required greater latitude in the certification requirements.

Unlike other professional groups whose members were claiming control over entry and oversight of their professions as their prerogative, teachers had to comply with decisions made by state and local educational administrators. From the administrators' perspective, teachers needed to be better prepared, but they also needed greater direction to achieve widespread, high-quality public education. One of the central aims of educational administrators was to develop an educational structure where the quality of education would not be affected by the short duration of many teachers' careers or the inherent weaknesses of women teachers. From the outset, teachers were viewed as public employees whose licensure and work were justifiably regulated by state and local mandates. Despite this, the experience of teachers depended very much on where they were teaching, as we will see as we continue to follow Florence Thayer's teaching career.

The Village School Teacher

The village of Fairport, where Florence began her teaching career, was a thriving community. Since it was located on two main rail lines, residents had ready access to the city of Rochester. The directory of the Fairport Classical Union School proclaimed: "The two school buildings, with their spacious grounds, are among the most attractive features of the place. They are heated by furnaces, and particular care is given to their ventilation. Great pains is taken [*sic*] in keeping the grounds and buildings in good condition, and in making the rooms attractive, by pictures, flowers, and other decorations." Fairport citizens had good reason to be proud of their schools, which were solidly constructed brick buildings. Although improvements were being made in village and country schools across the country in the late nineteenth century, many country schools were painted red because red paint was cheaper than white paint, or were not painted at all. Schools were often poorly equipped and teachers were expected to perform janitorial as well as teaching duties.[30]

The North Side School, where Florence taught, enrolled 128 students, from the first through the sixth grade. Seventy-five percent of the students in the village were in the elementary grades, with lower enrollments at the upper levels. Florence had a combined first- and second-grade class of 46 children. The school day was from 8:45 A.M. to 3:30 P.M., with a lunch period of an hour and forty-five minutes when most children returned home.

The course of instruction for the first and second grades included a curious mixture of specific directions for the teacher to follow—"Have pupils copy the words and sentences taught, using *long* pencils and holding them *properly*"—and the broadest of curricular outlines. For the first-grade reading course teachers were advised: "Develop the idea by use of objects, pictures, etc.: give word orally, then teach from blackboard. Read from charts and primer. Spelling taught with reading. Sounds and names of letters given. The teacher will tell class story of Red Riding Hood, Cinderella, Jack and the Beanstalk, and such other similar stories as she thinks best, and read to class from Snedder's Book of Fables, Aesop's Fables, Seven Little Sisters, and other books."[31]

Beginning in the second grade students were grouped by ability for arithmetic, reading, and geography. The other subjects, drawing, physiology, writing, spelling, and music, were taught to the whole class. Florence Thayer probably taught in the same manner that she had been taught at Brockport, with heavy reliance on recitations and drill. Without doubt, she was the central focus in a classroom where desks in neat rows were bolted to the floor, facing the front of the room.[32]

Florence's principal, William D. Manro, served as the administrative leader for the district, and also taught the Greek, history, and geometry courses in the academic department (ninth to twelfth grades). Manro, a Yale University graduate, led a staff of thirteen women, nine of whom taught at the elementary level. All of Florence's teaching colleagues had normal school educations, except for Manro's female assistant, a Mount Holyoke College graduate who also taught at the high school.

It is likely that Florence found that her new principal and the Fairport Classical Union School Board, whose members governed the school district, filled the guardianship role previously exercised by the Brockport Normal Hall preceptress, Miss Rhoades. Teachers' lives in rural communities at the turn of the century and in the early part of the twentieth century were restricted by community constraints as well as more general social expectations for young single women. Many teaching contracts governed teachers' behavior in such personal matters as religious activities, recreation, hygiene, relationships with men, and marriage.[33]

As highly visible outsiders, particularly in smaller communities where there might be only one teacher, young women teachers were under continual scrutiny and had little truly private life. Teachers often boarded with a school board member's family or the family of one of their students, and those teachers were always on duty.

In a wealthy community, like Fairport, Florence's circumstances would certainly have been better than those of teachers in more rural, less prosperous, areas. One of her contemporaries, who taught in rural Nebraska, commented, for example, that teachers might be willing to add agriculture to their curriculum, "were it not that they are overburdened, having 30 or more recitations to hear a day, from seven to eight grades; the sweeping, dusting, firing to do; a great many papers to correct; the lessons to plan for too many grades; going to a boarding place tired and finding no comforts there, children hanging about you; supper at 8:30 or 9; poor light, a kerosene lamp, a chilly room, destitute of any comforts whatever." This picture makes it easy to understand why most rural teachers stayed only a few years in their positions, seeking to move on to urban school districts when they could—unless they were required to leave teaching when they married.[34]

Rural teachers also had to respond to community expectations for service that extended well beyond the classroom. In accord with the domestic ideology of virtuous womanhood, schools were considered extensions of the home, and teachers the extension of motherhood. Teachers could be expected to teach a Sunday School class, to organize and carry out elaborate school performances involving singing and recitations by their students, or to attend to any demand children's presence might place upon a community. In her study of rural Vermont teachers, Margaret K. Nelson reports that one teacher summed her role up this way: "They expected the teacher to do everything and know everything. If . . . a child was sick, they'd send word down, want to know what to do. They'd send down the bottle of castor oil if they couldn't make the kid take it and wanted the teacher to make her take it." The lines between home and school, public and private, were blurred in villages and rural school districts, with teachers engaged as much in the act of parenting as in the act of instruction.[35]

Some teachers probably embraced these expectations of self-sacrifice and the domestic ideology of virtuous womanhood as part of their professional identity.[36] Extending the female sphere of influence beyond the home was extolled by some women as a strategy for improving women's status. In Rochester, the single female school board member and president of the Women's Educational and Industrial Union, Helen Montgomery, promoted the involvement of women club members in social issues with the observation: "It is not enough that the house is kept clean if the streets be wrong, and the ward unhealthful. There should be a broadened housekeeping, to extend out of doors and all over the city. All these things help women to gain full enfranchisement."[37] The historian Kathleen Weiler reminds us, however, that historical sources "do not provide a transparent picture of past lives." Our efforts to reconstruct teachers' experiences must acknowledge not only the prevailing beliefs about teachers, but also the individual circumstances which shaped their lives. Accepting the role of surrogate parent may have been the best alternative available, especially when teaching provided the sole source of a teacher's livelihood.[38]

The Spirit of the True Teacher

The connection between teaching and service was made most explicitly by educational leaders, superintendents and education professors from the university schools of education, who characterized the professional teacher as reflecting the "spirit of the true teacher," a combination of virtuous womanhood and professional altruism. The sociologist Lester F. Ward wrote about teachers, "The manner in which teachers are paid and the general attitude of society toward them clearly indicate that they are looked upon, to a certain extent, in the light of the philanthropists who should expect to fulfill their mission without much substantial aid . . . and [as] a mere 'labor of love.'" Although Ward's observation was intended to be critical, educational leaders wholeheartedly adopted the description of teaching as a "labor of love" to be performed by the "true teacher."[39]

The characteristics of the "true teacher" were multifold. "True teachers" had a love for human nature, reflected in sympathy for and gentleness with children. They were resourceful in finding ways to engage their students' enthusiasm. They demonstrated good judgment and set an example to be followed.[40]

The "true teacher" was born to the task. Formal education might perfect and enhance natural ability, but without inherent qualities, training alone was insufficient. Reflecting this sentiment, one educator wrote, "The specialist is seldom a good teacher, even though his specialty be the science and art of teaching . . . The elements of a good teacher are deep down in character; they involve the whole make-up of the man, his attainments, his ideals, his purposes and his energies."[41] Formal education could enhance the qualities of a good teacher, leading school men believed, but teaching required certain inherent personal characteristics. Failure as a teacher, therefore, was a matter of personal shortcomings.[42]

The ideology of the "true teacher" was intertwined with the language of professionalization in the name of altruistic service. Teachers were told that they should seek their reward in their service to others. Such reward was greater than any material reward and was recompense for any difficulty teachers might be asked to accept. Reflecting this spirit, William Maxwell, Superintendent of the New York City School District published an article in 1904 entitled "The Teacher's Compensation," in which he wrote: "The teacher must often work under oppressive and vexatious conditions, he must often endure poverty and even privation, he may often be subjected to indignity, but if he has the spirit of the true teacher, he will have compensation—a compensation that does not come in the same degree to any other profession—the compensation of seeing his work bear fruit in the lives and characters of his pupils."[43] The concept of the "spirit of the true teacher" emphasized personal sacrifice and pushed the element of service into prominence for teachers at a time when other professions were gaining control over their specialties with claims of scientific knowledge and expertise. By linking altruism to the "spirit of the true teacher" administrators effectively quashed any complaints from the predominantly female teaching force. Those who challenged the status quo were not "true teachers." The "true teacher," or in other words, the true professional, was the teacher who accepted and dutifully served in her prescribed role.

Just as females were subordinate to males in the rest of society at that time, women teachers were subordinate to male principals and superintendents. Four different male principals directed the Fairport Classical Union School between 1893 and 1898. At each change the female preceptress, the second in charge, and a college graduate herself, was passed over. The same pattern was true of teachers associations, which were generally headed by principals. This picture was writ large in urban school districts such as Rochester, where Florence Thayer would accept a teaching assignment in 1898. There, as in most urban districts, much of the reform agenda focused on creating an educational program that one historian, David Tyack, has called "the one best system."[44]

Teaching in Urban Schools

By the late 1890s dissatisfaction was growing among the Rochester city leaders with both school district and city governance. Rochester schools were controlled by twenty commissioners of education, selected as representatives of the city's political wards. The superintendent of schools, a businessman chosen from among the commissioners, viewed school business as a political power base. Teaching and administrative contracts, as well as other school contracts, were used as political favors. The accounting system for the district was haphazard, and commissioners were known to forge business contracts for their own personal gain. Teachers were poorly paid; salaries were lower than any other urban teacher salaries in the state.[45]

Leading Rochester citizens believed that the cure for this corruption, and the solution to improving education, had to begin with removing school control from the ward politicians and employing educational experts. A new school governance law, enacted in 1899, enabled reformers to create a five-member board of education, elected for four-year terms. The newly elected Board of Education of 1900 included five of Rochester's leading citizens, four men and one woman, reflecting the pattern of professional and business leadership that was developing nationwide.[46] The sole female board member, Helen Bartlett Montgomery, had been elected with the help of Susan B. Anthony, despite the fact that Rochester women still did not have the vote in municipal elections. Women had achieved suffrage in the states of Colorado and Wyoming by this time. The new Board of Education members ended the traditional pattern of selecting a school superintendent from among the board membership. The new field of educational administration offered great hope that education could be improved through more objective and scientific management. One of the first acts of the new board was to hire Dr. Charles B. Gilbert, a professionally trained educator, to reform Rochester's schools.

Like his counterparts in other cities, Dr. Gilbert wanted to create a system of schooling that could assure uniformity of quality and outcome. To accomplish this goal, Dr. Gilbert embraced scientific management, an approach that was quickly gaining credibility among educational administrators as the most effective way to organize schools. This approach, adopted from industry, focused on creating a hierarchical organization of schooling, which centralized decision-making. Quality education could be assured by standardizing instruction and providing teachers with specific teaching guidelines. Teachers were viewed as part of the reform problem. Increasing teacher training, standardizing teaching, and careful supervision were the solutions.[47]

Beginning with a new curriculum guide, revised requirements for teachers, and the building of two new high schools and six grammar schools by 1905, Dr. Gilbert's administration through 1903, and that of his successor, Clarence F. Carroll, aimed to achieve progressivism and efficiency. In his report for the years 1905–1907, Superintendent Carroll summarized the developments in Rochester this way:

> Perhaps no educational system ever had a more sudden, a more violent, and a more complete transformation than that witnessed in Rochester since the year 1900. The deplorable conditions that seemed to exclude all possibility of improvement; the rise of public opinion; the fearless championship of the highest ideals by men and women; the pioneer and unrivaled educational charter; the small school board which it provided and its work with an eye singly to the improvement of the schools; the uncounted changes in school equipment and teaching force; the most progressive course of study ever written; the steady and cooperative advance along well approved lines by the Board of Education and the community still in progress—all make the educational situation in Rochester a most interesting study to a much larger public, and to all students of education."[48]

Superintendent Carroll's zeal in touting his reforms might be viewed as self-serving at worst and celebratory at best. His self-congratulatory remarks, like those of most reformers, contained a mixture of truth and fiction that is best understood from the teacher's vantage point. Although we do not have the advantage of Florence Thayer's thoughts about her new teaching position in Rochester, we can learn a great deal about how these reforms affected teachers from her class lists for the years 1898–1905 and the curricular guide that she was supposed to follow.

With her move to Rochester, Florence was able to work in a fully graded school. She was assigned to teach first grade, instead of having to teach the combined primary grades, as she had at Fairport. As a first-grade teacher, Florence instructed her students in writing, reading, spelling, arithmetic, language, gymnasium, and drawing. Teaching only one grade did not necessarily reduce the challenge of educating her forty-five students, since their ages ranged from five to eight, and only fifteen of the forty-five attended school for the full year. The majority, twenty-seven children, were enrolled in her class for only a third of the year. Children entered school at different times in the fall, as early as mid-September and as late as the end of October. In addition, the district's policy of mid-year promotion meant that children could be moved on to the next grade in January. Teachers completed promotion lists in both January and June, evaluating their students in each subject area and recommending whether they be passed or not. Some of the volatility was also due to the mobility of students' families, since frequent moves were common.[49]

One of the key elements of the modernization of the urban school district was the development of the curriculum guide. Created by the superintendent and a staff of subject area supervisors, usually without the involvement of teachers, the curriculum guide sought to provide a uniform educational product. Educational administrators hoped that by carefully adhering to the curriculum guide, teachers from different schools across the city could end the year with the same results from their students. Soon after he was hired, Dr. Gilbert set to work to produce a new curriculum guide for Rochester's schools. The course of study was 160 pages of specific instructions directing teachers how to conduct the school day. The school day was divided into segments of ten to twenty minutes with activities outlined for each time period.

The assistant superintendent, Miss Ada Van Stone Harris, supervised the teachers who taught kindergarten through fourth grade, and was a firm believer in the advantages of the curriculum guide. "I am convinced that much of the waste in school life is due to the failure to arrange a scientifically constructed program. The time of the teacher and that of the child may both be made much more effective if properly planned," Miss Harris wrote in her annual report. Teachers were responsible for following the assigned schedule and building principals were charged with assuring that it was enforced. Miss Harris continued her report by adding, "The program calls for special drill exercises in phonics daily but unless our principals feel the vital importance of this exercise in its proper place and emphasize the necessity of it—teachers often thoughtlessly neglect it."[50] With the curriculum guide, Rochester's school administration attempted to achieve maximum efficiency and system-wide organization for its grammar schools. The difficulty for teachers was to implement this program in classes where there was wide variation in the ages and attendance of their students.

The impact of the course of study for the grammar school teachers can be better understood by comparing it with the high school curriculum for Rochester. Although it offered several different tracks of study, the high school program was outlined in one page. The language of the

high school principal in describing his teachers was qualitatively different from that used by Assistant Superintendent Harris in commenting
on the grammar school teachers. Rather than being "thoughtlessly
neglectful" of the schedule to be followed, the high school teachers
were "college graduates with few exceptions, broad-minded men and
women with no exception, who enter into the lives of our students."[51]

The course of study developed by Rochester was viewed as a model,
receiving awards for excellence in regional educational exhibitions.
Regarded as an educational innovation in 1901, by the end of the
decade, curriculum guides like Rochester's were the norm at both the
elementary and secondary levels.[52]

In the spirit of educational efficiency, the rationale for the carefully
prescribed course of study was that it was created in the teacher's best
interest. To develop an efficient teaching force teachers had to know
what was expected of them, to understand the best method for carrying
out their assigned tasks, and to be held responsible for specific outcomes. Writing on this subject, Dr. W. C. Bagley, of the nearby Sate
Normal School of Oswego, commented, "the most effective means of
improving efficiency is to build up in the young teacher the ideal of
responsibility for definite results. This ideal can be developed only by
setting definite tasks and hold the teacher to strict accountability for
'bringing the answer.'" Teachers needed to know what was expected in
very specific terms if educational reform was to progress.[53]

We can only wonder how this elaborate course of study was actually
carried out. During the 1902–03 school year, Florence Thayer had a
class of sixty-four children, whose ages ranged from five to nine, some
of whom were enrolled in her class for as little as one month and others
of whom stayed with her as long as three years. Crowding had become
such a problem that the Board of Education adopted half-day sessions
for kindergarten and first grade. By the end of the year, she recommended that only half of her students be promoted to second grade.
More than likely, the most significant improvement in Rochester's
public education came from building additional schools and reducing
class sizes. By 1906, six new elementary schools had been built, solving
the problem of overcrowding, and reducing Florence's class size to
thirty children. At mid-year, Florence recommended that twenty-four
of the thirty children be promoted.

The curriculum guide, created by administrators for teachers, reflected the belief of educational administrators that teachers were part

of the reform problem, and that the almost exclusively female grammar school teaching force needed close direction and supervision to be effective teachers. In accord with national demographics, 95 percent of Rochester's teachers were women. Of a teaching force of 663 teachers, only 34 were men, all of whom taught at the high school level.[54] Since only 10 percent of all students attended high school, high school teachers made up a small percentage of the total number of teachers. In Rochester, 15 percent of the teachers taught high school. Thus school reformers focused most on increasing the standards and training of the female grammar school teacher.

Although there were thoughtful critics of this movement toward standardization, including Rochester's Dr. Gilbert, who recognized that overregulation could have negative consequences and that there was a need for "freedom of teaching," standardization was clearly one of the goals of "expert supervision."[55] Rochester principals were to provide daily supervision of their teachers to assure that they were following the schedule. Teachers were responsible for monitoring the number of hours in each day that a child was in school, submitting weekly grade reports, and also providing a detailed record of their own attendance. Teachers' salaries could be withheld for failure to provide attendance data.[56] The training and credentialing process, the curriculum guides, and the emphasis on record keeping all reinforced the administrative oversight of teaching. As one commentator at the time observed, "Teaching has lost much of its directness and simplicity through the extreme systematizing and mechanizing of the educative process . . . With the large graded school, with its long rows of seats and the hierarchy of superintendent, assistant superintendent, supervisors, and assistant supervisors, principals, and, last, and least, the teacher."[57] Educational leaders created a system that, in the name of teacher professionalization, reduced teachers' autonomy and placed them at the bottom of the administrative hierarchy.

It is impossible to know if Rochester teachers felt constrained by the structure that was created for them or if they accepted it as the most "scientific" approach to teaching because we have no records of teachers' voices. We do know that the Rochester Teachers Association, unlike teachers associations in other cities, did not challenge administrative decisions. Established in 1894, the Rochester Teachers Association reflected the philosophy of the National Education Association, seeking to include instructors from every educational institution in

Rochester. Soon after its establishment, the association lobbied unsuccessfully to raise the revenue base for schools and to have teachers' salaries increased. In fact, Rochester teachers continued to be among the lowest paid statewide.[58]

More than a decade later, in 1905, the Teachers Association succeeded in establishing a teachers' pension fund, in large part due to the help of a sympathetic male principal. Gaining support from sympathetic male administrators to advance their causes was an effective strategy for teachers' groups at the turn of the century. In some cities, though, teachers were actively challenging the administrative hierarchy.[59] Margaret Haley, leader of the Chicago Teachers Federation and a national teacher activist, is a good example of just such a teacher.

Teachers' Activism at the Turn of the Century

In 1899, school centralization and scientific management were the educational reform choices for school leaders in Chicago as well as in Rochester. As spokesman for a local education commission, the president of the University of Chicago, William Rainey Harper, recommended hiring a superintendent of schools to manage the district and reducing the size of the Board of Education. The proposal, which was soon labeled the Harper Bill, called for hiring more male teachers, criticizing the increased number of female teachers in the district. Higher wages for male teachers and more rapid promotions were recommended to attract more men. In addition, Harper proposed that all teachers be college graduates.

Teachers, led by Margaret Haley, a sixth-grade teacher, and Catherine Goggin, a primary school teacher, organized a campaign to defeat the centralization plan. They gained the support of women's groups, such as the University Women's Club and the Political Equality Club, which condemned the proposal of unequal pay scales for men and women teachers. Through their efforts, teachers succeeded in defeating the Harper Bill four times between 1899 and 1909.

In 1899, Catherine Goggin was elected president of the Chicago Teachers' Federation (CTF). With Margaret Haley's help, the CTF soon chalked up another major victory. The organization won a tax suit against a number of Chicago businesses, and the money they had to pay generated sufficient revenue to increase teachers' salaries. This was the beginning of a nearly twenty-year campaign by Margaret Haley to achieve equal pay and equal rights for teachers.

Ella Flagg Young, a colleague of John Dewey's who would later serve as school superintendent, also joined this battle. Young was concerned about the negative consequences of scientific management and school centralization. Like Dewey, she advocated teaching methods that gave central importance to connecting students' experience with new learning and to fostering relationships between teachers and students. In her book, *Isolation in the School*, published in 1901, Young criticized the trend toward standardization:

> Unification was confounded with uniformity by the leaders, reformers, and organizers in their efforts to make that systematic which was to a considerable degree chaotic. The human mind, the most delicate, the most sensitive, the most complex of all organizations loses power, is arrested in its development, if its efforts are directed toward establishing unvarying conditions . . . For teachers and pupils to become part of an "incoherent homogeneity" is for them to lose from their school life that individuality which is the inherent right of every soul.[60]

As an alternative to administrative centralization, Young proposed the creation of teacher councils at the school, district, and city levels to involve teachers in educational decisions. Teacher councils would make schools more democratic, and as a result teachers would be more successful in educating students for democratic citizenship. Teachers' views about school decisions, Young believed, were an important component of a democratic organization.[61]

Margaret Haley, whose career as a teacher activist was interwoven with Ella Flagg Young's career as an educational leader, embraced the idea of teacher councils, arguing that teachers' involvement would enable them to discuss critical educational issues. Schools would become a democratizing institution for society, and teachers would become agents of genuine school reform and social change. This early conceptualization of shared decision-making was generally not implemented as Ella Flagg Young and Margaret Haley envisioned it, however. Rather, school administrators in a number of cities used the idea of teacher councils as a means to undercut teachers' activism by giving teachers a "legitimate" opportunity to have their views considered. At the same time, teacher unionization activities were labeled "unprofessional." By the late teens and twenties most unionization activity had been successfully squelched and teacher councils had been abandoned.[62] In Chicago, teachers defeated centralization efforts until 1917, when the Chicago Board of Education outlawed teachers' unions and the Illinois State Supreme Court upheld the exclusive power of the Chicago Board of Education to hire and fire teachers.[63]

In addition to their efforts in Chicago, Margaret Haley and Catherine Goggin helped organize women teachers' federations in a number of other cities, including Baltimore, Philadelphia, Boston, and St. Paul. These federations, plus those in Minneapolis, Atlanta, and Toledo, would become the charter members of the American Federation of Teachers. Margaret Haley, who was the more vocal of the pair, also challenged the leadership of the National Education Association (NEA). Like the women teachers at the state education association meetings, women teachers at the national meetings spent most of their time listening to male education experts.[64] Haley's hope was to create a national teachers' federation within the NEA that would focus, as had the teachers' federation in Chicago, on issues of teachers' salaries and working conditions.

At the NEA annual meeting of 1899, Margaret Haley and her followers began their campaign to get the NEA to address the economic conditions of teachers and to broaden the leadership to include women teachers. By 1903, at the annual convention held in Boston, Haley had rallied three thousand women teachers. Just before the convention, Margaret Haley visited and corresponded with Susan B. Anthony, then eighty-three years old, hoping to induce her to attend the meeting in support of the teachers. Despite multiple efforts, Haley did not succeed in convincing Anthony to attend, but ever the activist, Anthony did send several letters of encouragement to the group. The last letter, written after the teachers were assembled, included this message: "You teachers today will make a precedent for those of tomorrow, just as the teachers of the past made a precedent for you to be ignored on the program today. Had those of each year been true to woman's best interest you would have a great deal easier time in asserting yourselves now . . . Women should have equal pay for equal work and they should be considered equally eligible to the offices of principal and superintendent, professor and president. So you must insist that qualifications, not sex, shall govern appointments and salaries."[65]

At the 1903 convention Margaret Haley succeeded in getting teachers on the nominating committee and in having her delegation recognized. Hoping to contain the teachers' demands, President Nicholas Murray Butler appointed a committee to study teachers' wages, pensions, and tenure. Despite this action, the women teachers also insisted, successfully, that Margaret Haley speak to the general assembly before the meeting's end and be invited to speak at the 1904 national meeting.

Haley's success was shortlived, however. After 1904, in an effort to diffuse the women teachers' collective strength, the NEA leadership reduced the power of local teacher delegations and admitted a number of other women's groups, largely made up of upper-class women who had little knowledge of school life or teachers' working conditions. The NEA leadership acknowledged the teachers' economic concerns, but failed to address the issues of oversupervision and lack of job control. The question of school organization was left unanswered. Women were given the opportunity to be on the program and to speak from the floor, but this was more a token gesture than a real change. Although there were successes for women, including the NEA presidency of Ella Flagg Young in 1910, the control of the NEA remained in the hands of the overwhelmingly male superintendency.[66]

During the succeeding years the NEA leadership promoted membership in the organization as a demonstration of professional behavior, and teachers' membership in the NEA became an effective means of counteracting other teacher unionizing activities. "Loyalty to the school, loyalty to the country, and loyalty to the profession were manifested through the instrument of an NEA membership card. Membership in militant organizations was, by the same token, 'unprofessional.'"[67] So effective was this strategy that by 1925 the National Education Association had 150,103 members and the American Federation of Teachers had a membership of only 11,000.

Women teachers were also unable to maintain control over the teacher federations that they had begun. At the organizing meeting of the American Federation of Teachers (AFT) in 1916, the women elementary teachers and Margaret Haley were overshadowed by the male high school teachers, who argued that in the face of potential firing of teachers for union activity, strong leadership was required. Margaret Haley watched as a male high school teacher was elected president of the organization she had worked seventeen years to establish.

The historian Marjorie Murphy suggests that the choice of a male high school teacher as president of the AFT had profound consequences for the organization. The immediate consequences were the strained relations and subsequent break between the American Federation of Teachers and the Chicago Teachers' Federation, a rift that would have negative consequences for both organizations. The AFT lost substantial revenue from the large contingent of CTF teachers, and the CTF lost its voice at the national level. With the loss of CTF support, the male leadership set the tone for the American Federation of Teachers, rejecting the style and methods of the feminist Chicago Teacher's Federation leadership. In addition, the union became a high school teachers' union enrolling few elementary teachers for the next thirty years.[68]

With union activity denigrated as antiprofessional, and with the predominantly female, grammar school teaching force estranged from the AFT, educational administrators in the 1920s successfully overcame the AFT challenge and maintained firm control of the NEA. Despite their best efforts, activist women teachers were thwarted in their goal of developing a national voice. At the national and local levels, teacher associations would continue to be dominated by administrators until the 1960s. By the 1920s the organization of teaching created earlier in the century was well entrenched. Although there were sporadic efforts during the 1930s, 1940s, and 1950s to vary this structure, significant changes in the relationships that had been established would not occur until the renewed teacher activism of the 1960s. Education initiatives, framed with specific instructional guidelines for teachers, integrated the beliefs of progressive education and scientific management. Activist teachers were effectively muzzled, and school administrators consolidated their control of school operations.

6

Reforming Teaching in the Midst of Social Crisis: Andrena's Story, 1960–1990

Andrena Anthony's mother was a black Jamaican nurse who had come to upstate New York to work in a military hospital during World War II. There she had fallen in love with and married a soldier who had been wounded early in the war. Andrena was born in 1945. After the war the family settled in Syracuse, where her father found a job at the rapidly expanding Carrier Air Conditioning plant.

Andrena's mother enrolled her in Catholic schools through the eighth grade. Then her father, who had been working on an engineering degree at night school, insisted she attend the city's leading public school, Hamilton High, which had a reputation for an outstanding math and science program. They became one of the first African American families to buy a house in the Hamilton school district, and Andrena entered ninth grade there in the fall of 1959.[1]

There were fewer than a dozen blacks among Hamilton's thousand students. But Andrena did not feel like a token, perhaps because she had gone to the majority-white parochial schools and not the virtually all-black public grade schools in a city where many children still spoke of "nigger town" and "jew town." She was an extraordinarily beautiful young woman who soon overcame the prejudice of some of her teachers to earn a reputation as a strong student, although she did not shine as much in math as her father had hoped. It was literature and social studies that she loved, particularly her poetry classes with Kay Kastenmayer, who also drew Andrena into school drama productions. It was there she became close friends with a girl whose father was a liberal lawyer in Syracuse. Most Hamilton High parents of that era were pleased that their school was "integrated" and usually gave Andrena the longest and loudest applause for her roles, rejoicing in this evidence of their good intentions. They rarely if ever spoke of what all knew—that the drama club was one of the few places where cross-racial friendships could blossom. The fraternities and sororities, which established the dating hierarchies at Hamilton High, had never accepted a black student, and Jews had their own sorority and fraternity. Cross-racial friendships did not include dating, however. Andrena's first experience of an overt color bar came after an exchange student from Sweden had taken her to several films. When it became clear he had begun to develop a crush on her and might even ask her to the junior prom, the vice principal called him in and told him such behavior was not approved social practice. Schools in the northern United States did not exclude blacks like those in the South but interracial marriage and hence interracial dating was not tolerated. Andrena stayed home on prom night.

That experience partly influenced Andrena's decision to become a teacher. Perhaps she could help change those attitudes. Kay Kastenmayer encouraged her and helped her through the college application process. Andrena applied to two of the state teachers colleges and was accepted at both. She chose Brockport, which Kay Kastenmayer knew would be one of the first of the old normal schools to be converted to a general liberal arts college. Until that time, New York had no state system of free public higher education other than the teachers colleges.

When she arrived at Brockport in the fall of 1963, construction for the conversion had begun. But Andrena sat in classrooms not much different from those Florence Thayer had toiled in during the 1890s. The curriculum was not altogether different either; some of the courses, such as "The Child and the Curriculum," even had similar titles, although the content was updated. Most of the students were preparing to teach in elementary schools. Andrena enrolled in the early secondary program, which would certify her to teach up to ninth grade—the highest level of preparation then permitted to the teachers colleges. Part of the reason for the conversion was to enable the teachers colleges to compete with the state's private liberal arts colleges, which then had a near monopoly on the preparation of high school teachers.

Under the program being phased out as she enrolled, six courses, or twenty-four credit hours, were required in English, with only fifteen of these in literature and the remainder in composition. A total of thirty-nine hours was devoted to education courses, including fifteen hours of practice teaching. In the new program instituted by 1965 when Brockport officially became a liberal arts college, students like Andrena were required to take fifteen hours in literature and encouraged to use seventeen hours of electives to expand an English major to thirty hours of courses in English and American literature. The hours of education credits were reduced from thirty-nine to twenty-one, with twelve of these devoted to a semester of practice teaching in a high school.[2]

Andrena's years at Brockport passed largely untouched by the campus revolts that began at Berkeley in 1964 but did not spread to colleges in small towns like Brockport until the late sixties or early seventies, if at all. However, she had skipped part of her freshman orientation program to go to Washington with her parents to hear Martin Luther King make his famous speech from the steps of the Lincoln Memorial. And in the spring 1966 term she did her practice teaching in a high school in nearby Rochester, where African American parents were beginning to protest the slow pace of racial integration in the city's public schools.

In the normal course of things, Andrena would have started her teaching career in seventh or eighth grade and served an apprenticeship before being promoted to one of the coveted high school English positions. But these were not normal times. The 1960s brought the postwar baby boomers to high school, nearly doubling the number of adolescents. And in Syracuse, as in Rochester, the African American population had grown rapidly, doubling in the 1950s and again in the 1960s as southern blacks moved north in record numbers.

During Andrena's first year at Brockport, the mayor of Syracuse had appointed a special task force to investigate "racial imbalance" following a citywide protest by civil rights groups. The city school board at first resisted the findings of widespread racial imbalance in the public schools. But a new board and school superintendent accepted the findings, and admitted that so-called compensatory education in the predominantly black schools had not worked. While Andrena was doing her student teaching in Rochester, Syracuse began to implement a major desegregation plan that broke up the pattern of ghetto schooling for blacks. The city also began to send recruiters south to hire black teachers to diversify its faculty. Kay Kastenmayer wrote to Andrena before her graduation in 1967 to tell her that under these circumstances she might have a chance to begin her teaching career at her alma mater, especially if she immediately began to study for a master's degree in English. Andrena submitted her application for the master's program at Syracuse University the same day she wrote for the teaching job. She began part-time graduate study that summer and in August was offered a position teaching ninth grade English at Hamilton High.

She was the second African American hired at Hamilton High. The first, a black chemistry teacher from Georgia, darker in complexion than Andrena, had been hired the year before. They became good friends, although Kay Kastenmayer continued to hold first place in her heart. The Hamilton High to which Andrena returned in the fall of 1967 did not seem vastly different from the school she had left only four years ago. There were more African American students—about 10 percent of the 1,150 students enrolled, mostly clustered in ninth grade—but the rhythms of the school felt the same. Her first moments with the principal were awkward. She learned years later that he would not have hired her had not the school system's new affirmative action officer and Kay Kastenmayer used all the political clout they could muster. It was less a matter of race than of his skepticism about appointing someone so young, and passing over teachers who been waiting for an appointment to Hamilton. He had been there since the late 1940s, an era when high school principals were assumed to be appointed for life. Their decisions were rarely challenged.

Andrena knew the hierarchy at Hamilton and did not make the mistake that some new teachers had made of taking the parking spaces nearest the school that by custom were reserved for senior faculty. Space was getting tight inside the school, too, and it took several years for her to claim her own classroom. Like the students, she had to gather her books and move to whatever classroom was vacant during a given period.

She moved quickly through the glistening hallways, as they did. Students were seldom late to class and would not dare to throw a candy wrapper on the floor. Dress codes had begun to relax, however. Young male teachers, some of them avoiding the Vietnam War, no longer wore a tie and jacket—she heard that one or two had smoked marijuana. A few students adopted a hippy style, but most boys still wore creased khakis and the girls wore neat skirts and blouses. A letter in the school paper criticized girls who had dared to wear miniskirts. Many students were headed for Ivy League colleges, and more than four-fifths of Hamilton graduates went on to some form of postsecondary education. Hamilton students, competing with students in about twenty schools in the county, regularly won about a third of the college scholarships awarded by the state. Students were expected to do two hours of homework each night.

Andrena was doing four or five hours of "homework," trying to keep up with her classes. She had never worked so hard in her life. She had five classes, and a total of 133 students. If she assigned only one short essay a week—as short as a paragraph—and took only three minutes to read and comment on each one the task absorbed more than six precious hours. But she couldn't do justice to most of them in three minutes and often worked ten-hour days on Saturdays correcting papers. She had to drop the graduate course she was taking two nights a week.

When classes went badly—as they often did that year—she some-times felt like crying. Particularly troublesome was her sixth-period class, with a group of boys who seemed to delight in tormenting her and yet were clever enough to avoid doing anything so vile that she could eject them. Nor did she want to admit to the principal that she could not control her classes without his help. This was nothing like her student teaching, where the "real" teacher would step in and give students what-for if they stepped too far out of line. How did teachers learn to break these wild colts, she wondered one day as the sixth-period boys came loudly in after lunch mimicking Malvolio's speech in Shake-speare's *Twelfth Night?* She remembered when a teacher's stern look over the shoulder or simply flicking the lights off was all that was needed to produce silence. That didn't work for her. The boys cackled in the dark when she tried dousing the lights. She thought of her courses in educational psychology and the idealistic professor who had spoken of the need to find a way to motivate all students to learn. She would love to see him try to motivate these oafs.

Andrena's jokes fell flat. She stopped trying to humor them. She feared she might be turning into a grouch. Some days she felt sweaty and nauseous before a class that wasn't going well. Several times she simply abandoned the lesson plan she had thought great the night before and gave them makework—then felt ashamed of herself for not sticking with it. Even when a lesson was going reasonably well, she struggled for the right examples that seemed to fall so easily from Kay Kastenmayer's lips. Was that because Kastenmayer had read so many more books or lived longer or was just smarter than she was? Why did she get so flustered?

There were times she was thinking so much about how badly things were going or what to do next that she completely missed what a student had just said. Once a student had called her on it and she had truly felt like a fool, and a coward to boot, for not admitting immediately that she hadn't heard a thing the girl had said. Luckily the girl had accepted her belated apology.

What an art it was to ask the right question at the right moment! What were the essential questions to ask? How could she arrange them into themes and broad instructional goals? What should she be aiming at? Why should it matter if students knew the plots of Shakespeare's tragedies? Did memorizing "Ode on a Grecian Urn" make a better or a happier citizen? How could she develop the critical intellect and nurture the creative spirit? Curriculum guidelines helped some. She smiled inwardly to see how far some teachers bent them, with bird-lovers importing units about birds into the curriculum and golfers discovering short stories written about their game. Yet the best teachers put their mark on their courses in a serious way. They were not slaves to published guidelines but took the broad aims of the curriculum seriously—even as they disputed them—and developed units of instruction that would engage students and tap into their interests.

As the year went on, she began to look more closely at the New York State Regents' exams. Hidden there was one statement of the real goals of the curriculum. That was what students had to know, and their performance on those examinations would also be a measure of her effectiveness. She had long talks with Bill Beak, a young physicist who had done his degree at Brown University. He told her he had been enormously perplexed about what of physics to teach until he studied the Regents' exams and saw that they were what he should pay attention to. As the spring of 1968 began to unfold, she noticed that many of her colleagues required their students to buy paperbacks filled with earlier versions of the Regents' exams. She was uneasy in doing so but began to assign regular homework from those prep books. It was a lot easier than figuring out creative lesson plans. To her surprise, the students settled down, too. This was the real stuff. Now they knew what to memorize and what counted. No more struggling with Miss Anthony's intricate analysis of plot and motive, meaning and symbolism. No more weekly essays. She was able to take a few Saturdays off, too, because the students could correct each other's Regents' quizzes with a little in-class guidance from her.

Her basic class—the slowest track at Hamilton—was still a problem, however. These students were not required to take the Regents' exams. It was a small class, eighteen students, and all but three of them were black. Following an urban-renewal project to make way for a new interstate highway, public housing had been built on the border of the Hamilton district. The few black classmates she had had in the early sixties were children of ministers and nurses and postal workers. Now there were 150 black students at Hamilton, many of them poor children from public housing who had formerly gone to the black ghetto schools and then to Central High, where most of them dropped out at the age of sixteen, after which schooling was not compulsory. More would be coming to Hamilton as the new desegregation plan continued to change the feeder patterns. The class was not out of control. These students respected her. But it was not at all what she had hoped, either. Andrena saw fear and failure in their eyes, and she wanted to motivate these students. She assigned Ralph Ellison's *Invisible Man* and Martin Luther King's *Letter from the Birmingham Jail.* She was able to stir some lively discussions on several occasions. But she was less successful in getting them to analyze Ellison, or to write essays. Some of them had never written a paragraph and most were poor readers.

In May, several weeks after the assassination of Martin Luther King, Syracuse newspapers carried the first notice that all was not well at Hamilton High. The *Herald-Journal* reported that classes had been suspended while "some 200 or 300 students gathered in the school's auditorium to talk out racial tensions resulting from misunderstandings between Negro and White pupils." The article closed with assurances from the principal: "Everybody was very, very happy. Our school is as quiet as it has been since I've been here."[3]

Andrena was not reassured, however. She had never heard the word "nigger" from a teacher when she was a student in Hamilton High. But as the number of blacks from the housing projects rose, she had heard it in the faculty lunch room from a few faculty who were not aware of her sitting in a corner away from the smokers. And next year they would have more than two hundred African American students. Although she had initially seen nothing wrong with the placement of students in the lower track, Andrena was disturbed by the plan to slot most of these new students in basic classes. This was beginning to look like a "black track" to her, a kind of internal segregation and degradation she had never felt as a student. She was glad when she read that summer that her old principal had resigned. Riots had swept through the black ghettos of Detroit and Newark. Hamilton students had seen televised reports of the police "bust" outside the Democratic Convention headquarters in Chicago. That fall, some of her students watched Vice Presidential candidate Edmund Muskie struggling to be heard over antiwar protesters when he spoke in Syracuse.

The new principal, who was returning to Hamilton, where he had been an industrial arts teacher, was a lanky and genial man who was widely liked by both students and teachers. He immediately sensed the new mood in the school, as did the faculty, when a new student newspaper, the *Picayune Papers*, appeared. It grew out of discussions of racial tensions the previous spring, and its first issue carried a bold photograph of sixty black students with Afro hair styles wearing dashikis and African dresses. The days of quiet assimilation of black students were over. A spokesman for the students pictured explained that black students should identify with their own people: "Black people should be proud of themselves."

Desegregation brought to Hamilton not only more militant blacks but also more working-class ethnic whites. In a student poll on Presidential candidates, Hubert Humphrey outpolled Richard Nixon two to one, but George Wallace also received 5 percent of the vote. The new mix in the school came to a boil in late October when the first full-scale riot erupted in the school cafeteria. Chairs were thrown and tables were scattered across the room. When the new principal tried to stop it, he was clubbed over the head; he went to the hospital with a fractured skull.

A tremendous shock spread through the community but the worst was yet to come. Over the next three years outbreaks of violence became commonplace. Three or four police cars were often parked in the Hamilton driveway and a police officer was assigned full time to patrol the halls. Hamilton closed ten times in 1968–69, and went on block sessions so that the school could send students home for lunch rather than risk confrontations in the school cafeteria. Classes were frequently disrupted and several teachers were injured. Weapons were brought into the school, fires were set, and some white parents grew so alarmed that they chained the doors early one morning to publicize their feelings that the building was not a safe place for their children to enter. Teachers routinely locked their classroom doors after the bell and hoped they could get through each class without incident. The new principal resigned after two years and his thirty-five-year-old replacement had a bodyguard assigned to him; riots had become a way of life. One day he told the fireman cleaning up after a fire that he wanted them to put fans in the hall to clear out the smoke so school could go on. "We can't let them shut us down," he said.

After he resigned the principalship, the former industrial arts teacher defended the basic track as the best way to deal with black children "from Mississippi or Florida" who lagged three or four grades behind their classmates in reading abilities. "They lacked the computing skills, the reading skills—not because they lacked the intelligence but because they never really had an opportunity to have a decent education where they came from. Now do you cast them off to the winds? No. You put them in the basic classes. Some people didn't belong at the high school level." Yet most of these students had come not from Mississipi but from segregated elementary and middle schools in Syracuse, where their failure was nearly invisible. When they arrived they were given the message, as the former principal had inadvertently put it, that "some people didn't belong" here. Moreover, they were angry to discover how far behind their white classmates they really were. The tragic irony of desegregation in most American schools was that poor black students who had thought they were making good progress in formerly segregated schools—whether de facto as in Syracuse or de jure as in the South—were brought together with affluent whites to discover how far apart they truly were.

As she started her fourth year of teaching, Andrena was enthusiastic about her third principal, the first at Hamilton with a doctorate in educational administration. Although he had never taught, she liked his youth and his new ideas. He banned fraternities and sororities and held rap sessions with students, announcing that his philosophy would make the school "student-oriented rather than teacher-oriented." Most important, he moved quickly to abolish the tracking system and assign students randomly to classes. He broke the schedule into ten-week modules and expanded electives, enabling students to choose new teachers four times a year. He stripped privileges from what he called the "old guard faculty"—those who might have a telephone in their rooms and had the choice teaching assignments, some of them teaching only seniors or advanced classes. Now they had a mix of the best and worst students in all their classes. A teachers' union survey in the early 1970s showed he had one of the lowest principal ratings in the city.

An exodus of whites began. By 1972 white enrollment at Hamilton had declined by 350 students, and real estate prices in the district had fallen almost by half. The effects on the students—both black and white—were profound. The undoing of three hundred years of racial segregation in America left no one untouched. Except for prisons, no institution in American society bore the brunt of the racial revolution as much as schools. Some liberal white students became racists. Some middle-class blacks were torn apart by conflicting loyalties between the old world they knew and the demands of revolution.

Teachers, too, were battered and confused as the world they had known crumbled beneath them. They left in unprecedented numbers. In a five-year period, about 70 percent of the teachers retired, resigned, or transferred. Many of them felt an overwhelming sense of failure as teachers. The strategies that had been effective in the classroom no longer worked. Most teachers lacked the knowledge, the resourcefulness, the imagination, or the energy to teach the new black—often angry—students who sat in their classrooms. A school that had functioned so smoothly that student monitors had once kept order during the change of classes was now considered unsafe even with police officers patrolling the halls.

A few of the teachers were outright racists, but nearly all of the rest felt that their profession had been shamed by what had been revealed of the school system's complicity in sustaining previously segregated schools. Although the number of teachers who left Hamilton was above the average, even for urban schools in that period, the demoralization of teachers in America was widespread. Teachers were no longer sure of the grounds of their moral authority. School systems grew more centralized as they implemented desegregation plans. Traditional understandings and governance structures were swept away. Principals and teachers were stripped of their former prerogatives. Many urban school systems were being run under court order. School superintendents and principals often feared to make a move without first consulting lawyers.

While teachers were still reeling from the racial revolution, yet another was born that was nearly as profound in its effects—a radical reordering in the relations between children and adults that was brought about by a transformation in student rights. These changes stemmed from two Supreme Court decisions—the *Gault* case in 1967 and the *Winship* case in 1970—that began to have a dramatic effect on American public schools in the 1970s. In 1971 the Syracuse Board of Education adopted sweeping new due process requirements. Many matters once left to the discretion of the school principals or teachers now were subject to grievance and courtroom-like review. In *Gault* the Supreme Court established a new standard that juvenile court proceedings "must measure up to the essentials of due process and fair treatment." The *Gault* decision was later extended, in the *Winship* case, to insist that juvenile courts also meet the standard of proving guilt "beyond a reasonable doubt." In these two decisions the Supreme Court undid the work of an earlier generation of children's rights advocates who had established the juvenile court system in the early 1900s when ten-year-olds were still tried and sentenced along with hardened criminals. The intention was that a wise and kindly judge would consider a wide variety of evidence in dealing with juveniles, who might be straightened out with a stern admonition or referral to a foster home rather than with the imposition of sentences that might criminalize them. But the Court turned away from this view, concluding that "the essentials of due process" might now be better therapy for juveniles than the inconsistencies of "paternal advice and admonition." In sum, the Court was no longer willing to trust the discretion and judgment of the juvenile court judges. Little time was lost in applying this reasoning to attack the "paternalism" of the school principal. It was not long before all of the tests of due process enumerated in *Gault* were applied to schools, namely: notice of the charges, the right to counsel, the right to confrontation and cross-examination, privilege against self-incrimination, the right to a transcript of the proceedings, and the right to appellate review.

In the year following *Gault*, the American Civil Liberties Union (ACLU) published a widely influential document, *Academic Freedom in the Secondary Schools*. The ACLU statement laid down three principles, the first of which pushed academic freedom of students to a new limit by arguing not only that freedom implies the right to make mistakes but that students must sometimes "be permitted to act in ways which are predictably unwise so long as the consequences of their acts are not dangerous to life and property, and do not seriously disrupt the academic process." The second principle blurred the line between speech and action, arguing for "a recognition that deviation from the opinions and standards deemed desirable by the faculty is not ipso facto a danger to the educational process." Insofar as these principles were restricted to free speech issues, most school officials and most parents would probably agree with them—although they might not be happy with the relatively strong dismissal of "standards" of adults in the school. Third, the ACLU statement warned, "Students and their schools should have the right to live under the principle of 'rule by law' as opposed to 'rule by personality.' To protect this right, rules and regulation should be in writing. Students have the right to know the limits and extent of the faculty's authority and, therefore, the powers that are reserved for the students and the responsibilities that they should accept." In every area of discipline the ACLU statement took a lawyerly view of the need to reduce adult latitude and discretion in favor of specific definitions and rules.[4]

The recommendations of the ACLU statement became standard operating procedure in many urban schools, as they did in Syracuse, which often adopted the ACLU language verbatim. Henceforth, students could not be suspended without specifying their infractions in writing. The evidence against them would be provided to students or their legal representatives. Rules for student hearings were published. Students were to be given time to prepare their defense and the right to cross-examine witnesses. Records and transcripts of all hearings would be provided to students at school expense.

Students were emboldened and teachers were put on the defensive by this turn of events. They hesitated to act against even serious misbehavior unless they had "evidence that would stand up in court." Students from Hamilton and other Syracuse high schools were appointed to the Superintendent's Student Cabinet. They drew up a new grievance procedure, a five-step process that enabled students to bring a wide range of grievances to arbitration. It was adopted in 1972 and distributed to all pupils in a student handbook outlining their rights. The prologue sought to assure teachers that "the process does not seek to discredit staff members and administrators, or their position in the schools, but it does recognize that in certain instances a method of reconciling differences is necessary."[5] However, many teachers felt that if it did not discredit them, it encouraged harassment, particularly since the procedure mandated a hearing first with the principal, then with the director of high schools, and finally with the superintendent. It invited grievance on issues of grading and "when the behavior of any staff member willfully imposes upon a student(s) the ethical, social or political values of a staff member." The statement failed to make a distinction between socialization and indoctrination. Many teachers felt it put a chill on their freedom to establish ethical standards in the classroom.

Some embraced the statement, however. A drug counselor, asked why she and other teachers did not intervene when students were openly using marijuana, replied: "Who are we to say what is right and what is wrong?" pointing out that some of the faculty drank too much and were in no position to criticize students for abusing drugs. By the mid-1970s the violence had subsided, and teachers who had been united when they were under siege began to split into different factions. New recruits replaced teachers who had resigned and different political viewpoints emerged. Teachers who had fended off chair-swinging students in the cafeteria favored different policies than did those who came after the riots. Faculty meetings became donnybrooks over whether Eldridge Cleaver's *Soul on Ice* should be taught in English classes. The splintering of the faculty could be seen at lunchtime. Once they had all shared one lounge; now they ate in three different locations. Old guard males gathered in the room where the copy machine was located; these middle-aged white men had fared worst in the challenge to their classroom authority. Middle of the road and conservative female faculty ate in the home economics area. Andrena had so much work to do that she often stayed at her desk; when she had time she lunched with the younger, more liberal faculty, including some of the union organizers, in the old lounge.

The new faculty differed in their orientations. Some were deeply sympathetic to the escalating protest movements. A few had been involved in college demonstrations in the late sixties. They encouraged students to call them by their first names, actively opposed the Vietnam War, and since they smoked marijuana themselves were lenient with students who came to their classrooms in a drugged state. Young female faculty wore miniskirts. The winds of the cultural and sexual revolution abroad in the land stirred Hamilton High. Sexual affairs among the faculty became more numerous, and an occasional liaison with a student was overlooked. These teachers differed markedly from more traditional faculty in their expectations for achievement, their grading policies, and their tolerance for missed deadlines. Andrena disapproved of their tendency to go easy on black students out of what she felt was misguided liberalism. They angered older male teachers when they supported protests by female students about sexual inequality in the athletic programs and facilities (girls were given old uniforms and even used boys white socks; their teams had limited access to courts and playing fields). One outcome of such differences at Hamilton High and elsewhere was that teachers perceived, quite correctly, that they could no longer be sure that another faculty member shared their views about a basic matter of discipline or would support them if they challenged a student misbehaving in the hall. Faculty tended to withdraw from such encounters or not to see them. Once a car approaching the school was stoned by a group of students in full view of a number of faculty members, and no one attempted to stop the violence.

Andrena's loyalties were torn. On the one hand, she felt the pain experienced by decent teachers who, perhaps more than any other members of society, took the brunt of pent-up anger over generations of racial discrimination. She knew most of them were good teachers and was troubled by how confused and disoriented many of them had become—not only for their sakes but for the sake of the students, who were not being taught as well as some of these same teachers had taught her. She tried to listen sympathetically when they told her of name calling or other abuses. Even Kay Kastenmayer had been enraged when a student she had caught cheating had forced her to appear at a hearing. "I saw him with his open book on his lap during a test," she told Andrena. "They wanted documentation. 'How can you prove it? How did he cheat?' I said I am telling you that he was cheating. But the question now is, 'We've heard John's side of the story, what's yours?'. . . . The issue is the boy's cheating and now two hours later I'm in the principal's office discussing due process."

On the other hand, Andrena had herself been radicalized by the cascade of events. She also sympathized with students whose rights had been trampled on, reminding her of her own pain when the Swedish boy was told he should not take her to the junior prom. The protests in Syracuse had opened her eyes to the depth of racism and the way it had affected poor blacks more severely than it had blighted her life. School boundaries had been gerrymandered, and blacks had been overassigned to the lowest academic tracks, particularly in mathematics. As a teacher with access to files, she now read condescending comments by counselors, such as "Charles is a Negro student, but is accepted by all for the fine young man that he really is." Police response during the riots had been disproportionate. At Central High downtown, police had forced black students outside the school and cordoned them off more than a block away, while white students were allowed to stand in front of the building. At Hamilton, black students who were not participating in a riot charged that they were roughed up by police, whereas white students who were involved were ignored. One black girl testified that a policeman had shoved her up against the wall and ordered her to get out of the school. "But I'm a student here, I told him." Until 1972 no picture of Hamilton events in the *Syracuse Herald-Journal* had included any black students, and Andrena noticed that even as the number of black students approached 40 percent at Hamilton, there were few candid photos of them in the school yearbooks. As a teacher said many years later, "We treated them as though they were invisible."

Andrena was also radicalized in a pedagogical sense. Although many of her colleagues were opposed to the young principal's reforms, she was gaining confidence as a teacher and began to feel excited by the challenge of developing new courses. She had resumed work on her master's degree in English and thought she would adapt a course on African American writers to offer as an elective in the new modular structure. Although she was in a minority, she was not alone. Some faculty and some students (particularly the blacks) were energized if not exhilarated by the conflict. Some white students who had personal resources and the self-confidence to ride out the conflict also were imbued with revolutionary fervor. Several whites enrolled in Andrena's new course on African American writers. The civil rights movement that led to school desegregation coalesced with other movements protesting the Vietnam War and student demands for more voice in educational decisions. The move to abolish fixed requirements and increase student choice in the curriculum spread down from college campuses and affected the climate of high schools like Hamilton.

Hamilton yearbooks in the 1970s displayed exceptional vibrance and creativity. They also depicted the radical transfer of power to students. Whereas the yearbooks had always opened with pictures of the faculty and administration, now the faculty came last. The opening pages of one book featured students in revolutionary garb and a photograph of a student holding a sign that read, "Zoo: Do Not Feed the Teachers." Andrena supported the increase of student elective power as a way to demolish the tracking system, and she delighted in the ability of some of her newly empowered black students to take a leading role in classroom discussions, and not only in her African American literature class. A decade later, however, she was disturbed when research showed that these students were in a small minority. After tracking was abolished, the gap in scores between black and white students widened. The study of actual courses chosen showed that the majority of black students continued to track themselves after the abolition of formal tracking. That is, they often chose the softer options and not advanced courses in science, math, and foreign languages. She realized then that raising the achievement of all black students meant requiring more math and science of all students (although not reinstituting tracking) and reforming teacher training to give teachers more tools to be effective with a wider range of students. It also required paying closer attention to the preparatory courses in junior high school, particularly in math and science. She joined a committee that developed a new course-planning guide for students in the seventh grade, and supported proposals to require three years of high school mathematics of all students.

As the years passed, Andrena also began to take some graduate courses in education to expand her own repertoire of teaching skills. Unlike many young teachers who were left to sink or swim on their own, she had had the benefit of informal consultations with the master teacher Kay Kastenmayer. She trusted Kay and could share her anxieties with her and seek counsel about problems she was experiencing in the classroom. But she realized that Kay had her limits, too. Andrena was particularly interested in discovering how to make cooperative learning work in her classrooms. She devoured the work of Elizabeth Cohen, whose writings explained how to set up cooperative projects among small groups of students from differing backgrounds and ability levels in ways that maximized mutual respect and the possibilities of effective peer tutoring. For example, don't assume a Latino boy can teach a Spanish poem in a small group simply because he speaks Spanish. The boy may know little about poetry or how to teach effectively, and his stumbling attempt may confirm the prejudices of mainstream peers. Find out what interests him and what he could teach with some skill and enthusiasm. Coach and rehearse him privately in the development of a trial lesson plan so that his performance in the group builds his confidence instead of shaming him. Peter Elbow's engaging style in *Writing without Teachers* similarly appealed to her. Elbow helped her see the importance of continuing to write herself—writers are the best teachers of writers—and of responding with more enthusiasm to short passages students wrote that touched her emotions, even if those passages contained some grammatical errors or were embedded in essays that failed in other ways. She was also quick to put some of his inventive "free writing" techniques to work in her classes. She was amazed at how students she had nearly given up on began to write some powerful passages when she confronted the whole class with a simple question like "Pick up your pens and write for three minutes about whatever comes into your head about how you felt on your first day in kindergarten." Then she used some of the new peer tutoring techniques she had learned to put them in pairs and get them to appreciate and critique each other's writing. Voilà![6]

Her positive experience with those first education courses convinced her to make time for one refresher course at the university each year. One summer she enrolled in Greta Dershimer's seminar. She had heard Dershimer was a good teacher who showed a lot of videotapes. But the seminar was not what she expected. Dershimer went into classrooms and captured teacher-student interactions on video. The seminars were intense examinations of what was really going on between teachers and their students. This experience opened Andrena's eyes to the subtle messages teachers may communicate without ever realizing it: that they may respond to boys more than girls or avoid the eyes of black students; or that some teachers rarely wait for students to think about a question they have posed before they go on to answer it themselves—thus training the students not to think, not to engage, and not to take seriously the problems teachers are posing. She began to feel comfortable with longer silences and found that a wider range of students began to join discussions.[7]

Another eye-opener was a psychology seminar that Andrena took in the early 1980s, where she encountered the work of Howard Gardner, who completely altered her understanding of human intelligence. Gardner made her see that traditional intelligence tests primarily measured only one kind of "smartness," logical-mathematical skills, or linear thinking. That was important, but there were other frames of mind that were essential to human cunning and achievement. The mime Marcel Marceau, the jazz pianist Oscar Peterson, and the hockey player Wayne Gretzky all exhibit a high level of bodily-kinesthetic intelligence in the way that they coordinate one hand with another and exercise complete mastery over the manipulation of objects to produce stunning effects, just as did many of her students who might have been poor writers. Intelligence was multiple, not singular. It included the kind of intelligence that gives one greater access to one's own feelings—intrapersonal intelligence—and the kind that enables one to sense distinctions in the moods, temperaments, and motivations of others—interpersonal intelligence. Andrena thought of students of hers who had extraordinary "radar equipment" in just this sense, who were the ones who identified with a wide range of character motivations in a novel and who could act as skillful mediators to defuse tense conflicts among their peers. Altogether Gardner enumerated seven kinds of intelligence, including the spatial, musical, and linguistic in addition to those just mentioned.[8]

As an undergraduate, Andrena thought sociology was a pseudo-science for people who could not write good English. Now she discovered not only Elizabeth Cohen but others who could write and had something to say. Philip Cusick had spent a year of observation in an urban high school and wrote insightfully about the variation in student subcultures. Cusick got inside the heads of working-class white students, giving her more understanding of their resentments and resistance to schooling. Her favorite sociologist, however, was Sara Lawrence Lightfoot, from whom she learned how differently teachers construct their roles as teachers, both in their relation to pupils and in their relation to parents. It dawned on her in reading Lightfoot that although there were only eight teachers in her English department, they had different ideas about teaching English. Some saw themselves primarily as teachers of writing and grammar; others considered themselves conveyors of the great works of literature; and still others put much more emphasis on establishing relationships with students and saw literature almost as a way of giving therapy by discussing the human emotions. The last group tended to relate to parents in this way as well, and spent more of their time analyzing the psychic make-up or emotional problems of their pupils. She realized that she was less "motherly" in this sense, more didactic, more inclined to sit down with a parent to discuss a problematic essay than a personality problem.[9]

Andrena had now completed her master's degree, but continued to enroll in seminars that interested her. She had earned permanent certification and was respected by colleagues and parents alike. She was seen as a teacher with high expectations who demanded much of her students and of herself, but also as a person formal if not austere in manner, in part the careful engineer and in part the nurse who could be firm with a recalcitrant patient.

In 1981 her mother was found to have a devastating form of cancer. Over the next two years, Andrena corrected most of her papers at her mother's bedside. She was an only child, and her father relied heavily on Andrena, who could be there in the early afternoon to administer medication and change dresssings. It was an extraordinary role reversal for Andrena and also the occasion for deeper sharing with her mother. As her mother told her some of her secrets, and revealed aspects of her own struggles as one of the first black registered nurses to work in a Syracuse hospital, Andrena found that she was able to talk about some of her early defeats in the classroom that she had never spoken to her mother about before.

After her mother's death, while working through her own grief and a depression that led her to seek therapy, Andrena came to the realization that one of the ways she wanted to change as a teacher was to be more present as a person in the classroom. She knew it was neither desirable nor possible to establish the kind of intimate relationship she had had at her mother's bedside, but she realized that she had been most fully herself when she shared her doubts and fears with her mother, when she no longer presented herself as the perfect daughter. Now she began to see that maybe she did not have to present herself in school as the perfect teacher either.

She began to assign essays that encouraged students to be more revealing and introspective—something as simple as asking them to write about how they felt about their own given names. When she did so, following Peter Elbow's advice, she wrote along with them, expressing her ambivalence about the name Andrena and a great aunt she had been named after whom she never liked. She sought criticisms of her own essay, using it as an example on the overhead projector, editing it with a red felt pencil in response to some of the student's suggestions. After they had done some critiquing of each other's papers and had rewritten them, she rewrote hers as well, again sharing it with them.

She was also more inclined to express her feelings and reasons for things that mattered deeply. Whereas she had always treated any form of cheating or plagiarism with stern imposition of justice, she now spoke with some passion about the difficulty of establishing any trusting relationship without truth-telling, of the impossibility of science or even a good seminar if participants dissembled or misrepresented evidence. Perhaps most important, she said, they cheated themselves. They cheated themselves of self-respect. They cheated themselves of the opportunity to learn and grow. If they represented others' work as their own, they would never learn what needed improvement in their own writing. Her eye might fall on football star: "Would you want to examine a videotape of only another quarterback's passing game and never have an honest critique of your own?" Thinking of a time she had once cheated herself, and looking at some of those applying to the most select colleges, she might suggest that perhaps the worst motive for cheating is refusing to accept who we are, not believing we are worthy enough, fearing no one would love us unless we had at least an A-minus on this paper. "If you believe in human dignity, believe in it for yourselves. Your best honest effort will earn you the best reward."

She also spoke out more now in faculty meetings. At first she was surprised that the room grew quiet when she stood. It made her nervous. Then she realized that no one wanted to miss what she had to say, and that her opinion often influenced the outcome of the issue under discussion. She even got to the point where she could make a joke now and then. When asked if she would allow herself to be nominated as a union representative, she declined, pleading overwork. Asked again a year later, she consented and was elected by a large majority. As one of the four "building reps," she met frequently with the principal and began to have more voice in schoolwide policy. She also got to know her colleagues better as they brought their complaints and requests for intervention to her. Most of these complaints were justified: one teacher was denied a day of leave to attend her uncle's funeral, and another thought that a vice principal had been too lenient with a student who frequently disrupted a class. And these problems were usually easily resolved, although at times formal grievance procedures had to be invoked.

The most difficult cases involved firings. Andrena had no problem with young teachers who clearly were not fitted for the vocation by temperament or natural inclination; it was doing them a favor to get them started in a new direction early in life. She was troubled by cases where teachers were being dismissed for ineffective classroom performance that could have been remedied by better college training and more support and coaching in the first years on the job. Accusations of poor teaching by tenured colleagues were rare, and when made the union was often successful in defending a teacher on a technicality—a required observation had not been made or report not filed. And the union was prepared to make it expensive for the school district to press a case of teacher incompetence. This aspect of union philosophy—protect the weakest link of the chain at all costs—troubled Andrena. Most of these teachers should have been let go, and there were more whose teaching was clearly inadequate who were never challenged because principals did not have the stomach for it or the school district the purse. She sympathized with many of these failing teachers; she knew the family problems that had led some into alcoholism, and realized that others should have been advised not to teach when they were undergraduates. But she sympathized more with the students who were being short-changed in their classrooms. The students should not be sacrificed to incompetence. She wondered if the union could ever find a way to deal with this problem. Teaching would never be considered a worthy profession if teachers could not find a way to police their own ranks. Such oversight need not all be punitive, she thought. Some of the tenured teachers might be saved through better coaching, stimulating sabbaticals, and other opportunities to improve their practice.

As she listened to the lore of the old-time union reps, she realized how deeply their thinking was affected by their struggle for job security and basic rights. They reminded her that when she was a student in 1960 teachers' salaries were abysmal and teachers could be fired at whim. Teachers who became pregnant were expected to take leave as soon as the baby "showed." Teachers grew more militant and overcame their aversion to traditional blue-collar union tactics. New York state law barred public employees from striking. Yet it took strikes in Syracuse and Rochester and major legal battles to win contracts that protected teachers against arbitrary firings and gave them leverage when discussing salaries at the bargaining table.

Now in the mid-1980s teachers were beginning to push for a greater share in educational decisions. One of the forms this effort took was the formation of school improvement committees in many districts. At Hamilton High, the first such committee consisted of a dozen teachers and staff members elected by the faculty. Andrena was pleased to be among them. Perhaps this committee could tackle some of the issues that her experience as a union rep had made her aware of. Discussions of "school improvement" would not be limited to contract items in the way that union rep meetings with the principal were constrained. She was not naive, however. She knew that in some schools these improvement committees were a bone tossed to the teachers by administrators to delay more radical power-sharing moves by the union. Yet she was encouraged that the principal had agreed not to chair this committee, and in fact did not come to the first meeting so that the teachers could feel free to set their own agenda. The committee was representative of the diversity of the staff and included a core of the best teachers.

None of the teachers wanted to leave at the end of that first meeting.

Spirits were high, and most hoped that because this was the first elected committee of this type, things would be different. Still, the history of previous committees had not been encouraging. Principals tended to ignore teachers' suggestions that did not serve the administration's purposes. Committee work often seemed futile. Faculty meetings operated in a chain-of-command style, with suggestions being passed up by department heads. Even when principals had been sympathetic to teacher empowerment, "downtown" allowed the school and its teachers little autonomy. Central office personnel treated us "like children" and expected us to follow whatever schedule they handed out, said one teacher. "You have made so many requests and been turned down so much that you just give up and do your own thing."

Yet a candid tone was established early. Teachers did not just bash administrators. Heads nodded around the table when Andrena deplored the lack of collegial engagement on matters of substance and pointed out how few conversations she had had with her peers about either ideas or teaching. Another teacher, noting that her own daughter would enter Hamilton High in a few years, raised the question of how many of her colleagues would have high expectations for her. She had doubts whether most of them would expose her "in a positive way to learning that . . . is challenging to her, and that isn't always going to be pleasant." The librarian commented that Hamilton served the most disadvantaged students as well as the most able, but "I'm worried about the middle-of-the-road kid who is there every day, who does his homework, and who gets no extra attention." After some comments about widespread littering and students hanging out in halls long after the bell rang, a math teacher cautioned that Hamilton should not follow the lead of other high schools whose tough policies had led to higher dropout rates. A chemistry teacher responded firmly, "I don't really buy that bull because I think there are ways to keep kids out of the hall without leading to high dropout rates, and you don't have to have garbage in the hall either." Several teachers reflected on the lack of respect shown by the way the students trashed the school, and the school secretary pointed out that the faculty did the same thing in the teachers' lounge. The librarian made the point that change would have to involve the entire school community, students, parents, and teachers. The school counselor said that little things could add up to big changes, explaining that she always greeted all her advisees by name in the hall and expected them to respond with hers—"just that little bit of courtesy." Another teacher suggested that they all had a vested interest in change. "Why should any of us—teachers or students—work in an ugly and degenerative environment. It's depressing."

Faculty resentments about being treated as children were confirmed soon after that first meeting when the committee learned that their principal had been called to the superintendent's office and told that the teachers should not meet without the principal and that the principal should chair the group. The teachers were not opposed to his participation and had discussed ways to involve him at that first meeting, although they also appreciated the opportunity to have a teachers-only discussion. The superintendent's action was an irritating reassertion of hierarchical control. "It really insults your intelligence [to be treated this way]," said one of the science teachers at the next meeting. "What does the superintendent think we're about? What are we going to do that he's afraid of? We only want what's best for the school." The teachers protested the oppressive uniformity they felt the central bureaucracy was imposing on all high schools. They felt central control meant that all schools "had to be absolutely the same," when the real problem was how to achieve a unique spirit in each school.

They invited the principal to the next meeting, and some were surprised to hear him agreeing with them. Being called downtown or overruled by the central office was fairly routine. "Every time I make a decision, I turn around and get my hand slapped for not communicating with the central office." The desire for equality was too often wrongly turned into pressure for uniformity because those in the central office "don't want one school to lord it over another, fearing if we're unique we're better or different."

The teachers pointed out that his disillusionment was not so different from their own feeling of disempowerment. They often felt like clerks at the end of the chain of command rather than like partners in the firm. Faculty meetings were characterized more by dissemination than by discussion. As a math teacher put it, the meetings were "lists of points A, B, C, D," when the issue ought to be, "Are we going to make decisions together as a faculty?"

The principal granted that the school was too bureaucratized and admitted he was discouraged to the point of having considered resigning. He felt that teachers did not trust administrators and he was not sure what to do about it. Although teachers talked about wanting change in the school, he felt that too many "did not give a damn" and most were individuals pursuing their "personal agendas." They might give lip service to the idea of school improvement but their bodies were not there in the hall confronting students who would not go to class. "Everybody operates as an individual . . . It's very difficult to get a faculty this size to sit together and say we're going to come up with some commonalities and say we're all going to get behind this."

Andrena felt it was possible to reach some common ground and create a different world for both students and faculty at Hamilton. But she also knew it wouldn't be easy because teachers would have to believe in those commonalities for them to make a difference. She looked at the principal but she was talking to everyone in the room: "Maybe some no longer believe what they do in the hall or inside their classrooms makes any difference. Maybe they're as disillusioned as you are. We need to do something about those people, too."

Two themes were interwoven throughout this quite remarkable exchange. The first was that there had to be a space for genuine dialogue. It had to be "a place where teachers feel comfortable and secure expressing their concerns without feeling that someone is passing judgment on them." Second, genuine dialogue implied some changes in the structure of the school. More time would need to be provided for teacher-to-teacher interaction and continued opportunities for teachers' growth. Teachers needed to be able to participate in decision-making and in creating their world, "because there's no sense to continually brainstorming ideas and using your energy in a bureaucracy in which you're going to have to do exactly what you've done before." By the end of the two hours, the principal said he was "going to hang my hat on the future of this committee," adding that he wanted to be a co-participant, not the chairman. He knew that real change had to come from the faculty and that difficult issues had to be put on the table. The librarian cautioned the group that change would not come about easily. "There's a lot of self-defense. We can blame others for our problems. Arriving at consensus is a very arduous process," requiring honest self-examination.

The teachers met frequently over the next year and that self-examination sometimes proved searing. Andrena noticed that, contrary to the experience with any previous committee, teachers arrived early and absences were rare. Nothing was sacred. They talked about widespread cheating in the school, the rise in drug use, and the increasingly aggressive demands by parents to pick the teachers they wanted for their children. Negotiating for your child's program or a specific teacher had become an accepted way of life at Hamilton, especially when it was a middle-class white parent who threatened to withdraw the child if demands were not met. The teachers complained about the profusion of special programs funded under various mandates, and the lack of influence they had in choosing the teacher's aides with whom they had to work in these programs.

One night a remark by the special education teacher sparked a heated discussion about mainstreaming of disabled children into regular classes. More than 10 percent of the students at Hamilton were now officially classified as disabled. Some of them were in special classes, but many more were now spending a good part of the day mainstreamed into regular classes. Teachers felt underprepared for the students assigned to them, even when aides accompanied the students, some of whom had multiple disabilities. A social studies teacher turned to her colleague in special education and said: "I don't understand your program. I don't understand the learning disabled. I don't understand what's going on with them yet I have to teach them." She was supported by a biology teacher, who said one day a guidance counselor came in to give her a pamphlet on Tourette's syndrome and the next day the child was in her class. "I really didn't feel I had enough information to handle it. Here's the pamphlet, here's the kid . . . We need more in-servicing or something."

Teachers began to bring research to the meetings, and some of them shared student surveys and other data they had gathered over the years. A social studies teacher brought in a questionnaire completed by 750 students showing that the longer they had been at Hamilton the less they liked it. Those who responded "I do my very best" dropped from 57 to 36 percent in four years, and the percentage of those who felt it was important to be on time to class fell from 52 to 34. It was not all bad news. At one meeting they discussed some university research that charted the gap between black and white Hamilton students on standardized test scores from 1965 to 1985. As noted earlier, the gap had grown in the decade 1965–1975 after tracking had been abolished and student choice expanded. The data showed that black students took proportionally fewer courses in math and science and that their achievement declined. It was also the time of greatest turmoil and highest teacher turnover in the school. By 1985, after the imposition of better middle school advising and the strengthening of core requirements for all students, the gap had been reduced markedly. Andrena also thought the stability in the school encouraged better teaching as more teachers figured out how to do a better job of reaching all students in untracked classes.

Putting the sensitive topic of race in a historical frame, which showed that they had made some progress after all, encouraged the first open discussion of what had almost been a taboo in the group up to that point. Partly to explain the drop in achievement for blacks in the first decade of desegregation, one of the white male survivors of that era said he just didn't know how to describe the trauma and tension he had felt then. "At the end of the day you were just exhausted . . . You'd just go home and go to bed . . . Teachers gave up trying to control what went on in the halls . . . There was no backup . . . It was like gasoline being poured on the fire and it just kept going." He was supported by other teachers, and Andrena felt that they told the truth of what they had experienced. Yet she also knew that that period was one of the most exciting and fulfilling of her teaching career. She had developed new courses, become a spokesperson in some ways for the African American students, and felt energized as never before. She was also glad that the science teacher who had been the first black hired spoke up, saying she doubted that many minority teachers would have been hired if it were not for the protests. "But when kids started demanding and tearing down things, they decided to hire more black teachers to control the black students." As a girl, this teacher had gone to school in Mississippi, and she asserted that the black students had no other release for their frustrations: "It was like those of us in Mississippi—we had no outlet, we had to do it. And they had to do it, there was no other way, because nobody listened." One of the white males who had spoken earlier, a social studies teacher who had been clubbed in the back of the neck and rendered unconscious in one of the first riots, interrupted her: "I don't believe that wanton violence, that tearing through the place is the answer. If you say, 'This is the only outlet they have,' it's a copout. You're rationalizing. You're saying, 'Hey, it's OK, tear the place apart, we understand.'" She replied: "What else could be done? To get attention that I'm hurting, that you're discriminating against me, that I'm not a worthy person, that you're not teaching me, you have no expectations for me . . . That I'm in a foreign land. How do I get you to listen to me?"

The room fell silent. The gulf between blacks and whites two decades earlier had been recreated in the room. The librarian, who had served in the Peace Corps and had come to Hamilton after the riots subsided, broke the tension by saying she did not know if she could have survived in that era. Then she turned to the black science teacher, speaking slowly: "You've got the vocabulary. You say, 'I'm hurting; you're not teaching me.' Often the adults don't have the words." Would it have been any different if they had been more prepared for the changes that swept over them, she asked—if they had had the math workshops and supportive services that were now provided? A math teacher recalled the painful truth: "We had absolutely no training, virtually no skills, it was a situation we were not able to deal with in any effective way. The kinds of things we tried in the beginning to get things jelling the right way just did not work." Yet who would have given the "training" for a revolution, Andrena wondered. These teachers had been through a series of social revolutions. They had put their lives on the line. While she pitied some, she admired the courage of many others, of the math teacher who had just spoken, for example. He was one of those who had helped hold this society together, who had faced some of his own unconscious racism and who had changed as a teacher. Despite their pain and some of the differences just expressed, none of these teachers wanted to resurrect the Hamilton High of the 1950s or the inequalities it embodied. "Wouldn't it have been much better if we had had the courage twenty years ago to meet like this and talk?" the science teacher asked. "Yes, if it had been possible," Andrena replied.

This thought kept recurring in the coming months. What kind of reform was possible through a teachers' committee of this kind? Could teachers ever take charge of their practice in the same sense that doctors and lawyers did? Andrena wondered. Or was it just a lot of talk that would fade away? The committee was still meeting in the spring of 1986 when one of the guidance counselors brought a copy of a just-published report by the Carnegie Foundation to their attention. "This report recommends what we're doing," she said. "Schools ought to be run by teacher committees!" She summarized the main theme of the report, which was that "teachers are not treated as professionals and not listened to as professionals and a lot of teachers resent this." The math teacher agreed, adding that real change in schools would never come until "teachers play a considerably more active role in running schools."[10] With a brief apology to the principal sitting to her left, the guidance counselor reflected that like her and Andrena, several of the teachers in the room had been at Hamilton for nearly twenty years. Principals had come and gone every three or four years. Some were innovators, some quite conservative. Each of them had felt he (and they had never had a "she") had to "turn the school around" or "turn it in some new direction or turn it back." There was some assumption that principals had a special wisdom, she went on, "but we know different," pointing out that some Hamilton principals had never been regarded as successful teachers and that the best of them succeeded in drawing on the wisdom of the teachers. That was where the real wisdom lay, she concluded. "We really do know what is best for kids."

The Carnegie report was widely publicized and read, in part because of the prestige of the Carnegie Foundation and the blue ribbon committee of prominent Americans who signed the report. It was well argued and well written. It dramatized what many were beginning to think and synthesized the arguments supporting teachers' empowerment that were being raised in different sectors.

Organizational theorists were persuaded that the key to greater productivity lay in greater worker participation and reduction of hierarchy. Feminist scholars wrote about the formation of the teaching profession as a classic example of patriarchal domination of women; teachers' work was organized in a way that would have been unthinkable in a predominantly male profession like medicine. The second wave of reforms that had followed the 1983 publication of the Reagan Administration's *Nation at Risk* report emphasized the need for school restructuring and more democratic forms of governance in schools.[11] Teachers' unions pressed for more voice at all levels of educational policy-making, and for granting teachers more say about the curriculum and the power to decide who was fit to teach, who should be hired, and who should be tenured or fired.

These reform currents came to a crest in the late 1980s as many school districts began to grant teachers more professional authority. In some cases, as in both Syracuse and nearby Rochester, progressive superintendents broke the usual pattern of negotiations to hold summit meetings with top union leadership in which they agreed to new principles of shared management by which both would be bound. In Rochester, the result was a breakthrough contract that received front-page attention in the *New York Times* in 1987. As we will discuss at greater length in Chapter 7, Rochester established a new career ladder for teachers modeled in part on the medical profession. Newly hired teachers served as interns under the supervision of expert lead teachers, who would be paid up to $70,000, then an unheard-of salary in large urban systems. Moreover, the teachers themselves had a significant voice in determining who were chosen as lead teachers, and in deciding whether the intern teachers would be reappointed and eventually tenured.

Teachers everywhere were cheered by the news in Rochester. But Syracuse teachers, including Andrena, negotiated a less radical contract a year later. They got big raises, although about $10,000 below Rochester's top salary, and avoided the quid pro quo that was implicitly contained in the Rochester contract: that teachers would justify their raises by achieving better outcomes, as measured by standardized tests and dropout rates. They did create a range of new roles for teachers in policy-making, curriculum development, and mentoring, although without a formal career ladder of the Rochester type. Syracuse established the Professional Responsibilities Committee, soon known as the PRC, in which teachers had equal representation with "management" in choosing the occupants of these new roles, who would be paid a 10 percent salary bonus while serving in them.

During the semester that she considered applying for one of the new roles, Andrena enrolled in a seminar that examined the causes of inequality in schools. It was her first brush with the neo-Marxist analysis of the economist Samuel Bowles, who argued that equal educational opportunity was a myth perpetrated by a capitalist society to create an illusion of fairness. In reality, Bowles said, schools in America reproduced and maintained inequality by having lower expectations for lower-class students and by tracking them into programs of study that led to low-status jobs. Andrena thought Bowles overestimated conspiratorial design in the system, and underestimated the amount of upward mobility schools in America had achieved for many youths born into poverty. Yet he had also put his finger on a contradiction that troubled her, though she had never put it as concisely as he had. Was she part of a system of schooling that strained "to justify and reproduce inequality rather than correct it"?[12] She had tended to see inequality in schools through the frame of race; now she also saw it as a matter of social class. Although she did not accept all of Bowles's analysis, she began to think differently about the growth of suburban schools and the differences between schools that served rich and poor children. She also wondered how much schools could do to overcome the ravages of poverty that blighted the lives of some of her own pupils, even if schools were not as guilty of justifying inequality as Bowles seemed to think.

Schools alone could not create a level playing field. But there were some things they could do. The analysis she found most persuasive was Linda McNeil's *Contradictions of Control.*[13] Andrena had more faith in McNeil's analysis, in part because, unlike Bowles, McNeil had modified her thesis on the basis of her observations in classrooms. McNeil's book evolved from a project in which she attempted to find out what teachers actually taught in social studies, especially economics. She suspected that many high school teachers presented a very conservative economic ideology, if they were not guilty of outright capitalist indoctrination. What she found was that most teachers, regardless of their ideology, presented a shamefully oversimplified version of their subjects. And they elicited almost no sense of genuine inquiry. There was little dialogue or questioning of minds. Instead of educational exchange, they provided lists to be copied and facts to be memorized. Andrena thought of that passage as she walked down Hamilton's halls during her free periods, hearing teachers drone on, sliding down a cover sheet to reveal the next item on the overhead projection screen.

When McNeil interviewed teachers she found that their shortcomings did not derive from a lack of knowledge of their subject. They said they taught that way because that was what the controllers of the system wanted. Administrators didn't want teachers who rocked the boat or contravened centralized controls. What the system aimed at was not justifying inequality but simply moving kids through as efficiently as possible. Keep the dropout rates down, turn out graduates with certificates. The system didn't especially want teaching people to think. Teachers wouldn't be rewarded in their paychecks or in any other way for crafting stimulating lessons. McNeil argued that most schools produce "school knowledge," a thin gruel which is an exchange of facts and lists without much real learning or engagement on the part of students.

Yet some schools seemed to establish a different belief system. Instead of that thin gruel they served a feast of learning in many classrooms. One of the four schools McNeil studied was so blessed. It had a principal who valued intellectual engagement and worked with teachers to put educational goals ahead of control and "efficient" production of diplomas. He helped teachers get grants to develop new thematic curriculums, opened up the schedule so they would have time to meet and plan together, made sure they had some funds to buy the latest books and materials, and enabled them to visit other schools and classrooms where they could discover ways to improve their practice. He cared about ideas himself and was eager to listen to the teachers' plans as they developed them. This school was saved from the deadly cycle of what many students experience year after year, the "exchange of one body of facts for another—an inert transmission, the delivery and redelivery of segmented and self-contained dates and formulas" that leaves them with a restricted sense of intellectual work.[14]

Although her now retired mentor Kay Kastenmayer was skeptical, Andrena decided to put her name in for one of the policy-making roles delineated in the new Syracuse contract. Kay scoffed that the administrators were inviting the teachers to take over the helm of the *Titanic* as it was going down, battered by a decade of criticism and complaints of failure. Nonetheless, Andrena accepted an appointment in 1990 to serve on a citywide task force charged with rethinking the district's language arts curriculum.

A dozen teachers from all levels of the system had been selected by the Professional Responsibilities Committee to serve on the task force. They met one afternoon a week and sometimes on Saturday mornings as well. Although a few of the members seemed to have been selected more for union loyalty than for teaching talent, on the whole Andrena felt good teachers had been chosen. She was disappointed early on when one frustrated member of the task force suggested that they needed to hire a curriculum expert, but at least the suggestion had generated a useful discussion about their own competence. The consensus achieved was that they had the knowledge required to develop the curriculum, although they might want to call for expert help on some issues. Andrena was stimulated by the opportunity to think about the sweep of the curriculum, to consider how what her colleagues taught in sixth or seventh grade related to what she did in the eleventh. Another member of the task force irritated many of the members with her insistence on defining outcomes for students. Andrena at first dismissed her as a zealot, but as the members loosened up and got more comfortable with each other, she found that they all began to think more seriously about the goals of the curriculum. What were they aiming at? How were Andrena's students changed by what she taught? What did they know and what could they do that they did not know or do before they took her course? Why did it matter that they spent a year in English 11?

Even though two of her colleagues disappointed her—they had been very erratic in attending, contributed little, and did not deserve the 10 percent bonus—the task force seemed to making good progress. It was at the end of the first year that Andrena discovered how difficult it was to make any changes in the system. Not that it was much of "system." As she soon discovered, there was no real vision and little coherence. The English curriculum was a conglomeration of subjects driven by teachers' inclinations, state-level Regents' tests, and administrative mandates. The members of the task force had been told early on that they could not "touch" the middle school curriculum. That was a pet project of one of the assistant superintendents who had labored to put it in place, and it was not to be disturbed. When they called assistant superintendents to discuss drafts of the task force report, they found they had not been read. One central office administrator bluntly told Andrena she had no time to read the report with all the paperwork she had to do. She expected Andrena to call her and tell her what was in it. It took the task force two months to get on the calendar for a meeting with three administrators whose approval they needed. Little was approved and the task force received very little helpful criticism. Finally, it dawned on Andrena that this committee was doing some of the things that the middle layer of the school bureaucracy was hired to do. The more successful teacher committees like this became, the more in jeopardy those administrators felt their jobs to be.

At the end of two years, with Syracuse facing major reductions in the school budget and new negotiations with the union about to begin, the superintendent mailed a survey to all teachers asking them to rank potential cuts. The policy-making roles developed by the Professional Responsibilities Committee received the least support from the teachers. Initially, Andrena was astonished. Then she realized that if the other task forces were like her own, they spent more time dealing with the middle bureaucracy downtown than communicating with teachers about the work they were trying to do. Although they had some positive feedback from teachers about new exams members of her task force had written, she knew that most teachers had little idea of the good work they had done. Many teachers also apparently felt that if they were going to get any raises at all the elimination of the 10 percent bonuses for teachers in the new mentoring, curriculum development, and policy-making positions (about two hundred of a total of about sixteen hundred teachers) would be a small price to pay. These positions, including those alloted for Andrena's task force, mostly disappeared in the new contract. And all teachers received a cost-of-living raise.

The task force conversation about how to teach in ways that developed a wider range of student competence lingered on, however. Andrena decided to teach a course in journalism, which she had previously scorned, and to take over the nearly defunct student newspaper. She planned to teach a series of skills that students would have to demonstrate: interviewing, analysis of data, persuasive writing (editorials), descriptive writing, humor, computer skills, graphic design. More than in any other course she had ever taught, Andrena found herself coaching students in small groups and rarely lecturing to the whole class. Students interviewed the principal, learned how to make up pages of the newspaper using computer graphics, brought the math teacher in to help them figure out how to analyze survey data, worked in teams to develop special writing projects, and published a real paper for a real audience. And the paper staff was as diverse as the Hamilton student body. The paper was read avidly and won a sheaf of prizes.

Andrena loved the course, and found she bonded with students in a new and more satisfying way. She was still the teacher and knew she had more than ever to teach. But she was also a co-learner, working alongside students who were trying to get the Pagemaker computer program to wrap type around a photograph. She felt as excited—and as vulnerable—as her students when a new issue was being devoured by readers in the cafeteria. Her reputation was on the line, too.

Andrena was so preoccupied with developing and teaching this new course that she lost interest in the school improvement committee. She rejoined it in the fall of 1992, however, when the first African American principal was appointed to Hamilton High. He impressed her immediately. He carried a large plastic bag filled with beer bottles to his first meeting with the faculty. He had broken up a seniors' "welcome back" party behind the school. He said the school had a problem with both alcohol and drugs and asked for their help. He met with each class of students on the first day, announcing that hats had to come off and stay off once students entered school. The ninth-graders accepted this decision with hardly a murmur, but the seniors harangued him, and some jeered. A few of the girls who wore baseball caps explained that this was the fashion and they had laid out big bucks for these new outfits. He listened to their complaints, insisting that rowdy students be quiet so that they could hear them, too, then explained why he thought his policy would make a difference in establishing a more serious learning climate in the school. If there were no improvements in a year's time, he would reconsider. The next morning and every morning thereafter he was at the front door politely asking students with hats to take them off. Andrena was as amazed as nearly all her colleagues when the hats disappeared by the end of the week.

She felt he was one of the few principals she had known who really did listen and who welcomed strong women into his inner circle. He also was the first to share the power of the purse. It was a small step, but seen as important, when he turned over the budget for "teacher in-servicing" to the school improvement committee. The teachers divided into subgroups to develop a "curriculum" for things they felt the faculty needed to learn about computers, school restructuring, cooperative learning, and better discipline. They assumed responsibility for planning what had been called "superintendent's days" for staff development. Instead of hiring outside speakers, they had teachers read a provocative article about student peer tutoring and then meet in small groups to discuss whether this would work in their classrooms. Some of them, Andrena was pleased to note, kept talking about what they had read at lunch.

One of the positions that had not been eliminated in the recent cuts that had decimated many of the new teachers' positions was that of staff development coordinator. The coordinator's program was not formally set up as a mentoring program for new teachers, as it had been in Rochester, but it was an avenue for peer mentoring and teacher development. The new principal turned over selection of the staff development person to the teachers on the school improvement committee, another first. Three teachers applied and were interviewed by the committee; Andrena was chosen.

Andrena developed her concept of the staff developer's role after reflecting on what teachers had experienced since she came back to Hamilton High. It was not an exaggeration to say that they had been through a series of social revolutions and that some of them had lost faith in themselves and each other. Their recovery had been slow and sometimes painful, but now trust and some self-confidence had been restored. They had been through the necessary process of reconstituting themselves as a community of teachers. Although some of the new committee work and power-sharing had been a waste of time and a bore, teachers had begun to come out of their classroom nests and to assume more responsibility for the school as whole. It was years since anybody had heard the door locks click as classes began. The teachers had begun to reflect together, to engage in diagnosis of what might be wrong and what they might do about it. And they were beginning—just beginning—to inquire more honestly into their own classroom practice and seek ways of improving it. These teachers had chosen her to help.

She was a realist, however. She was aware that the teachers sometimes took three steps sidewise and two back for every one forward. Syracuse was now in the midst of school site planning under the aegis of a citywide strategic plan. Teachers, parents, staff, and community members met to hammer out their goals for Hamilton High. It was a politically driven process that kept participants locked up in hotel rooms to grind out plans in a fill-in-the-blank manner. She worried that some of the goals were so unrealistic that they would lead to cycles of hope and despair, or cause some teachers to "cook the books" to meet the targets. For example: "By June 1998, the percentage of students achieving a final grade of 70 or above in all of their subjects will increase by 50 percent."[15]

Yet she recognized that such plans did mobilize political will and draw parents and community members into supporting roles. Some of the tactics developed to meet the broad objectives made sense to her, such as creating programs to maximize peer tutoring, to form student study groups, and to provide more students with mentors. She worked hard to get a commitment written into the plan that would require "all staff to improve their instructional and interpersonal skills." The action plan appended to that goal specified that all teachers would develop personal portfolios reflecting on their teaching and what they were doing to improve it, and that the staff development coordinator would encourage the organization of voluntary peer coaching teams among teachers.

This was hardly a revolution, or if it was it was slow and erratic. Yet she doubted that it could be stopped. Teachers were a long way from assuming full responsibility for their practice. Meaningful change in practice would only be brought about by slow and patient work. But many more teachers would now have the benefit of the coaching and mentoring that she had acquired only by the fortunate accident of her student relationship with Kay Kastenmayer. Nor was there any magic knife of "school restructuring" that would enable teachers to cut through the thick crust of school bureaucracy and save the public schools from years of suffocating regulation. But teachers would never again tolerate the kind of autocratic principals she began to teach under.

"Now that I control my destiny more, it will be hard to silence me," she reflected. "I feel it's like a women's movement, it's the civil rights movement, it's typical of all the movements that we will not be denied." In her more cynical moments working on the school site plan, she felt she was just playing a game. "In many ways it's a horrible document." But her steadier self admitted that this was the kind of politics whereby changes are made, one piece at a time. The action plan gave her some leverage in her new role; now she had to rise to the challenge of how best to use it.

She was convinced that the focus on improving instruction and classroom practice was the most important piece of the reform effort. "I hate to see a teacher go bad . . . selfishly because then I have to live with them for thirty years, and idealistically because I know most of them can be saved with the right kind of help." Andrena threw herself into her new work with enthusiasm. It was set up as a half-time position, so that she spent half a day teaching and had the remainder free for mentoring and staff development efforts. She knew that she was a good teacher and that she had a vision of what good teaching was that encompassed a variety of teaching styles. Or as she concisely summed up her expertise: "I know good teaching and I know good learning and I know good results." One of her first challenges was to work with a new teacher in deep trouble. With the principal's cooperation, she cleared the teacher's schedule for a week of afternoons of intensive work one on one. Andrena found videos relevant to units the novice would be teaching in coming weeks in the ninth-grade general science class. Andrena explained that it was generally not a good idea to show a film for the whole class; instead the teacher should use ten minutes of a video to illustrate a concept and build a structure to achieve a particular learning outcome. Andrena helped her to develop creative ways of teaching discrete skills without relying on lectures, overhead projectors, and endless note-taking, which simply isn't effective: "Not that you don't need to do some of that. But she needed to know how to achieve a balance of activities that allows kids to be out of their seats and more engaged in doing science. I put her on one chair playing the left lung while I got on the other and played the right lung. It was something she could use and build her confidence with these kids. By the time we got done the kids did well."

Andrena spent most of her time in classrooms, helping and encouraging. She wrote notes to teachers about all the positive things she saw.

She established herself as one who was ready to help good teachers get better and not just a one-person rescue squad. "You want to go visit an exciting school—I'll make it happen. You're a physics teacher who wants to go see how they do physics at Bristol Labs—not hard to do. You want me to cover your classes while you're having unit tests so that you can sit in on classes with a teacher who's doing great thematic instruction, I'll do it for you."

At the end of the first year she convinced the principal that teachers should not just drop portfolios about their teaching on his desk. Instead they scheduled half-hour exit conversations with every teacher in the last weeks of the year. Each teacher was asked to reflect on three questions before the conference: What are you most proud of having achieved this year? What goals are you setting for yourself for next year? And given those goals what are your development needs and how can we help you to fulfill them? That first year Andrena and the principal mostly listened. "We didn't insult anybody. We heard some of the finest lies you have ever heard in your life, but we didn't call them on it." Most of the teachers were thoughtfully self-critical. The feedback was very positive. Often teachers said, "You know, nobody ever asked me to reflect on my goals before." The second year they didn't let any lies slip by and pushed those few teachers who had not taken any steps to achieve the goals they had set. Those who had said they would join a seminar on teaching skills and then missed four of six meetings found out their absence had been noticed and wouldn't be tolerated next year. Andrena felt that she had developed the language to encourage teachers to reflect on their teaching. "Too many teachers aren't reflective practitioners—we haven't been taught to do that, and weren't ever given time." She recalled conversations with teachers she had helped to be more reflective who said, "Hell, why didn't somebody tell me that ten years ago." And these were not "huge things" I was telling them, Andrena went on, "but new ways of engaging kids that make you feel better as a teacher and that's how you come to be a better teacher. We never had those honest exchanges before."

At the end of three years in her new role, she had so clearly justified her usefulness that she was doing it full time. Teachers saw her as an instructional leader and not a "fink or a spy for the principal." It was no longer a one-way street. Teachers sought her out to talk about their teaching. It was no longer just her stuffing notes in mailboxes. Teachers wanted to share interesting things that were happening in their classrooms. Sure, some teachers ribbed her when she walked into the lunch-room, and one dropped the sports pages and announced in a loud voice, "Now as we were saying about the best way to improve classroom practice . . ." She smiled. She knew that teacher had done little to change his practice. Yet although a change in lunchroom language was not a change in classroom behavior, it was a step toward it.

7

Teachers' Struggle to Take Charge of Their Practice: The Rochester Story, 1987–1997

The Mapledale Party House was a buzz of voices. Rochester teachers had been reading the news reports and hearing rumors for several weeks about the new three-year contract that Adam Urbanski, the president of the Rochester Teachers Association, had negotiated with Superintendent Peter McWalters. Now, finally, they would hear more about the contract's details and hold the contract vote.[1]

Marie Furnelli, a special education teacher in a middle school, could hardly contain her excitement. Since she had first heard there might be the possibility of teachers taking on new responsibilities, she had known she would vote for the contract regardless of the salary increase. Having taught for fourteen years, she was ready for a new opportunity, but she had no interest in becoming an administrator. Maybe this idea of having lead teachers to mentor newly hired teachers, but still teach part-time, was the answer.

In another part of the room, Nancy Collins, having finished her twentieth year teaching high school math, was far more skeptical. The new contract eliminated the seniority system and automatic salary increases for additional years of service, so who knew what that would mean in the long term? Sure, the salary increase, 40 percent over three years, was phenomenal, more than she had ever expected to make as a teacher. But so far the talk had been long on idealistic slogans and short on specifics. Despite the partnership between the superintendent and the Rochester Teachers Association president, Nancy was not convinced that any real change would result from this high-flown talk about teacher professionalization and shared decision-making. What's more, it was beginning to sound as if she was supposed to become a social worker, or something akin to it, being assigned to keep track of twenty students' progress and communicate with their families. Who wanted to do that?

As she listened to the voices around her though, Nancy soon realized that her misgivings were clearly not shared by the majority. Most teachers seemed caught up in the enthusiasm of the moment. Just think of the salary increase! Who could turn that down? Shared decision-making in all schools: Wasn't that what teachers had been talking about for years, less direction from administrators and more autonomy? Finally, an end to the "snoopervision," as Urbanski had called it.

The Career in Teaching Plan would help new teachers, who would now have an internship year with a mentor to guide them. It was about time to end the "sink or swim" induction process they had all endured. Even if the specifics weren't spelled out, Urbanski had led them well for six years and teachers trusted him. The contract was approved in August 1987 by an overwhelming vote of 1,109 to 169. Nancy Collins voted against it, convinced that the contract committed teachers to too much, without being clear how the promises would be kept.

Rochester's contract was big news. *Newsweek* magazine ran the story under the heading, "Raises, Reform, and Respect." The *Washington Post* proclaimed, "Changing Children's Fate by Changing Teaching: In Rochester Experiment, Educators Pay and Responsibilities Grow." Featuring a two-page picture of all the community leaders who would be involved in making the reform ideas reality, *U.S. News & World Report* began a series to report on the progress of Rochester's reforms. Albert Shanker, president of the American Federation of Teachers, of which the Rochester Teachers Association is a member, heralded Rochester as "the educational flagship of the United States."[2]

The news reports focused heavily on the substantial salary increase. New teachers' salaries were to jump from $23,000 to nearly $29,000 in two years. By the second year of the contract, more than half of Rochester's teachers would make $45,000 or more, with the possibility for teachers to earn as much as $70,000. Nationally, the average teacher's salary was $29,000 in the late 1980s, and in New York the average was $35,000. Rochester's contract made its teachers among the highest paid teachers in the country.[3]

Beyond the salary increase, though, the contract incorporated many of the educational reforms policy experts had been recommending to improve schools. A career path with multiple levels based on experience was created, culminating in a lead teacher position for which teachers would be selected by a joint committee of teachers and administrators. Shared decision-making would be adopted by all schools. Teachers would have the largest number of representatives among the constituent groups of teachers, administrators, paraprofessionals, and parents on school-based planning teams, the district's name for school-based shared–decision-making committees. The intent was to change the existing school district organizational structure by giving much greater authority and autonomy to the schools. Additionally, the contract called for more involvement of teachers in communicating with students' families through the establishment of a homebase guidance program for all secondary students. Each teacher would be responsible for keeping track of twenty-five students' progress and communicating with their families. The district also planned to involve industry to make better transitions between school and future employment. Social service agencies were to be more closely connected to schools to provide better support for students and their families.

Suddenly Rochester had recast the structure of the teaching profession in ways other districts had only begun to talk about. So much so that the National Center for Education and the Economy, an education think tank, decided to relocate to Rochester, to be part of its heralded reforms. Marc Tucker, president of the National Center, commented that no school district had gone as far as Rochester in adopting the reform recommendations of the Carnegie Commission's 1986 report, *A Nation Prepared: Teachers for the Twenty-First Century*. Adam Urbanski and Peter McWalters became educational celebrities, touting their reforms in speaking engagements all over the country.

Despite the instant attention, the Rochester contract reflected two decades of effort by the Rochester Teachers Association (RTA) to achieve more power in district decisions. Since the 1960s, the RTA had struggled with the district to extend the parameters of teachers' authority. Following years of conflict and an unproductive teachers' strike in 1980, the union leadership turned in a bold new direction.

Elected in 1981, Adam Urbanski proved to be a visionary union leader. The thirty-four-year-old high school social studies teacher, himself a graduate of Rochester's schools, had arrived in Rochester as a teenager following his family's exodus from Communist Poland. An excellent student, Urbanski had gone on to complete a Ph.D. in American history at the University of Rochester. Despite his fondness for saying he was just a "poor Polish boy," Urbanski quickly came to the attention of union leaders looking for change. Urbanski defeated the previous Teachers Association president in a five-way race. It soon became clear that he had a different vision of teaching and teachers' unionism. If children were to receive the kind of education needed in a great democratic nation, teaching should become a profession, with the autonomy, authority, and rewards of other respected professions. Urbanski knew unions would have to change from focusing almost exclusively on bread-and-butter issues and on protecting the weakest teachers. He was convinced that schools could not improve unless teachers were unshackled from the bureaucratic fetters that had hampered them for nearly a century. An articulate spokesman, and persuasive writer, Urbanski explained in op-ed pieces why professionalization of teaching and greater autonomy for teachers were necessary to improve Rochester's schools. His goal was to educate the public as well as skeptical teachers about the need for fundamental change in the way schools and teaching were structured. Within a few years, local newspaper editorial writers began to agree with him, increasing public support for teachers.

At the same time, Urbanski pushed for changes within his union. He succeeded in establishing a peer intervention program so that the weakest teachers received peer assistance to improve their teaching skills or, if necessary, were dismissed. Innovations such as the dial-a-teacher program to help students with homework problems gave the Rochester Teachers Association a more positive image.

By the early 1980s, it was increasingly clear to everyone that Rochester's students were failing in large numbers, particularly at the secondary level. Only 24 percent of those who graduated were receiving the Regents' diploma, awarded for having successfully completed a college preparatory course and having passed a series of state-level exams. Worse, nearly a third of Rochester's students were not graduating at all. The president of the Urban League of Rochester, William Johnson, published a report that was sharply critical of the schools and called for community-wide involvement to address the problem.[4]

With growing local consensus that radical change was required to improve Rochester's schools and the national reform agenda's focus on teachers' professionalization as the solution to school improvement, the

Rochester contract became a possibility. Rochester's superintendent, Peter McWalters, was a strong supporter of local school authority, having taught in an innovative middle school before moving to central office administration under the previous superintendent. Only a few years had passed since he had been on strike himself as a teacher. McWalters viewed the contract as a way to give schools more autonomy while at the same time increasing teachers' accountability for student outcomes. Urbanski saw the contract as a way to increase teachers' professional authority and to substantially increase their salaries.

In negotiations, Urbanski proposed a 40 percent increase over three years and said, "What do you need to sell it to the school board?" McWalters asked for teachers to work an additional five days. Urbanski replied, "Done." McWalters asked for teachers to take more responsibility for working with students' families. Urbanski agreed. McWalters asked that a new teacher evaluation process which held teachers more accountable be created. Urbanski said, "Done." As the next request came, Urbanski's negotiating team argued that they needed to discuss these promises. But Urbanski was determined to agree to McWalters's demands in order to achieve a breakthrough. In the early morning hours the contract agreement was sealed.

Teachers like Marie Furnelli were ecstatic. Finally they would be recognized for their professional expertise. The heavy hand of bureaucratic control would be lifted and teachers could decide what was best for their students. They were willing to take on the challenge. Leaving the meeting, Marie exclaimed to a colleague, "I felt the membership was very daring to say, okay, we will give up seniority and some other things, but we're going to pursue professionalism in education." Nancy Collins left unconvinced by her colleagues' enthusiasm. As far as she was concerned, she had always been a professional. "What difference is this going to make?" she thought to herself.

Hector Diaz was looking forward to student teaching in the spring of 1988 at Genesee Elementary School in Rochester when he learned about the newly signed contract from his education professor at Brockport. Although he didn't know all the details, two aspects immediately drew his interest: the salary for beginning teachers and the fact that if he taught in Rochester he would have a mentor his first year. Hector had heard horror stories from other graduates of how they had struggled their first year in the classroom, and he was worried about whether he could really be successful. The idea of having a mentor seemed like the answer to his prayers. Right then he determined that he would be one of the new teachers hired for the fall of 1988.

The first month of student teaching Hector was so busy learning about how to get his fourth-graders to behave while he was trying to teach them about the Iroquois Nation and how to add fractions that he didn't give the new contract a second thought. He had no idea teaching could be this hard or this time consuming. Just trying to keep track of everything, like attendance and lunch vouchers, seemed to be a full-time job. Most of all he was overwhelmed by the needs of the children. Genesee School was located in one of the poorest neighborhoods in Rochester. It was kept locked at all times because of problems with theft in the building and the drug houses that surrounded the school. Nearly all the children received free breakfast and lunch, and the school counselor reported that three-quarters of the children had some member of their family who had a substance-abuse problem. The students' test scores were well below the scores in other schools in the district.

As Mexican immigrants, Hector's parents had worked hard to leave the migrant camps of western New York and settle permanently in Rochester. With both of them working they had managed to purchase a small clapboard house in a working-class Rochester neighborhood. Hector and his sisters had all graduated from the Rochester city schools and gone on to college. Hector had thought his family had to struggle. Now he realized that his circumstances growing up had been far better than those of most of his students. He had had a secure childhood in a stable working family that had high expectations for him. Most of his pupils were poor enough to qualify for free lunch and came from homes where parents had no work. Drugs were constantly present in many families.

Hector had learned a lot from his college classes, but nothing could have prepared him for these children. Fortunately, the teacher whom he was assigned to work with, Beth Michaels, was both an excellent model and an effective coach, a fact that got Hector thinking again about the idea of having a mentor for his first year of teaching. He was astonished when he learned from Beth that the Rochester administrators' union had filed a law suit to stop the mentoring program from taking effect. Beth explained that the administrators' union was claiming that teachers did not have the authority to evaluate other teachers and that the mentoring program would impinge on the administrators' responsibility to evaluate teachers.

"How could this be?" Hector thought. He had only seen the principal once since coming to Genesee School. It seemed to him that
administrators were so busy they would welcome the involvement of
lead teachers. In talking to Beth further, he realized that she didn't
think all administrators would be against the idea. In fact, the teachers
at Genesee School had a good relationship with their principal, George
Martin. They were proud of the fact that they had organized a school
advisory council made up of teachers and parents five years earlier.
Even though Mr. Martin was the final authority, the teachers felt that
what they said did make a difference in how he made decisions. Beth
thought this cordial relationship would help them implement shared
decision-making more easily.

By the end of the semester, Hector had learned a lot more about the
Rochester City School District. Sitting in the teachers' lounge at lunch
gave him a chance to hear other teachers' perceptions. In contrast to
Beth's optimistic comments about creating a school-based planning
team that would make all the important decisions, other teachers wondered out loud if the central office would ever really turn decision-making over to the schools. Even a Rand Corporation study of Rochester
had concluded that the district was more bureaucratic than many others
and that decision-making was highly centralized.[5] At that time, the
whole district was being turned upside down with a school reorganization plan for the next year that would create four middle schools for
sixth- to eighth-graders. Students would have a chance to say which
school they wanted to attend. At Genesee School, the sixth-grade
teachers were waiting to hear whether or not their building was going
to keep the sixth grade. Despite this uncertainty, Hector hoped he
might be hired at Genesee School. Beth Michaels had told him that he
had done a great job. Everything looked positive. Now he just had to
wait out the slow process of hiring, which he had been told might take
until the first week of school in the fall.

Marie Furnelli learned at the end of the school year that she was
going to be reassigned to one of the newly created middle schools. Her
elementary school was losing its sixth-grade classes, and Marie's special
education students were going to join their classmates at George Eastman Middle School in the fall. Marie wasn't sure this was a good idea
for her students or for herself, but there wasn't anything she could do
about it so she was determined to make the best of it. Her school hadn't
done anything to implement a school-based planning team, and per-

haps with all this shifting around it would be a good time to begin at Eastman. She also hoped that teachers at Eastman might be open to the idea of creating a blended classroom to include her special education students in a regular classroom setting. And she hadn't forgotten about being a lead teacher, but it seemed that she should wait a few years to get settled in her new location.

Nancy Collins was relieved that she did not have to move and was planning to return to Susan B. Anthony High School in the fall. What a chore it would have been to pack everything up and relocate! She empathized with several of her colleagues who had not been so lucky. At least seniority still had some benefits.

Not much had changed at Anthony High School in the 1987–88 year. There was talk about creating a school-based planning team and organizing homebase classrooms, but no one seemed in any great hurry to actually do anything. Mostly people were beginning to talk more and more about how much the students had changed. When Nancy first started teaching in 1967, after her daughter entered kindergarten, the students were primarily from the surrounding white, working-class neighborhood. Now the students were mostly black and came from families where high school completion was the exception rather than the rule. Many students did not seem to have any real support at home; some were already living on their own or had their own children to care for. Although she thought she was a good teacher, Nancy found herself wishing that her current students were more like the students she used to have.

The other big change was that the new contract had eliminated the position of department chairperson. From what Nancy could see so far, the loss of the department chairs meant that no one was spending much time working on curricular issues. The vice principals who had been assigned this duty were overwhelmed with other tasks, and there was no one who was getting the math teachers together. Nancy had a feeling that this lack of communication was going to create real problems.

By the end of the 1988–89 school year, the school reorganization was in place. School-based planning teams had been established at most schools, and the Career in Teaching Panel had selected the first group of forty-one lead teachers. The district and the union had worked to fill out the contract's vision and at least on paper it sounded promising. The new guidelines for school-based planning even said, "Needed change will come about only through a collective action of the school community working to restructure schools in ways that give them the capacity to respond appropriately and quickly to the needs of the students they serve."[6]

Press reports about Rochester were turning critical, however. *U.S. News & World Report* gave the district a grade of C when it analyzed the Rochester reforms in June 1989. The local papers were even more critical, picking up on a front-page *New York Times* article on Rochester teachers' resistance to assuming greater responsibility for advising students and raising achievement levels. The Rochester Urban League president, William Johnson, told the press, "We're still at a stage where the troops—the teachers—have not gotten the religion yet." Doubts were increasing about whether decentralized decision-making would really lead to improved schools. Concerns were also mounting that many of the school-based planning teams did not reflect the constituents they represented, particularly in terms of racial diversity.[7]

With the reorganization, which eliminated the sixth grade at Genesee School, Hector Diaz ended up substitute teaching in two long-term assignments for a year before being hired as a third-grade teacher at Genesee Elementary School for the 1989–90 school year. The administrators' suit challenging the organization of the mentoring program had been dismissed, so he was looking forward to working with his mentor teacher, Susannah Brown. Marie Furnelli had settled in with her twelve students at Eastman Middle School and was continuing to get acquainted with her colleagues. Overcoming her doubts, Nancy Collins had agreed to run for the school-based planning team and was elected for a two-year term. She remained skeptical, but had decided that as a professional she had an obligation to make an effort.

For all three teachers the 1989–90 school year proved to be demanding, with scarcely a free moment. Hector was both pleased and nervous, at first, to work with Susannah. She seemed so sure of herself. No matter what was happening in his classroom, she always seemed to know what to do—whether it was dealing with the whole class or solving an individual student's problem. As the year progressed, Hector realized that Susannah's involvement had made a world of difference in his skills as a teacher and in his learning about how to work in the district. He became less and less concerned about her evaluation of him and more and more eager to share his new ideas each week during her visits. He was also grateful for the professional development workshops that she alerted him to, and even arranged for him to attend by taking his class from time to time. Hector was impressed by how much the district had invested in the mentoring program. Susannah told him that she had completed a two-week training program for mentors and was attending regular monthly meetings with other mentors. Hector also liked the idea that he could give his own evaluation of Susannah when she completed her evaluation of him at the end of the year.

Susannah's evaluation and Hector's principal's evaluation gave him high marks. He would be reemployed as a resident teacher until he obtained tenure and permanent certification by completing his master's degree. At that point Hector would become a professional teacher in the Career in Teaching Plan. At the end of her last meeting with him, Susannah told Hector that he should begin thinking about what kind of professional involvement he wanted to have beyond his own classroom. Becoming a good teacher was still his most important work, but teachers needed to help improve their schools as well. Hector promised he would, but knew that for the present he needed to stay focused on his own classroom. There was plenty of time to get involved in other professional activities. In the meantime, he was glad to know that he could call Susannah any time he needed advice and that he had met several other colleagues he could consult.

Marie Furnelli felt as if she was starting at square one once again as she struggled to get acclimated to a building twice as large as her previous school. For most of her first year at Eastman Middle School, she was preoccupied with learning how the school worked. She missed the informality of a smaller school and felt, at first, that she would never get to know any other teachers. It seemed just what she needed when she heard about a proposal from a local college to be involved in a curriculum project for the homebase class. At least, she would have a chance to talk to other teachers and to have something concrete to do with the students in the class. Despite what the newspapers had said, the Eastman faculty had embraced the homebase guidance idea. The teachers arranged their schedules to meet with their student advisees at the beginning of the day for thirty minutes and then again at the end of the day for ten minutes. There was now a form that teachers signed each period to indicate that students had been to class and to note any problems. It seemed to be a perfect way for the homebase teachers to keep track of how their advisees were doing. The plan was for teachers to keep the same advisees for three years so that there would be continuity.

As a special education teacher who worked with the same students for several years, Marie thought she had a lot to contribute to this effort. She wondered, though, how the decision to involve the school in the curriculum project had been made. When she asked the teacher representatives on the school-based planning team, they had no idea how it had happened. The team was trying to sort out what should be addressed under the school-based initiative and what was beyond its mandate, but did not seem to be making much progress. Apparently, the principal was still operating the way that he always had, consulting only other administrators and a few trusted teachers. "Oh well," Marie thought, "it will take a little while to sort this out but before long school-based planning should really be making a difference in how we do business here."

Before she knew it, the school year was over. Marie left for the summer feeling that she had finally settled in. The curriculum project was off to a good start, and she was looking forward to having the same students in her homebase the next fall. She planned to take a summer course about how to create blended classrooms to include special education children in regular education classrooms. In an essay that was printed in both the Teachers Association newsletter and the newspaper, Adam Urbanski had written about creating blended classrooms as a way to reduce class size and move the reforms to the classroom level. Perhaps she could convince some of her colleagues to try this innovation.[8]

Nancy Collins looked back at the school year and thought that she had never in her life spent so much time in meetings. What was worse, they were meetings that seemed to go nowhere. What had she been thinking when she agreed to serve on the school-based planning team? First of all, it was clear that Simon Walker, the principal, saw the team as a hindrance and was doing everything he could to hamper it, including withholding information and controlling the agenda. Moreover, everyone seemed to have a different idea about what the team should be doing, or not doing.[9] Each person had a pet topic he or she wanted the team to address. The discussion went around and around, accomplishing little. Finally at the end of the year the district agreed that it would provide some training for the team. Nancy hoped that this help would make a big difference in her second year. If it didn't, she knew serving on the team was going to drive her crazy. The team members even wanted to meet during the summer. For what? Nancy did not feel guilty about saying that she couldn't meet. After all, she was teaching summer school and she did deserve a little vacation. What did they expect?

At the same time, Nancy wasn't willing to give up. She had made this commitment, and some of her friends were indicating that their schools were having some success. They talked about creating a schoolwide discipline plan and increasing parents' involvement. Some even said that they were really beginning to work with their principals and the adversarial relationship was beginning to change. But they weren't sure if the central office was really going to turn over the power to them or not. It was the third year of reform, and they still had no real authority over personnel decisions or budget allocations. As Adam Urbanski had said, "It's just not going to happen without some pain. We're talking about getting some people to let go of control, of power. We're talking about listening to constituents who haven't been listened to before."[10] That summed up the situation at Anthony High School pretty well.

By the spring of 1990, the Rochester Teachers Association leadership was turning its attention to the upcoming contract negotiations. Already it was clear that the progress of the reforms was going to be a major issue. It did not seem to matter that everyone was finding out that district-wide reform was going to be much more difficult and take much more time than anyone had at first envisioned. The public and the School Board wanted some tangible evidence that student performance was improving, and aside from some improvements in elementary test scores, there was not much to suggest any real improvement had been made. A 1990 poll had found that 69 percent of Rochestarians thought that teachers' and administrators' salaries should be tied to the students' performance. The Urban League president, Bill Johnson, and other community leaders were becoming more vocal in their criticisms of the failure of the reforms to hold teachers accountable.

What was becoming increasingly clear was that there was no consensus about what was meant by accountability. For many School Board members and community leaders, accountability referred exclusively to teachers, and specifically to the teachers' accountability for test score results. What mattered were those performance indicators which were being reported in the newspaper. If educational outcomes were going to improve, teachers' salary increases needed to be tied directly to how well or poorly their students performed. Parents should be viewed as customers of the schools, and if they weren't satisfied with the product, teachers should be held accountable.

Adam Urbanski and the Rochester Teachers Association leadership, however, argued that teachers could not be held accountable for what they could not control. Test scores were not solely affected by teachers. Too many other factors, such as whether the children were getting support at home and whether teachers had the resources they needed to be effective, influenced test scores. Besides, educational experts were increasingly critical of norm-referenced, multiple choice tests that measured only basic skills. Why should teachers be held accountable for such a flawed measurement of their performance? Student performance might be a part of that assessment process, but should not be the only way of measuring teachers' performance. Rather, teachers should be held accountable for fulfilling a set of professional expectations that outlined what teachers should do as professionals—expectations such as knowing their subject matter and knowing how to teach effectively, being involved professionally beyond the classroom, and being involved with their students' families.

The Rochester Teachers Association leadership thought that new teachers were already being accountable through the evaluation by mentor teachers, as well as principals, before they were rehired. There was also the intervention program, which had been created even before the 1987 contract, and addressed the issue of teachers who truly were ineffective either by helping them to improve or by requiring them to leave the district. What was needed now was a peer evaluation program to help tenured teachers be more accountable as professionals. In addition, the notion of accountability should not apply simply to teachers. What about school administrators, the central office, parents, community members, colleges and universities, and businesses? If teachers were going to be held accountable, why not the other constituents involved?[11]

Since the district and the Teachers Association recognized that reaching agreement about what teachers' accountability meant was central to the contract negotiations, they agreed to create a joint district-union task force to address the issue. The resulting report reaffirmed the union's focus on the development of a professional accountability system based on peer review. It further framed accountability in terms of schoolwide progress based on a multiyear school improvement plan the school would develop.[12] The task force rejected, however, the idea of specific rewards and sanctions for schools based on standard test score results, a measure that had been adopted by the Kentucky legislature in its statewide school reform legislation.

One of Nancy Collins's friends had been involved as a teacher representative on the shared accountability task force, so Nancy knew about the report before it was made public in August 1990. From what she had heard, it seemed to make sense. Nancy liked the idea of being able to set her own expectations for her performance. And she certainly did not want to be judged just on test scores, although she recognized that parents had a right to know how their children's tested ability in math or reading compared with the abilities of others of the same age. With her students, there were even more basic issues such as getting them to attend her class every day. Since the school attendance rate hovered around 75 percent, all the teachers were concerned about reducing students' absences.

In early September the Teachers Association announced that it had reached a contract settlement which tied teachers' salary increases, in part, to their rating on a four-part scale as "superior," "very good," "good," or "unsatisfactory." The specifics of the evaluation process had to be worked out, but Adam Urbanski assured the teachers that they would have control over it. Teachers rated "superior" would receive significant salary increases. Despite the shared accountability task force, the School Board still wanted some version of pay for performance. The day of the teachers' contract vote Superintendent McWalters was quoted in the paper as saying that he didn't think many teachers would be rated "superior." At the meeting Urbanski tried to persuade teachers to vote for the contract, telling them he would "give them the moon and the stars if he could," but this was the best he could do.

Nancy was flabbergasted. What had happened to all the talk about professional accountability and teachers setting their own professional goals? This time she was in the majority. Teachers rejected the contract. Pay for performance was not going to be accepted in Rochester.

At Anthony High School, Nancy Collins found that she had a new principal. Simon Walker had been reassigned downtown. No one was sure what he was supposed to be doing there, but it was well known that ineffective building administrators usually disappeared downtown until they retired. The new principal, Roger O'Laughlin, seemed nice enough, but it was clear that he was feeling pressure to raise test scores. As far as the school-based planning team was concerned, Nancy didn't think the members were really dealing with how to improve the students' performance. But at least the team members were doing a few things, agreeing to have teachers be in the hall to get stragglers to class, for example, and they were talking about how to create an incentive program for good grades.

At Eastman Middle School things weren't turning out as Marie Furnelli had expected either. She returned to find that the group of homebase students she had worked with the previous year had been reassigned and she had a whole new group to get to know. When she asked why this had happened, she received a vague answer about scheduling problems, but she suspected that the registrar just didn't want to be bothered with trying to keep the same groups together. Since the whole curriculum she had worked on last year was based on keeping the same students for three years, she couldn't have been more frustrated. What was worse, except for a few other teachers who had been deeply involved, no one else seemed to care. The system of having students get their teachers' signatures was beginning to fall apart because some teachers were no longer bothering to follow through. Marie wondered whether the problem stemmed from anger about the contract or whether teachers were just getting tired of never-ending increases in paperwork. It was also demanding to do a good job with homebase. It was really an extra class. More and more teachers were calling families directly if there were problems, but that did not provide the kind of sustained involvement with a teacher that the homebase plan had intended.

As the year went on, it became increasingly clear that the contract was not going to be resolved any time soon. A new proposal that eliminated the pay for performance requirement had been approved by the Teachers Association's members, only to be rejected by the School Board. Rumors were also flying about a $2 million budget shortfall caused by a reduction in state funds. New York's economy seemed to be heading for a free fall. Teachers were getting more and more frustrated about working without a contract and the Rochester Teachers Association leadership called for teachers to fulfill only their contractual obligations until the contract dispute was resolved. At Eastman Middle School and most other schools, school-based planning teams were unable to meet because the teachers on the teams refused to participate.

Finally, in April 1991, a two-year contract for 1990–1992 was agreed upon by both the teachers and the School Board. The contract outlined professional expectations for teachers, incorporating language from the newly developed National Board for Professional Teaching Standards. The contract also endorsed and formalized a new teacher evaluation process called Performance Appraisal Review for Teachers (PART) that would allow teachers to choose how to be evaluated. Lead teachers would be responsible for developing the PART process. But all that did not satisfy skeptics on the School Board. The painful conflict over teacher accountability as measured by student performance remained unresolved.

The year-long contract dispute irrevocably changed the partnership forged by Adam Urbanski and Peter McWalters. Improved relationships among the adults in many schools were shattered. Parents were outraged that the teachers had boycotted the school-based planning process. Urbanski was seen as returning to old-style protectionist unionism, and teachers were seen as not willing to be held accountable because they had rejected the pay for performance contract. Rochester's mayor, Thomas Ryan, long a critic of the school district's agreement with teachers, succeeded in having legislation passed that permanently reduced the city's fiscal obligation to the district. Commenting on the newly agreed upon contract, which increased salaries 7.25 percent each year, the mayor observed, "They have signed agreements over there in the school district that by any standards are excessive. They act like these funds are an entitlement."[13] The fragile trust upon which school reform depended had been broken.

From Marie's perspective, however, there did seem to be some good news to balance the bad. As school began in 1991–92, Marie's principal announced that the school-based planning team had agreed that the school should participate in a five-year school reform project. The aim was to keep more students engaged by integrating academic subjects, including special education students in regular classes, maintaining continuity with students over their three years at Eastman, and developing strong parental involvement. Participation in the project was voluntary, but the team members hoped to group involved teachers together so that they could support each other. The first year, teachers were to work with two university researchers to plan the curriculum. The grant was to pay for substitutes so that the teachers could have release time during the day to work together and to learn more about how to make these changes. This was what Marie had hoped for and more. Now she could finally begin to create the kind of education she thought children with disabilities should have. She was one of the first to sign up.

Marie also decided to document her involvement in the project as part of her performance-evaluation portfolio. She had heard some grumbling among her colleagues that the new teacher evaluation process was too confusing, that there were too many ways to organize and document teaching performance. Among the many possibilities, teachers could continue with the existing administrative evaluation, develop a professional portfolio, engage in peer review with a group of colleagues, or videotape and analyze their teaching. But as far as Marie was concerned, being responsible for setting annual performance goals and determining how to document one's progress was the next logical step for teachers who wanted to take charge of their practice. Everyone knew that the old administrative evaluation checklist was a joke. For the last few years, her principal had asked her to fill it out herself, and he had signed it. So Marie thought the idea of setting her own professional goals and documenting them in a portfolio was a big improvement. She planned to have a section for each goal with examples of how she had met it.

At Genesee School, Hector Diaz remembered his mentor's advice about broader involvement and decided that maybe it was time to act. His first two years of teaching had been wonderful. Now he felt that he had a little extra time, even though he knew that doing the cooperative learning and project-based instruction he found worked best would still take a lot of energy. Hector decided to run for the school-based planning team and soon learned that he was running unopposed. Other teachers told him that it just took too much time without producing much in the way of results. Despite their efforts, little had changed. If he wanted to do work on the team, more power to him.

Now that the contract was finally settled, the plan for a school improvement process was resurrected. Schools were supposed to create a three-year school improvement plan. Each school was to issue an accounting at the end of the school year to inform the public of its progress. It seemed that this was something the district was really serious about. It made a lot of sense to Hector, and he thought it was a worthwhile activity for the team. Perhaps now the reforms would finally begin to produce results. Hector hoped so, since many of the students at Genesee School scored below the district's norm for reading and math.

It came as a shock that not all of his colleagues shared his perspective. At the first school-based team meeting, two senior teachers immediately began complaining that formulating a plan was just a bunch of paperwork that no one was ever going to look at. Even if they did create a plan, they still had to get central office approval, which was just one more proof that the central office was really running the show. Every time they turned around something had to be done for downtown. What really rankled the most was that Genesee School was supposed to be piloting site-based budgeting, to give them more autonomy over how they spent their money. What happened, though, was that the district never gave them enough information to make thoughtful decisions. Even worse, the district usually expected a response in a week or less. Sometimes the team hadn't even been scheduled to meet before the central office demanded a response.

Hector wasn't quite sure what to think after this outburst. It did seem that some of what these teachers had said was true; but on the other hand, they were often so negative. It always seemed to be someone else's fault when there were problems. He remembered overhearing one of these teachers complaining bitterly about parents in the faculty lounge, but he had been having some good luck getting parents more involved. One project he was particularly proud of was an "Author's Day," when the children invited their families to come and hear them read a book they had written. It had been a great success. Hector decided he had better keep a low profile for a while, until he had a better idea of how the team worked. At the same time, he thought the team should make a real effort to create a plan and was going to do all he could to help get one written.

The team members began meeting twice a month for most of the fall. They brainstormed ideas, listened to a central office person who explained test data to them, met with a person who was trying to get social service agencies more involved in schools, and talked for hours about what they could or could not do. Through it all, Hector tried to focus on what would have a positive impact for students and kept trying to remind his colleagues to think about that too. Somehow they just couldn't get the plan written, and finally the assistant superintendent in charge of Genesee School wanted to know why. The meeting was not pleasant. There really weren't any good answers for why it had taken so long to produce nothing. As Hector thought about it later, he decided that in some ways they were their own worst enemies. Here was central office telling them to develop a plan for their school. Their principal was supportive and involved as a member of the school-based planning team. They even had one active parent member. The only thing that was holding them up was themselves, their own past frustrations and fears that no matter what they did it would make no difference.

As fate would have it, these feelings were to be reinforced by the news delivered at mid-year that the district was facing a $10 million dollar budget deficit. Peter McWalters had departed for a new position a few months earlier, leaving the newly appointed superintendent, Manuel Rivera, to deal with the crisis. Rivera, who had spent his entire career in Rochester and had been the natural choice for the superintendency, would later acknowledge that when he learned of the deficit, he tried to get out of his contract. Pressure from School Board members persuaded him to stay. Desperate to avoid mid-year staff cuts, Rivera requested a 1 percent wage concession from both the administrators' and teachers' unions. In response the Teachers Association ran a full-page ad listing administrative salaries with the slogan, "Chop from the top: furlough the bureaucracy. Spend on students."[14] Adam Urbanski would agree to wage concessions only if the district would agree to a 40 percent cut in administrative positions and an extension of the teachers' contract to 1993. Urbanski proclaimed that this was a "battle to the death" to dismantle the district bureaucracy. Since Manny Rivera could not even tell him what some of these administrators' jobs were, why not use this opportunity to address the problem?

The district's Parent Council urged the Teachers Association to reconsider. The acting chairman said, "We pay them professional salaries. They can afford a 1 percent giveback and still go home smiling."[15] As parents learned that their children's schools would lose their librarians, they organized protests outside the district central office and at local libraries.

It was a battle that Urbanski did not win. One hundred and ninety employees, including elementary librarians, school counselors, teachers' aides, building and central office administrators, and maintenance staff, lost their jobs. Many of those let go were recently hired minority staff members who had been actively recruited by the district.

At Anthony High School, the students walked out, disrupted classes, and refused to return to the building. The firing of the only African American school counselor caused frustrated students to erupt in anger. Suddenly Nancy Collins and the school-based planning team had a major crisis to manage. Over the next few weeks the team met in extended sessions to hammer together a plan to address the students' concerns. A student forum and a parent forum were held to air complaints, and the team got an earful. Students complained that they didn't think most teachers cared about them and that many were racist, that the building facilities were badly in need of repair, that the curriculum did not reflect their interests or concerns, and that there were too few minority staff members. Knowing that these were issues that would take time to resolve, the team focused on trying to bind the racial wounds. After much debate, Brotherhood Week was planned for the end of the year. Nancy Collins was deeply shaken. She was sure she was not a racist. How had this happened in her building? She knew that even though things were better on the surface, the problems remained.

Over at Eastman Middle School, Marie Furnelli was also struggling to understand the events of the spring. What was causing her consternation, however, were her own colleagues. Her reform team, "Eastman in Action!" had worked hard all year to develop a plan for a school-within-a-school involving about a third of the Eastman teachers. She was very excited about the possibilities it offered and was sure that the school-based planning team would endorse it wholeheartedly. Instead, the team wanted to examine every bit of the plan, finding omissions—such as how testing would be handled—and demanding more specifics about a curriculum that was not yet fully developed. Marie and her reform team were frustrated. As far as she was concerned this was not what school-based planning was about. She told the principal, "What is School Base going to do? We are going ahead, no matter what they say." In fact, Marie decided, after four years the team still wasn't clear about its role. As far as she could see the team members did not have any authority to stop this project so why were they acting like this? It was only when she talked with one of the teacher team members that she began to see that they did think they had the authority to approve or disapprove whether the project would go forward.

What a mess! How ironic it was, Marie thought, that the New York Board of Regents was going to require all districts to have shared decision-making teams made up of teachers, administrators, and parents by 1994. It was a great idea in principle, but if they were not clear about what authority the teams had, it wasn't going to work much better than it did at Eastman.

At Genesee Elementary, Hector Diaz waved the completed school improvement plan, shouting, "We finally did it!" at the last school-based planning team meeting. Every member had signed it and so had the assistant superintendent. It had been a challenging year. Losing their librarian because of the budget cuts had been a blow to everyone's morale, but they had finished. Hector hoped people would come back in the fall ready to work on making the plan a reality.

After the Genesee Elementary teachers had weathered the horrendous mid-year budget cuts in 1991–92, the 1992–93 budget announcement that two-thirds of the school librarian positions were to be restored was welcome news. They would be able to open their library again. They hadn't forgotten how angry they felt when the decision to cut the position was announced. Weren't they supposed to be in a site-based budgeting school? If they'd been given the chance, they might have figured out a way to save the position. There was also universal grumbling that the budget did not include any money for salary increases. How did the district expect to negotiate a new contract if it was saying there was no money?

Genesee teachers were also surprised to find that they had a new principal assigned to their school. George Martin had been given a special curriculum development assignment at the central office for the year. His replacement, Corinne Moore, let it be known that she was not going to be George Martin's surrogate. She had her own ideas about how to run a school. For one thing, she wasn't going to let the members of the school-based planning team drag out their meetings before making a decision. If they couldn't decide, she was more than willing to make the decision for them. This did not go over well with teachers, most of whom had been at the school for years. Who was this person to come in and shake everything up, especially when she had only a temporary appointment?

Hector wanted to get started on implementing the school improvement plan. As far as he was concerned everyone had been able to participate, so it was a surprise to find that, all of a sudden, other teachers were questioning it. He would go to the faculty lounge and teachers would say, "Now, Hector, why is this in the plan?" By the time the school-based planning team elections were held in early October, Hector had been told by other teachers that the ones who were running "were on a mission to destroy." Well, Hector thought, maybe we just have to wait for George Martin to come back, and he decided he would put his extra effort into getting more parents involved in his own classroom. He didn't want to put in a whole lot of work on school-based planning if it was going to be one battle after another. This year he had more boys than girls in his class, and he realized, more than ever, how important it was for him to be an effective role model. Just the same, he wondered what it would be like to start a new school, as some of his colleagues had finally been able to do this year. Two teacher-led elementary schools had opened, each with a distinctive vision created by the teachers.

The "Eastman in Action!" teachers had worked all summer to get ready for their first year. After much struggle, they had finally convinced the school-based planning team to let them have a whole floor so their classrooms could be together. Three teacher teams, each with five teachers, had been formed. Each team would have responsibility for 125 students. They would also have the support of two lead teachers involved in curriculum projects at Eastman; one would help teachers to infuse writing into all subject areas and the other was an expert in technology. They had not succeeded in getting parents to sign an agreement of participation, but they could work on including parents later. Right now they had to get to know their students and figure out how to make time to continue working together so that they could integrate the curriculum the way they had planned. They could no longer take full days for planning because the grant funds for substitutes had been spent, so they would have to find common time over lunch or before or after school.

Marie was so busy that she wondered if her husband and children would forget what she looked like. But she was exhilarated, collaborating with her team members, as her twelve learning disabled students were integrated into the regular English, math, social studies, and science classes. It was a joy to be out of the self-contained classroom. They had a long way to go before everything would work smoothly, but they were finally trying something different. It looked as if the district was going to have to begin to make this shift too. The class-action suit filed by parents of students with disabilities in 1981 was under review. Everyone anticipated that the judge was going to mandate that more students must be included in regular classes.

Despite her busy schedule, Marie had not given up her interest in becoming a lead mentor teacher. She was worried that the program might disappear because the budget for the Career in Teaching Program had been reduced. If these budget troubles continued, it was a likely place to cut. She couldn't wait any longer; if the program was offered the next year, she was going to apply.

Marie also decided to add a peer review component to her performance review proposal for 1992–93. Now that she was going to be moving with her students into regular classrooms, she would have a chance to get some feedback on her teaching from others. As she listened to her colleagues she realized that many were not taking the process as seriously as she had. Some had not even done a report at all last year. It was disappointing that some teachers weren't willing to put in the time required, since she had gained so much from her own reflection about her work last year. It was the first time in years that she had made the effort to think systematically about her successes and failures with her students. When she mentioned this to one of her good friends, Melanie Wentworth, a social studies teacher at Eastman, she learned that Melanie was critical of the process. From Melanie's perspective the performance appraisal was just more paperwork and the teachers already had too much. Besides, some people had more of a knack for presenting themselves on paper than she did and she wasn't about to waste her time trying to create a glitzy-looking portfolio. It was hard for Marie to reconcile this view with Melanie's performance. She knew Melanie was a superb teacher who was constantly changing what she did in the classroom depending on her students' needs; if anything she was more naturally self-reflective than Marie. Why had the performance appraisal become just one more bureaucratic task for her friend?

No sooner had classes begun at Anthony High School than the worst happened. A student was shot by another student in the upstairs hallway over a dispute about a tape cassette. The bullet hit the boy's arm. Everyone was grateful the student had not been killed, but feared a future incident might result in a fatality. For years, teachers had been calling for stronger regulations on school violence, ever since a teacher had been stabbed to death by a student in 1983. Nothing had been done, however, and in the succeeding decade student assaults against other students, resulting in suspensions, had doubled to over nine hundred in 1991–92. The increase in assaults against staff members by students was even worse; assaults nearly tripled to almost three hundred in 1991–92. The School Board had never been willing to adopt a tough weapons policy, and some school board members had tried to minimize the problem of school violence. Enough was enough; it was time to deal with school violence, and the issue would become a central theme in contract discussions.[16]

Coming on the heels of the unresolved racial conflict of the previous spring, this increased violence made teachers uneasy about what might happen next. As the fall progressed, Nancy Collins found herself embroiled in a growing controversy over the representativeness of the school-based planning team. A group of African American teachers charged that the team was not representative of the larger school community because there were only a few African American teachers on it. They believed that none of the concerns from the previous year had been addressed. Tempers rose and they charged the white teachers with racism. By December the building was a racial tinderbox. Racial fights and harassment among students grew. Teachers had an increasingly difficult time getting students to follow their direction. Nancy was one of the few teachers who was still trying to get students out of the hallways during class, but she simply did not know what to do when a tall black student just walked away from her when she asked him where he was supposed to be. By the December school-based planning team meeting, feelings ran so high that it deteriorated into a shouting match. Finally, Superintendent Rivera announced that he was going to have an outside fact-finding team come in to investigate the racial charges and recommend what should be done. Nancy Collins put up a sign in her room which read, "I've been beaten, kicked, lied to, cussed at, taken advantage of, and laughed at, but the only reason I hang around this place is to see what happens next."

At the district level, contract negotiations stalled and then were declared at an impasse by the Teachers Association. The continuing dispute was about teachers' accountability. In an attempt to buy some time, a tentative agreement was reached between the superintendant and the Teachers Association to extend the existing contract until the end of the 1993 school year, pending the approval of the Board of Education. This approval was not forthcoming, however. The board defeated the agreement in a six-to-one vote. Public sentiment against the Rochester Teachers Association had strengthened. Before the vote Rochester's mayor once again lambasted the agreement. The Parent Council president commented, "Here we have another automatic pay raise for breathing." The Rochester paper ran a cartoon of a sinking ship named *City School District* with the caption, "Captain Rivera! Mr. Urbanski is demanding *more* deck chairs."[17]

Adam Urbanski and the Teachers Association leadership were outraged. There would be "no business as usual." Teachers were advised that they should not participate in any noncontractual school activities. Two thousand teachers signed a petition of no confidence in Superintendent Rivera. More than eight hundred teachers attended the next School Board meeting to demonstrate their dissatisfaction.

Soon after, the Teachers Association received unexpected support for their claim that reform was being strangled by bureaucratic bloat. In an audit report, the New York State Comptroller cited the Rochester City School as the worst in the state in excess administrative costs, an estimated $15 million overexpenditure per year. Now it was the district central office staff who felt the heat as the Rochester paper editorialized, "City Schools' Fiscal Mess Mirrors Poor Performance." A local magazine ran a cover story featuring a color picture of a bound and gagged teacher, "The Rochester Teacher: Bound by the System," describing a central organization of out-of-touch, unfocused, highly paid bureaucrats who did not serve schools or teachers.[18]

The school year ended with the announcement of further budget cuts for 1993–94. The Rochester City Council succeeded in changing the funding formula to further reduce the city's contribution to the school district budget by nearly $6 million.

Anthony High School was a mirror of the district-wide meltdown. The long awaited fact-finders' report was released. It expressed serious concerns about the level of racial tension, the poor quality of education, school safety, and school leadership. As a result, the principal, Roger O'Laughlin, was removed from his position. Any value that might have been gained from the fact-finders' report was lost with O'Laughlin's dismissal. Most white teachers believed Roger O'Laughlin had been made a scapegoat. From their perspective, the real problem was the small group of African American teachers. They should have been transferred because they were stirring up the students and spreading racial unrest. For their part, the African American teachers believed that radical change was needed if students were going to be successful. Susan B. Anthony High School needed to be shut down and reorganized.

In addition to removing the principal, Superintendent Rivera tried to disband the school-based planning team and replace it with a new team charged with creating several small schools to be housed at Anthony. The Teachers Association objected to the unilateral effort to redefine the school-based planning team, and this led to more conflict. Nancy Collins was reeling. Enough was enough. She resigned her position on the team. As far as she was concerned, shared decision-making had been a disaster. The only hope now was the appointment of a strong principal who had authority to make decisions as he or she saw fit. Nancy was worn out from the stress, and like most of her colleagues, retreated to her classroom and quietly closed the door. It was the only way to survive.

At the national level, Albert Shanker, president of the American Federation of Teachers, was also having second thoughts about shared decision-making. Shared governance could not work, he had decided, unless there was clear agreement about national standards and assessment. The experience of Rochester and other AFT districts which had been in the vanguard in the late 1980s had convinced Shanker that teachers were no more able than administrators to change schools. The AFT would still support efforts to redesign schools, but the central focus would now be on how to improve schools as they were.[19]

Adam Urbanski had also concluded that the outcomes of Rochester's reforms were not what he had hoped. He was not willing, though, to give up on the idea of democratically governed schools. He believed that teachers felt they needed strong principals because they were used to the way schools were organized. They had been trained to follow directions and perceived themselves as lacking power. Perhaps, he thought, school-based planning teams should be reconfigured into instructional design teams, as had been done in Los Angeles, but they should not be abandoned. What was needed, Urbanski believed, was to expand the 5 percent of teachers who had strong leadership skills so that teachers could truly take charge of their practice. With that in mind, Urbanski began to refocus the Teacher Association's efforts on strengthening teacher leadership and to encourage teachers to prepare for certification by the National Board for Professional Teaching Standards.

But there was the more immediate problem of the contract dispute. As the 1993–94 school year opened Urbanski commented, "I seem to be watching myself go more and more towards the old unionism." His observation would become reality as the Teachers Association raised the possibility of a strike, enacted work-to-rule, began picketing the homes of the superintendent and the School Board president, and voted unanimously for binding arbitration. The *Rochester Democrat and Chronicle* again took teachers to task, writing, "Most people consider themselves lucky to have a job, let alone one with even a modest annual raise. Why on earth should they support the teachers' demands?" "IT'S NOT THE MONEY" was the reply from the Teachers Association in a large ad a few weeks later. Rather than money, the conflict dispute from the teachers' perspective was about school safety and classroom resources. Teachers in the Rochester city school district were no longer the highest paid; in fact six nearby suburban school districts had higher teacher salaries, averaging $50,000.[20]

At Genesee Elementary School Hector was totally frustrated. The principal, George Martin, had returned and now the school-based planning team was not supposed to meet. Hector understood the need to press the district to settle the contract but his school and his students were being hurt. Test scores had not gotten any better, and now the teachers had been told that they should plan to have special education students included in their regular classes for next year. None of them knew anything about kids with special needs. How could they get ready if everyone was leaving school at 3:15 P.M.? One of the things George Martin had told him after his year at the central office was that everything was so chaotic downtown that a school could probably do whatever it wanted, if it could just get organized. With the contract dispute, though, it didn't look as if Genesee Elementary was going to make much progress this year. Hector couldn't help agreeing with another third-grade teacher who commented, "This school is going down and people are not willing to face the fact that these kids are in need. There are teachers who think these kids cannot learn because they are minority kids. At the same time I blame the Board of Education. Classes are too crowded. We have some very bright students here, but we don't have the proper resources. The city school district doesn't seem to care." There was enough blame to go around for everyone, Hector concluded. Oh well, there was always plenty to do in his own classroom. He had managed to get a grant with the other third-grade teachers to incorporate more literature into the reading program. He was also getting increasingly good at diagnosing students' learning difficulties and knowing how to move them to the next level of skill. There was also his master's degree in reading to finish.

Over at Eastman Middle School, the second year of "Eastman in Action!" had gotten off to a good start. Despite the contract dispute, the teachers had decided to meet on their own time during the summer. They couldn't imagine how they could plan intelligently for the new year otherwise. The teachers had agreed that they were going to move up with their students, so that the sixth-grade teachers would have the same group of students for the three years they were there. This made sense to Marie. So much time was wasted at the beginning of the year learning what the students could already do. It meant that the home-base guidance idea could finally work, too. This might really make a difference in the progress the students could make. She just wished that there was a better way to share what they were doing with the other teachers at Eastman. Many teachers were critical from a distance, but really didn't know much about what the team was trying to do. Since "Eastman in Action!" was on the top floor, other teachers were calling it the penthouse, as if they thought there were all kinds of luxuries available. If only that were true!

Marie was also excited to have been chosen to be a lead mentor teacher. She had gone through the selection process of submitting an application with letters of recommendation, followed by an interview with the Career in Teaching Panel, the previous spring. She felt being chosen was an honor and wanted to do her best. Granted, the program had been scaled back considerably because of budget cuts, but at least it had not been eliminated. She was concerned, though, that she had received only two days of training, just a tenth of what lead teachers used to get when there was more money for the program. The most worrisome part was that there had been little time to talk about what constitutes good teaching. It seemed that everyone had their own ideas, but the group had not developed their expectations for interns very well.

Marie was assigned to be a school-based mentor in her own building to two new special education teachers. She had already met them and thought that they were both going to be good. She hoped she would be able to give them the time they deserved. With the reduced budget, it was no longer possible to release every mentor teacher from part of her teaching day as had previously been done, so Marie would have to meet with her interns during her planning and lunch times.

As 1993 ended the contract dispute was finally resolved. Teachers would receive a 3.5 percent increase in each of the next three years and a lump sum for the 1992–93 school year. The contract also contained provisions for a three-year, summative evaluation for teachers, not tied to any salary increases, which required teachers to complete a peer review process with two colleagues and gain their administrator's endorsement. In addition, there was a strengthened policy on school violence and a commitment to establish a million dollar classroom resource fund to support effective teaching practices that would be managed by teachers.

The resource fund was never established by the district. As the year wore on, it was clear that there would be another budget crisis, a spring event which had become as predictable as the lilacs blooming. In June the School Board president advised the City Council that it could not afford the teachers' contract it had agreed to and acknowledged that the board had not been able to afford the two previous contracts either. City Council members were amazed by the admission, which confirmed what many of them had long suspected. The School Board was unable to manage the city school district. When Superintendent Rivera announced his resignation, the press blamed the School Board. Not only had the board failed to give Rivera the support he deserved, its constant interference with day-to-day operations sabotaged his best efforts. This time the editorial cartoon portrayed Rochester city schools as a plane in flames, with the School Board as pilots and Superintendent Rivera bailing out before the crash.[21] An acting superintendent was appointed for 1994–95, and plans were announced for a national search for a new superintendent.

Inclusion of special needs students in the regular classrooms was shaking up Genesee School as the 1994–95 school year began. The Teachers Association had called for a moratorium on full inclusion because of the haphazard way it was being implemented and the lack of training for teachers. But Genesee School had a hundred new students with special needs to educate. Hector was delighted with the new arrangement; with a special education teacher he had a blended classroom of thirty-seven children, twelve of whom had learning disabilities. He wished they had been able to work over the summer, but as usual Samantha Henessey, the new special education teacher, had been hired at the last minute. At least she was one of the teachers the school-based planning team had recommended hiring. Since tenured teachers could voluntarily transfer to other schools and final hiring decisions were made by the Human Resources Department, they had not always been so lucky. Samantha's eagerness reminded him of his own naive enthusiasm of just a few years ago. It seemed hard to believe he had already been teaching for five years. Hector was also impressed by Samantha's mentor teacher, Marie Furnelli. It was good to know that she had been working in an inclusion setting at Eastman Middle School, and he was delighted when Marie agreed to be a peer reviewer for his performance appraisal plan for 1994–95.

At the same time Hector knew that Genesee School had reached the point of no return. Test scores had fallen again the previous year, and there were rumblings that Genesee might be put on the state's list of low-performing schools. George Martin had been replaced as principal. Their new principal, an energetic woman named Virginia Welch, had begun their first faculty meeting by playing the theme song for *Mission Impossible*. It was silly, but it got their attention.

When the school-based planning team meetings began again, Hector and several other teachers who had served for several terms proposed that they create committees to better organize the team's work. They hoped that all teachers would serve on a committee as part of each one's professional development plan. Maybe with these committees they could finally make some progress. With Virginia Welch's support the team identified four standing committees: budget; standards and assessment; learning environment; and community service and support. Each committee had defined responsibilities tied to the school improvement plan. The school-based planning team was responsible for monitoring the progress of each committee. Finally, the shared governance process was beginning to make sense.

Marie Furnelli sensed the energy as soon as she walked into Genesee School to see her interns. She was going to mentor five new special education teachers in other buildings this year, while still teaching in the mornings with her team at Eastman Middle School. She was glad there were two interns at Genesee School, Samantha Henessey and Clarence Nichols. It looked as if Samantha and Hector Diaz were going to work together quite well. Both of them were very positive about creating a blended classroom. Hector had told her he hoped she would be willing to give him suggestions too. She was looking forward to her relationship with him.

Clarence Nichols, her other intern, was another story. She could tell already that he was not strong in classroom management skills and decided that improving them would be the first focus of her efforts with him. He had no experience working with more than twelve children at a time, so helping him learn how to manage a class of thirty-eight students was a top priority. Unfortunately, the teacher he was paired with was not being helpful. She had already cornered Marie to complain about Clarence and about inclusion. What a difference it made, Marie thought, when regular classroom teachers and special education teachers both volunteered for inclusion. It was hard to get a teacher to be enthusiastic about a program that she resented having to participate in. Marie hoped she could make a difference, but she knew how hard it would be to change a negative attitude.

Marie also realized that she was going to have to be careful not to get so involved with mentoring that her own teaching suffered. She did not want to shortchange her own students or let down her team members; it was going to be a challenge to balance all her responsibilities. On top of her work, she needed to spend more time at home too. At ten and twelve, her children were at the ages where they needed nightly help with their homework as well as constant chauffeuring between Scouts, music lessons, and sports events. Thank goodness her husband had a flexible schedule; otherwise, she could not possibly juggle all her obligations.

Both Hector and Marie were bemused when they saw the newspaper headline "Take Charge for Change" in December 1994. At the request of the new mayor—the former Urban League president, Bill Johnson— and the county executive, a group of civic leaders had issued a new report, *For All Our Children . . . No More Excuses.* The report began, "Rochester has suffered from a surplus of educational rhetoric and a scarcity of implementation of educational change." It went on to summarize the lack of improvement after eight years of reform and indicated that in some respects things had gotten worse. Only 13 percent of high school graduates were receiving Regents' diplomas, compared with 24 percent in 1986, when Bill Johnson as president of the Urban League had published his critical report *A Call to Action.* School violence and disorder had increased. Forty percent of the long-term suspensions for weapons possession were in the elementary schools. The report claimed that the average high school student attended school only four days per week, had a D grade point average, and was a year older than most students at that grade level. Elementary student performance had remained stagnant.[22]

A host of solutions were proposed by the authors of the report. Academic success should be the first priority and all current efforts should be evaluated in terms of student success. Parent involvement should be gained through having parents agree to a teacher-family-student performance pact. Teachers should have more say over how money was used and have more authority over instructional decisions, but they should be held accountable by being paid according to their performance. Tenure for teachers should be eliminated. The central office should be reorganized to serve schools better, but a strong superintendent needed to be hired and given authority to implement districtwide policy. At the same time a school choice plan, including as options new charter schools and possibly private schools, should be implemented. Social service agencies needed to be better coordinated with

[handwritten margin note: Every idea ever created!]

the schools. Finally, an independent, unpaid group should be created to monitor and report on student performance.

Where had all these ideas come from? wondered Hector and Marie. Some of the ideas were good, ideas that teachers had urged for years, but others made no sense to them. To think that a performance pact was going to make any difference as far as parent involvement was concerned just showed how far removed the report's authors were from the day-to-day life of Rochester's schools. It was also clear that teachers would never agree to pay for performance, so why did it keep coming up? As far as they could tell, this was a political ploy by the mayor and the county executive. The School Board members thought so too. Having been excluded from the report's development, School Board members refused to endorse it. The Teachers Association took a similar position, but agreed to participate in future planning efforts.

The significance of a report by a group of community leaders, two of whom were on the New York State Board of Regents, could not be dismissed, however. No matter what measure was used, according to the report, district-wide outcomes had not improved. Marie and Hector knew that they were working as hard as they could, and were making progress at their schools, but such progress did not show on a district-wide basis.

Despite the report's call for a recommitment to improving schools from all parts of the community, as the year went on support for the school district dwindled. A ten-year-old nonprofit organization that supported reform by operating a teacher resource center and a library acquisition project closed because of loss of corporate funding. The National Center for Education and the Economy, the think tank that had relocated to Rochester in 1988 to help support Rochester's reforms and extend them throughout the nation, lost its state funding. Soon after that, the National Center announced that the Rochester office was closing.[23]

By the end of the 1994–95 school year Marie found herself in the dual role of evaluating her interns and completing her own three-year summative evaluation. Despite her best efforts, Clarence Nichols had not been able to develop the classroom management and planning skills that he needed to be successful in a blended classroom. After long discussions with Marie, Clarence had decided that he did not enjoy managing the complexity of the blended classroom and that he was much more effective with children in less structured situations. He had decided to seek employment elsewhere for the fall, perhaps at the Mary Cariola Children's Center, an organization which served children with profound handicaps, where he would work with only a few children. Knowing how much effort Clarence had made to provide individualized instruction for the special education students, Marie felt that he would be much more successful in this setting. She was glad he had come to the decision on his own, so that she did not have to recommend that he be terminated.

Marie's own summative evaluation had been an interesting experience. Marie felt that it was important for her three-year evaluation to include both the teaching and mentoring aspects of her work. She had chosen one of her team members from Eastman and one of the teachers of the Career in Teaching Panel, the committee that oversaw the lead teacher program, to complete her review. Marie presented her portfolios and peer review reports for the past three years to her colleagues. She was pleased that someone else was going to look at her portfolios because no one had reviewed them since 1991–92. The Career in Teaching Panel had read all the peer review reports that year but soon discovered that it was impossible to read nearly two thousand reports every summer. The decision had been made to return the performance appraisal review process to the school-based planning teams. Unfortunately, most schools did little more than collect the reports and send them to the Human Resources Department.

The summative evaluation called for the reviewers to interview the teacher about her previous three years of work. Over coffee, Marie and her two reviewers had a wide-ranging discussion, giving Marie the opportunity to talk about her portfolios, to answer questions about how she had worked to include special education students in the regular classes, and to reflect on her role as a mentor. Following this discussion, the reviewers were asked to indicate whether Marie met professional standards as described in the contract. As a final step, Marie's principal was asked to review both Marie's work and the reviewers' comments and sign off on the report. Failure to receive a successful summative evaluation meant the withholding of a salary increase for the subsequent year, so it was a serious matter. Marie felt a strong sense of satisfaction when she received a favorable review from her principal. She knew she had been doing a good job, but it was important to get external recognition. She had only one criticism of the performance assessment process. It didn't seem to matter how much effort the teachers put into it. Many of her colleagues had done far less than she had. As long as teachers did something, they were almost guaranteed a satisfactory assessment. Marie was sure the process did nothing to improve teaching when teachers were not investing any effort in it.

As Nancy Collins got ready for school in the fall of 1995, she increasingly thought about retirement. After two years, the new principal had managed to quell most of the racial unrest at Anthony High. Tension persisted, but many of the most vocal critics had either left or been silenced by the strict procedures adopted for discussion at all meetings. The effort to create small schools at Anthony had been abandoned, and the principal was trying to focus on departmental improvement plans as a way to reinvigorate the school. These plans didn't seem to be making any difference as far as Nancy could see, but at least people weren't feeling as stressed as they had. White teachers no longer felt they had to watch their words whenever an African American staff member was present. Other efforts were under way at the school as well. A wellness center, staffed by the county health department, had been established. Funding from a federal grant was providing additional counseling and tutoring for students. And a schoolwide violence prevention program had been established.

But student attendance was still terrible, with about 25 percent absent on any given day. Many of Nancy's students didn't seem to have any interest in being at school no matter what she did. She believed that they had given up long before they reached her classroom. Nancy watched the state education commissioner's September school address on television and shook her head. Within the next few years all high school students were going to have to meet more stringent math requirements to graduate, with more challenging standards in the other core subjects as well. The commissioner seemed to think that teachers were just not trying hard enough to challenge their students. New standards would raise the bar for everyone. Maybe, thought Nancy, but will we lose six years' worth of kids who weren't prepared for higher expectations in the transition? Retirement looked better and better.

Rochester's new superintendent, Clifford Janey, an African American who had been an administrator in Boston, was talking about higher standards too. Curriculum and instruction should drive all budget decisions. Principals should have more authority to make decisions in their schools. With clear benchmarks for student achievement, everyone would know how well the district was doing on improving students' learning.[24] The only problem was that Superintendent Janey seemed to have made no effort to include the Teachers Association in his new initiative. Nancy wondered how the superintendent thought he was going to get anything accomplished without union leadership support. This looked like trouble.

A year later, while leisurely reading the newspaper, a retired Nancy Collins sadly learned that her prediction had been true. Once again relationships between the Teachers Association and the superintendent were deteriorating. Just as there appeared to be consensus on a new contract agreement, the district reintroduced a pay for performance proposal. Superintendent Janey argued, "Success must be measured before it can be rewarded." Adam Urbanski was quick to point out that none of the superintendent's unilaterally determined academic goals for 1995–96 had been met. In contrast to the B+ the superintendent had received for his first year from the press, teachers gave him a C–/D+.[25]

Although the superintendent had been effective with his business and community constituents, his negotiations with Rochester teachers were even more disastrous than the strife-filled negotiations with Superintendents McWalters and Rivera. In December 1996 teachers crowded into the School Board meeting to protest the slow progress of negotiations. Once again there was "no business as usual."

This time the district took action against the union. Adam Urbanski was accused by the district of shoving a security guard aside so that teachers could flood into the meeting. Disciplinary action was threatened. Relations between the union and the district had come full circle from the landmark partnership between Adam Urbanski and Peter McWalters in 1987. Urbanski contemplated what it would mean to be arrested, as Albert Shanker had been over thirty years ago when he began the fight for teachers' rights in New York City. Teachers were about to vote "no confidence" in Janey when he and Urbanski agreed to meet to address their differences.

As the 1996–97 school year came to a close, a tentative agreement was reached, but it soon fell apart, over the question of parents' evaluation of teachers. The district wanted a standardized questionnaire for parents to be incorporated into the revised teacher evaluation plan. The union thought each school should determine how to survey parents and wanted parental responses to be used only by teachers.

Hector Diaz decided to ignore the conflict. He had too much to do. His school was finally making some long-needed changes, thanks to the

[handwritten marginalia: Just 10 yrs later — ups & downs]

[handwritten note at bottom: how much things change w/ different administrators.]

work of the school-based planning team committees. Some of his colleagues remained critical, feeling that they had been given authority over the unimportant decisions while the administrators downtown still pulled the strings; but the majority of teachers were involved in trying to do what they could to improve Genesee Elementary School. This was Hector's second year with a combined third- and fourth-grade classroom, and he was proud of how much progress his students were making. The children with learning disabilities were sometimes hard to distinguish from the rest of the children. His partnership with the special education teacher, Samantha Henessey, was finely tuned. Each depended so much on the other that they couldn't imagine teaching in isolation again. The school had also created partnerships with several businesses and a civic group, so that there were many volunteers helping with tutoring and other activities. Test scores had improved for two consecutive years. Whatever happened between the district and the union, the teachers had to protect the progress they had made.

Marie Furnelli also knew that, despite all the negative assessments, progress had been made over the last ten years. The year before, Marie had been assigned to work with a veteran teacher who, after being reviewed by the Career in Teaching Panel, had been required to enter a formal intervention process because her summative evaluation had not been approved and she had a history of being ineffective. More than sixty underperforming teachers had been required to go through a formal intervention process in the past ten years. Half of them had improved, but the rest had left the district. Most left voluntarily, but a few were dismissed after intervention efforts had failed. In addition, more and more tenured teachers were requesting assistance from mentor teachers voluntarily; more than two hundred were helped in 1995–96.

Marie spent six hours each week with the teacher whom she had been assigned to assist, more than she spent with her interns. She identified a number of major weaknesses: lack of short- and long-term lesson planning, ineffective classroom management, poor communication with parents, and failure to keep commitments. As she did with her interns, Marie developed an action plan with the teacher and tried to help her improve. She knew how difficult it must be for a tenured teacher to have to agree to have a mentor, but she also knew that this teacher could not continue to work in the way she had been. She was hurting children. Unfortunately, as the year came to a close, it was clear that the teacher continued to blame everyone besides herself for her poor performance. Marie felt she had no choice but to recommend that the teacher be dismissed, and she was fired by the district. Marie thought what a major change it was for a teacher to be dismissed with the involvement of the teachers' union.

Marie had learned a tremendous amount about how to assist her fellow teachers over the past three years. This year was the end of her second two-year term as a lead mentor teacher, and she had to decide whether to apply again. On the one hand, she loved what she was doing; it had been tremendously fulfilling to work with other teachers while continuing to teach on a reduced schedule. On the other hand, she could see that more of her effort was needed again at Eastman Middle School. Her team had broken up, with one teacher moving to the high school level and another deciding to retire. They had accomplished their goal of staying with their students for three years, and those whom they had taught seemed to have benefited from the continuity. Now, though, new teachers had been assigned to the team and the cohesiveness had been lost. It was amazing how much the team dynamics were affected by the talents and personalities of the individual teachers involved. The central office never seemed to appreciate this fact in assigning teachers. Such well-integrated teams as Marie's had not yet become part of the school culture, and now they were in danger of disappearing.

Three hundred and fifty new teachers had been hired to replace those who had retired. This was just the beginning of a wave of projected retirements that were expected over the next five years. It was hard for Marie to know how she could be most effective, by continuing her mentoring, for which there was certainly a need, or by returning to teaching full-time to maintain the success of her team's efforts over the past three years.

She cared most about the children. They, after all, were what kept her and most of her friends going, no matter what happened. The hardest part was that so many more of her students now came from impoverished families. Where only one in four qualified for a free or reduced-cost lunch in 1987, now more than three out of four did. The New York State Education Department had ranked Rochester as the second neediest school district in the state. This ranking seldom got talked about when the reforms were evaluated by the media, but perhaps the teachers had not done so badly in the face of dramatically increasing poverty.[26]

By early 1998 the teachers' contract dispute had been resolved. For the first time, parents would be able to evaluate how well they felt teachers were communicating with them. The evaluation forms would be returned directly to the teachers, but the parents could send a copy to the principal if they chose.

Marie joined Hector Diaz, Nancy Collins, and Ray Bowen, a high school principal, as panelists at a community forum to review and assess the reform efforts since the historic 1987 teachers' contract. Panel members had been asked to share their perspectives about the past ten years of reform, especially the efforts at professionalizing teaching.

Marie began by reminiscing about how excited she had been to learn about the contract's provisions for lead teachers. Being a lead teacher had given her the opportunity to grow professionally without abandoning the classroom. Even more significant was the fact that teachers were evaluating other teachers as part of the internship reappointment process. Ten years ago the administrators' union had sued to try to prevent peer evaluation. Now mentor teachers worked collaboratively with principals, and the principals' evaluations of the mentor program were exemplary. With confidence Marie declared, "I am sure administrators will rely on what I've written because they don't have first-hand information like I do." Tenured teachers had also benefited from the mentoring program. More were requesting help, and the intervention process was a way to deal with the most ineffective teachers.

Marie went on to say that Performance Appraisal Review for Teachers, the teacher peer evaluation process, was not regarded by all teachers as useful; but it had been important for her own professional development. "You know," she said, "the performance assessment process gives us a chance to set our own goals and it helps us be more thoughtful about what we do. I couldn't imagine going back to the charade of the old evaluation checklist. I wish, though, that more teachers would invest more effort and not treat it like one more bureaucratic requirement. How can we claim to be professionals if we won't take our own work seriously?"

Finally, Marie admitted her frustration that, despite the efforts of many teachers, student performance had only recently improved at the elementary level.[27] She told the audience how she felt about the dramatic increase in the number of children living in poverty. "It has made me wonder if Rochester really cares very much about these children." Marie concluded her remarks by suggesting that the changes teachers had made in their profession were important, but were not enough. She thought teachers would need to organize and exert political pressure to gain improvements in other areas that affected their students' lives, such as better coordination with social service agencies and more educational and employment opportunities for parents.[28]

Ray Bowen, who had been a high school principal since the early 1980s, said that while he certainly agreed with Marie about students' needs, in his view the reforms had been a disaster. Much of the time the school-based planning teams had merely served as a forum for a number of very poor teachers. Most teachers had recognized that school-based planning was a waste of their time; it detracted from their teaching and just created more paperwork. Parents were not equally empowered, but were more distanced. As far as he was concerned, the Rochester Teachers Association had succeeded in sabotaging the reforms, and rhetoric aside, the real purpose of a teachers' union was to maintain the status quo. Teachers might think the bureaucracy downtown stifled reform, but from his perspective, the teachers' contract demands were a greater problem. What was needed was to grapple with teachers' avoidance of the real issue—that students' success or failure was fundamentally the teachers' responsibility.

At the secondary school level, he believed one of the worst decisions had been the elimination of the academic department chairpersons. Without these positions, there was not nearly enough attention being given to instructional issues. The vice principals, who were responsible for two or three subject areas, in addition to a lot of other duties, just did not have the time. With hundreds of new teachers coming into the schools, who was going to give them support once their internship year was over? Perhaps the former structure had problems, but what they had now was no improvement.

Hector Diaz began his remarks by discussing the struggle to create an effective shared decision-making process at Genesee Elementary School. The district and the Teachers Association had underestimated the magnitude of this major organizational change and had not provided the support schools needed. He wished it had not taken so many years to create an effective governance process. "It has been a lot of effort, but the committee system we developed has worked," he said. "Despite the struggles we have had, school reform has helped give me a sense that what I choose to do is up to me. The reforms have given me options."

There was still an uneasy tension between the school and the central office. Some of his colleagues, he acknowledged, were far more negative, believing that they had never been given any real authority. One of his colleagues had just complained to him that "teachers never had any real power; administrators just made people think they had. It's fine for us to write goals, but the central office just does what it wants to do anyway. Decentralization has not happened." At this remark, many teachers in the audience clapped in agreement. Hector said he thought people could look at the reforms differently, but he continued to believe the possibilities were greater than the obstacles.

Hector finished by commenting on how much had changed since 1987. There had been four superintendents; he had worked with three different principals; his school had enrolled children with special needs and reorganized to include them in regular classrooms; the teachers had received new curriculum guidelines and standards from the state of New York; they had created a portfolio assessment process for students; and the list went on and on. In some respects, he said, it was amazing that the 1987 reforms had survived at all, given the fast rate at which educational reforms come and go. Using the collective bargaining process to negotiate reforms had assured that the changes could not just disappear.

Nancy Collins opened her comments by observing that having been away from the daily life of schools for nearly two years, she had come to some different conclusions. First, Adam Urbanski had been right when he commented years ago that reforming schools was all about power. One way to describe the past ten years was as a continual power struggle: between the union and the district, between teachers and administrators, between the School Board and the superintendent, between the mayor and the School Board, between the Urban League president and the union, between parents and the union, between parents and the district, and on and on. Shared decision-making often seemed to be part of the problem rather than part of the solution. She recognized that this was part of the price we pay for democracy, but wondered when all concerned would see beyond the conflict to focus on children's learning.

Nancy also observed that as far as she was concerned teaching had always been a profession. She was not convinced that any of the reforms had made much difference, although she did agree with Marie that the mentoring program for new teachers was worth keeping. She did not agree about the changes in the evaluation of teachers though, commenting, "It doesn't tell anybody anything. There is too much emphasis on a lot of paper and none of it affects the students."

Nancy said that she realized, now more than ever, how little time she really had had as a teacher to do anything besides keep up with her classes. She wondered if it had been reasonable to expect all these reforms on top of everything else teachers had to do. Perhaps if the reformers wanted to make a real change for teachers they would reorganize the teaching load to give teachers more time to prepare and collaborate.

Finally, Nancy congratulated her former math colleagues for successfully increasing the number of students who were taking and passing the Regents math course that would soon become a graduation requirement. And then she wished them all well, saying she would continue to watch what happened from her porch swing.

8

The Progress of the Slow Revolution throughout the Nation

The accounts of Florence Thayer, Andrena Anthony, and Rochester's teachers attempt to capture the sweep of historical change over the last hundred years as teachers struggled to take charge of their practice. We have called this struggle a slow revolution. In this chapter we will move beyond portraiture to assess the outcomes of this revolution on a broader scale by looking at a wide range of recent research. Most of this research, including our own longitudinal study of nine schools in four school districts, began in the late 1980s in response to breakthroughs in the teacher empowerment movement that gave teachers new roles and increased authority.

As in most reform movements, enthusiasm for the cause, and belief in imminent change, were pervasive at the outset. For many teachers, the call for teacher professionalization in the educational reform reports of the 1980s was the outcome of years of struggle to gain greater working rights for teachers.[1] Teachers would finally have an equal voice in important decisions about their work, their students, and their schools. The overly bureaucratic, hierarchical model of schooling would be replaced by a collegial, professional model that would enable teachers to more readily benefit from their colleagues' wisdom. Teachers would be recognized for their training and expertise in their dealings with administrators, parents, and the public. Teachers would be able to make schools better for students.

Like the Rochester and Syracuse districts, many school districts have attempted to act on this vision by adopting school-based shared decision-making. Many schools have also been involved in restructuring efforts to increase teacher collaboration in the classroom and to broaden the involvement of parents and community members. Efforts have been made to redesign the teacher evaluation process based on a collegial, reflective model. Some districts have given teachers a voice in hiring and promotion, and many more have created mentoring programs for new teachers. Fewer districts have taken the step of creating a differentiated teaching structure like Rochester's Career in Teaching Program. However, there have been parallel job-enlargement efforts in other states, such as the Missouri Career Development and Teacher Excellence Plan and the California Mentorship Program, which offered teachers extra compensation for activities involving professional growth, faculty collaboration, school-community involvement, and the mentoring of new teachers.[2]

What can be said about the outcomes of this slow revolution? Teachers, even those at the same school, offer widely varied, sometimes contradictory, responses. "Reform never happened," a reading resource teacher concluded sadly. A few doors away the perspective shifts dramatically: "Reform has given me the ability to challenge myself. I can dictate what I want to be." On the floor above, a third teacher commented, "For the first time I feel that I can tap any part of the community; I saw things come together for the first time." Despite such varying opinions, we have concluded that slow but permanent change is under way in the teaching profession. Although there is often a sense of zigzag progress, taking one step forward, followed by two steps back, teachers at all but one of the nine schools we studied report that they believe real change is occurring and they are moving in the right direction.

In our last set of interviews in the late 1990s, we asked teachers to estimate the current status of the teacher empowerment reform effort at their school in terms of its incorporation into current practice.[3] Two-thirds of the teachers responded that the reforms had been incorporated either in a robust and major way or in a partial but still significant way. The remainder responded that the reforms had largely atrophied, although significant traces remained. No teachers said that reform had never been seriously attempted, or that if it had been tried, it had been dropped and had disappeared. A majority of teachers in the schools we studied indicated that they and their colleagues would continue to support the reform initiatives. This picture was repeated at the national level. Over 70 percent of teachers reported that their schools were engaged in a variety of reforms, including greater involvement of teachers in decision-making in curriculum, personnel, scheduling, and budgeting matters. These reforms have been either partially or fully implemented.[4]

This endorsement comes with caveats, however. Teachers were clear that reforms which were jointly developed and implemented with teachers at the school level were more likely to succeed than those imposed upon them.[5] There was greater success in schools where a majority of the teachers took on some aspect of the new roles. Engaging a majority of their colleagues was often problematic. Even when reforms were contractually negotiated or created by a joint committee of teachers and administrators at the district level, there was no guarantee that teacher involvement at the district level would be perceived as teacher involvement by individual teachers. Many teachers had little awareness of the work of other teachers at the district level. The quick demise of Syracuse's professional responsibilities committees and the lukewarm endorsement of Rochester's teacher evaluation process are good examples.

We found no evidence suggesting principals should be eliminated, although teachers seek leaders who manage more collaboratively. Teachers at all the schools spoke to the need for effective administrative leadership from their principals. There was a direct correlation between the quality of leadership and the vitality of the reform effort. The Hilltop Elementary School faculty in Syracuse, for example, lost much of their momentum when the principal was replaced with a principal who did not share their vision and, in the eyes of the teachers, did not have adequate leadership skills to sustain the effort.

Teachers experienced obstacles that discouraged involvement in new roles. The rigid structure of the teachers' work day, which allowed little time for planning or collaborative work, was a continuing concern.[6] As we observed in Chapter 2, American teachers spend more time actually instructing students than do teachers in most other countries. Often, initial enthusiasm for new roles waned with the day-to-day struggle of trying to carve out time for new collaborative work within an inflexible, overprogrammed day.

The question of whether teachers had genuine authority to make decisions or merely advisory powers was a second issue. As the Rochester story exemplified, many teachers were not convinced that real power shifts were occurring at the building and district level. And with good reason. As we noted in Chapter 4, in a comparison with schools in thirteen other countries. American schools were among the least autonomous, with only 26 percent of the key educational decisions being made at the school level. Most of the significant decisions are made at the district and state levels. The psychologist Seymour Sarason observed, "The problem of change is the problem of power, and the problem of power is how to wield it in ways that allow others to identify with, to gain a sense of ownership of the process and goals of change."[7] Teachers often feel little of that ownership within the existing bureaucratic hierarchy of public schooling. And they are right. In most cases, power over budget, hiring, and curriculum remains tightly held by the central office. Major devolution of power is the exception, not the rule.

A third concern is the capacity and willingness of more teachers to become engaged in taking responsibility for their practice. The lack of organizational resources to support them in these efforts is part of the reason. The low quality of many professional development programs for teachers has been so widely recognized that improving teachers' professional development has been included as one of the eight national education goals endorsed by the Clinton administration. Teachers reported that although professional development support in the form of release days to work with other teachers or extended training opportunities was initially available, resources for such activities diminished and then nearly disappeared as grant funding ended and districts experienced budget reductions. The budget for Rochester's Career in Teaching Program, for example, declined from $3.3 million in 1991 to $1.4 million in 1997. Lack of adequate resources confirmed the skepticism of those who questioned the genuineness of the reforms. Lack of resources aside, though, many teachers were unwilling to assume any serious role in evaluating their colleagues. This position is grounded in part in traditional unionism, but it also reflects long-held beliefs about equality among teachers and concerns about the potential negative impact of peer evaluation on teachers' relationships with each other.

Despite these realities, in five of our nine schools teachers estimated that 60 percent or more of the teachers were significantly involved in new roles. They were the teachers who described themselves as having gained more control over their own work, who became more concerned about how to define good teaching, and who broadened their frame of reference to include consideration of issues outside the classroom. Admittedly, these were teachers in the most progressive school districts.

They were unwilling to return to the role of being closeted in their classrooms. As one quietly said: "I could never, ever, go back. I could never again be without a voice."

In this chapter we will more closely examine the outcomes of the slow revolution in terms of two central issues. First, what have we learned about teachers' efforts to take responsibility for the quality of teaching? And second, what have we learned about teachers' efforts to take responsibility for the quality of their schools?

Taking Responsibility for the Quality of Teaching

The work of teachers was traditionally done in relative isolation behind classroom doors. Teachers often knew very little about the work of fellow teachers and had little say about who was chosen to teach. The negative impact of teachers' isolation on the quality of teaching and the schools is so widely accepted that it has become part of the conventional wisdom about the teaching profession.[8] Reform efforts have focused on increasing collaboration among teachers and giving them more responsibility for the quality of instruction, including the mentoring of new teachers and the evaluation of other teachers' performance.

There is substantial evidence that teacher collaboration can be a source of teachers' professional development, and schools where extensive collaboration is the norm are often more successful than those where teachers collaborate less.[9] Reform initiatives of all types, from the open schools of the 1970s to work-redesign plans for teachers and strategic planning processes, were intended to bring teachers out from behind closed doors into a more collaborative work setting.[10]

Beneath this easy assumption about the value of teacher collaboration is a far more complex picture, however. First, collaboration may take a variety of forms. Teachers engage with each other in numerous ways, for multiple reasons, for differing lengths of time, both within and outside their schools. One way of considering teacher collaboration is in terms of schoolwide collegiality, or developing shared norms of collective responsibility for student learning. In this view teaching is conceived as a joint enterprise occurring in a collaborative culture.[11] Successful restructuring efforts, such as that undertaken by the Coalition for Essential Schools at Brown University, have stressed the importance of collaboration based on commonly held principles as a central organizing framework for schoolwide reform.

Teacher collaboration also has a more intimate aspect, however—small groups of teachers who come together because of shared interests in their discipline, in teaching strategies, or in specific students. A three-year study of sixteen public and private secondary schools concluded that the academic department was the professional community of greatest significance to secondary teachers' beliefs about their practice and attitudes toward teaching and students. Moreover, departments often varied substantially in terms of the degree of professional collegiality within the same school. Teachers in cohesive departments where there was a capacity for reflection and problem solving were more likely to share a high commitment to helping all students learn.[12]

In addition to forming collaborative subgroups within the school, teachers often collaborate with like-minded colleagues at other schools. Professional associations and unions provide formal, organizational frameworks for cross-school collaboration, and teachers also create their own informal connections.[13]

Another aspect of teachers' collaboration is the degree to which their relationships are significant for teachers and promote professional growth. Andy Hargreaves has argued that much of what passes for teacher collaboration is in fact "contrived collegiality," administratively mandated and expected to achieve some specific outcome, such as implementing a new curriculum or instituting required peer coaching. True collaborative cultures emerge from and are primarily sustained by teachers themselves. They are voluntary associations, focused on developing initiatives that teachers support, and are deeply entwined in the daily work of teachers. Such relationships require constant effort to develop and sustain. This depth of collaborative work is found infrequently in schools.[14]

In all collaboration there is a tension between collegiality and individualism. There is value in solitude. Teachers need time for thoughtful planning and assessment, much of which must be done alone.[15] Individualism also allows teachers to separate their own work from the organization and from the work of other teachers. Teachers are proud and satisfied when their own classrooms are effective, regardless of what is happening outside their doors. As the conflict at Rochester's Anthony High School worsened, one of the highly regarded African American teachers resigned from the shared decision-making team and withdrew from schoolwide involvement saying, "I stay in my room with my kids.

It's just when you go out there that it gets crazy." Keeping one's door closed is also an effective response to one new reform after another.[16] In some instances, detachment is not professional isolation, but professional survival.

Finally, the question of "collaboration about what?" must be addressed. There is no guarantee that greater teacher collegiality will improve teachers' professional work or make schools more effective unless the collaboration is grounded in knowledge about successful teaching and learning. Gaining such knowledge can be a challenge. Educational research is often not written with teachers in mind. As a result, a multimedia, highly profitable industry of magazines, books, and videos for teachers has evolved to fill the gap. Some of these products are of high quality and genuinely help teachers improve their practice, but many of them reduce complex research to cookbook suggestions, frequently fed to teachers in one-shot in-service workshops offered in the name of professional development. Teachers are often at the bottom of the research food chain and much of what they receive is very thin gruel.[17] Commercial curriculum developers are also guilty of promoting their products with no evidence of their effectiveness. A survey of five hundred curriculum contractors conducted by the Kentucky State Department of Education found only sixty-four contractors could produce any evidence of improvements in students' learning.[18]

Despite the abundance of thin gruel, we found that teachers are increasingly critical consumers, demanding more substantial fare. By and large teachers rejected the one-shot workshop format for professional development. Twenty years ago the Syracuse School District rented the Syracuse University Field House, with seating for ten thousand, and required every teacher to spend the day being talked at in the name of teachers' professional development. It is hard to imagine teachers agreeing to such a use of their time today. At all of our schools, and in comparable research, teachers were taking over the role of deciding what professional development opportunities they needed and negotiating with consultants for their services. Instead of being passive recipients, they have become critical consumers of what the "experts" offer.[19] One teacher who was instrumental in this change at her school commented, "Staff development days are more useful because we all recognize the need to make changes, and are involved in planning the kind of changes we will make." In some schools, teachers and university professors have collaborated to create professional development schools, providing a forum where teachers and student teachers can read research and discuss how it can be used in their teaching.[20] Professional development less often takes place in a vacuum now, and it is increasingly tied to teachers' efforts to improve their schools. This shift is critical in a time when multiple reforms are being implemented simultaneously in schools.[21]

Another collaborative effort by teachers is doing research, either with university researchers or independently. The term "teacher research" has been applied to a wide range of teachers' activities, the central characteristic being systematic, thoughtful inquiry about teaching.[22] There is a growing body of published research by teachers, and increasing numbers of teachers' groups are gathering to share their experiences and learn from each other. At Crestview Elementary School, one of the nine schools in our study, teachers formed action research teams to conduct research on how to involve more parents in shared governance and how to use multi-age grouping in their teaching. The findings from the research teams were reported to the faculty at town meetings, which often generated new questions. Teachers in another district we studied, Pleasant Valley, spent three years reviewing the research literature on the evaluation of teachers. They surveyed teachers and administrators about peer review, and visited other districts with model programs, before developing their own professional evaluation model, which they called Supportive Supervision.

All of the nine schools we studied developed new collaborative cultures to some degree. The most robust schoolwide collaboration occurred at Crestview, located in a Rochester suburb. Before the school even opened the planning committee—made up of teachers, parents, the principal, and the superintendent—spent a month sharing their personal educational visions and reaching consensus on a strong set of guiding principles. These principles laid the groundwork for all further collaborative work and schoolwide decisions. Two other elementary schools, Hilltop School in Syracuse and Genesee Elementary in Rochester, also began to move, both with difficulty, toward schoolwide collaboration.

At the secondary level, although there were many collaborative subgroups, there was far less success in achieving schoolwide collaboration. In fact, initiatives proposed by smaller groups of teachers were sometimes weakened, and even sabotaged, by lack of collegial support. As we described in Chapter 7, the "Eastman in Action" team's efforts were frequently met with hostility by other Eastman teachers. At Raintree Middle School in Syracuse, another group of teachers working to create an interdisciplinary, theme-based curriculum were jokingly referred to by other teachers as the "Dream Team." Resentment of the Dream Team teachers increased when their students' test scores improved. Uninvolved teachers often believed that these change-oriented teachers were receiving preferential treatment, which they felt was unfair, but at the same time they were unwilling to join a truly collaborative effort, or even be informed about their colleagues' work. Without some degree of schoolwide collaboration, it is usually very difficult to sustain subgroup initiatives.[23]

One of the most comprehensive research projects on school restructuring drew on data gathered from more than fifteen hundred schools throughout the United States and field research done in forty-four schools located in sixteen states. This multifaceted, five-year study concluded that schools which functioned as professional communities were most likely to create high-quality learning for their students. Researchers concluded that four interconnected factors were critical for successful school restructuring. First, there had to be a commonly shared focus on high-quality learning, defined as learning that deeply engaged students in developing their own knowledge and skills through disciplined inquiry and interchange with the world outside the school. Second, methods of teaching and assignments had to be carefully designed to foster high-quality learning. Third, there had to be adequate time for planning, and sufficient technological resources, to support collaborative work among the teachers. Finally, external professional networks, including district personnel departments and state education departments, had to support the work of the school staff. In schools where these factors were present, the students gained greater knowledge and understanding, and scored better on standardized tests than did other students. Furthermore, this held true across schools with a wide diversity of students.[24]

The creation of professional communities in schools is a key variable in improving students' learning. But it must be driven by a vision of high-quality teaching that engages students in work that is complex and meaningful. The superior learning that results from this shift in the relationships between teachers and students and among students cannot always be measured on standardized tests. Some teachers in our schools reported that as a result of their own experiences in new roles, their students were more engaged, had learned to work together, and were assuming more responsibility for their own learning. But there was also ambivalence about whether these changes really counted, because they often did not affect test scores. Observed a Hamilton High math teacher, "I have been hoping someone I respected would teach differently than I do, using some of the new methods, and have significantly better scores than I do so I would be pushed to change. It's never happened. Using class projects and manipulatives will go into more depth but it happens at the expense of other material." This is the present dilemma for teachers and keeps many from changing their practice as long as standardized test scores remain the sole measure of teachers' success.

What is needed for teachers to create collaborative cultures, as opposed to "contrived collegiality"? The case of Hilltop Elementary School offers further insight. Hilltop School is a kindergarten through grade 6 elementary school with an enrollment of 450 students nearly equally divided between white and black children. Many children came from low-income families with needs the older, predominantly white, middle-class, female faculty were unprepared to meet. Test scores were low, teachers were frustrated, and teachers' attitudes were negative in 1990. One of the teachers described her relationship with other teachers this way, "It was everyone for herself. We didn't respect each other. You knew things weren't working but if nothing is working, there is nothing you can do about it."

In 1991, a new principal and vice principal arrived who were known as strong leaders with collaborative skills. The teachers were challenged to consider candidly how well their school was serving both students and themselves. The principal opened the dialogue by sharing his feelings about the negative environment. A highly respected teacher responded, "We're afraid. We don't trust the kids." Then other teachers began to acknowledge serious concerns that needed to be addressed if they hoped to improve their students' learning.

The teachers' recognition that they had a common problem and a shared need to address it formed the basis for genuine collaboration.[25] The Hilltop teachers came to recognize that their well-honed traditional teaching strategies were no longer effective; something else was needed.

Acknowledgement of a common problem was only the beginning. The subsequent interactions during the attempt to solve the problem were critical for the development of collaboration among teachers. Where teacher collaboration has been most successful, relationships are characterized by mutual respect, a sense of fairness and democratic decision-making, a willingness to tell the truth, the ability to resolve conflicts, genuine support for the development of new teaching skills, and shared belief in experimentation. The importance of human dynamics cannot be underestimated.[26]

The administrators at Hilltop proved to be masters at fostering relationships with and among teachers. They concentrated on encouraging leadership by teachers and a collective responsibility for learning. Over the next three years, teachers increasingly worked collaboratively to reframe their work around children's development and a thematic curriculum. The vice principal characterized the transformation this way: "I have vivid memories of walking through these halls when I first came here. Everybody was in rows, working individually, silently on basal text books. Kids had stopped achieving, test scores were pretty low. It was like knowledge was being forced into the kids. Now children are interacting and learning from one another. Teachers are making things more interesting for children so they want to learn." Through their collaborative efforts, teachers improved the learning environment for their students and enhanced their own sense of professional status. Interest in professional growth was widespread among Hilltop teachers. One, for example, observed, "When I began branching out of the classroom and getting others' respect, I saw myself as more of a professional." Another commented, "I am not as intimidated by administrators. The distances have shrunk and I am not down here and they are way up there."

Unfortunately, Hilltop could not sustain this level of success. After three years the principal and vice principal were replaced, and some of the progress the teachers had achieved was lost. The strong sense of commitment, previously fostered by the administrators, began to wane. The new principal was not perceived as sharing the teachers' vision and was not viewed as a leader. No external support was provided by the state or professional school linkages. Collaboration among teachers began to diminish. Test scores, which had risen, dropped again. Teachers have persisted in their efforts, but collaboration has become more difficult. Still, the teachers' isolation has ended; as one teacher observed, "We can talk with each other now about teaching and about how to deal with kids, and we couldn't do that five years ago."

Effective administrative leadership is critical for schoolwide teacher collaboration.[27] Teachers at Hilltop, and at our other schools, were in firm agreement that effective leadership by the principal was essential. The Hilltop principal who promoted collaboration described his role this way. "It is no longer, 'I know more than anybody else and I need to impart that knowledge' . . . You cannot have a bunch of master's degree people sitting in front of you and tell them how to act." Administrative leadership alone cannot create collaborative relationships among teachers, but it seems particularly difficult for teachers to create schoolwide collaboration without it.

The degree to which teachers value collaboration and invest in it is also important. Teachers face a three-part test in deciding whether to invest in any collaborative venture. First, will it help their students? Second, will collaboration make a positive difference in their teaching? And finally, is there adequate support for the work? If the answer to any of these questions is negative, teachers' support will fail to materialize or will quickly wane. In all of our schools, teachers were struggling to carve out the time to work together, in most cases with little organizational support.

Another central issue with regard to teachers' taking responsibility for teaching quality is how teachers will be held accountable for their work. Historically, teachers have been expected to meet externally established requirements. Good teaching meant covering the prescribed curriculum, demonstrating appropriate teaching behaviors, and more recently, having students achieve acceptable scores on standardized tests. Teachers were not expected to set their own professional goals or be concerned about how other teachers were teaching; that was the administrator's job. Teacher evaluation was largely a bureaucratic process that teachers and administrators alike knew had little real legitimacy and that many teachers found to be of little value.[28]

We have argued that teaching is a complex, multiskilled occupation. Good teachers are able to teach an entire class of students as well as meeting the needs of individuals. Additionally, their focus extends to help support the success of the whole school.[29] The National Board for Professional Teaching Standards has identified five key elements of outstanding teachers: commitment to students and their learning, knowledge of the subject matter and subject-specific pedagogy, effective management of student learning, systematic teaching practices, and membership in a learning community.[30] With this model of teaching, bureaucratic evaluation methods will no longer do. As Adam Urbanski, president of the Rochester Teachers Association, quipped, "It is no longer okay for teachers to say, 'I taught them, but they didn't learn.'"

Peer review by teachers has been advanced as an alternative to administrative oversight. Professional collective responsibility would replace bureaucratic compliance. Is this vision of collective responsibility truly plausible or merely a reformer's pipedream? Teachers in our study were about evenly split in their opinions. Half believed that evaluation was not the teachers' job, but the other half felt it was a necessity. A Crestview teacher said, "I believe we have to do it. If we don't it will come from outside and then there will be hell to pay." A 1997 American Federation of Teachers member survey suggests that there is growing support for greater teacher involvement in addressing poor teaching. Seventy-seven percent of the respondents supported peer evaluation and assistance for new teachers and sixty-three percent supported peer evaluation and assistance for tenured teachers who had received poor evaluations.[31]

Teacher peer evaluation raises a number of issues for teachers and their unions. These must be resolved if this fundamental shift in the authority relationships among teachers and between teachers and administrators is to be widely adopted.

First, although the national policies of the American Federation of Teachers and the National Education Association endorse the concept of peer evaluation, a significant minority of union members view it as a direct threat to union strength. The power of both the AFT and the NEA has been achieved by maintaining a clear distinction between management and labor. Teachers' working rights have been defined and protected through collective bargaining. New policies must not conflict with the preservation of this heritage. This requires teachers' unions to fulfill the dual role of maintaining and defending teachers' due process rights while at the same time insisting that teachers be held accountable for their teaching.

Second, peer review assumes a redefinition of teachers' relationships with each other. Although there are many teachers who believe teachers should assume responsibility for teaching quality and for each other's practice, there may be as many or more who do not perceive this as their role. They may be willing to assist other teachers in improving their practice, but draw the line at being their evaluators.

Several reasons can be offered for this reluctance. Teachers wonder who should decide what constitutes good teaching. Some argue that effective teaching is such an individualized enterprise that it is not appropriate for one teacher to judge another. An individual teacher's bias might prevent objective evaluation. The norm of equality among teachers also is called into question when peer evaluation is introduced. Although there is a growing acceptance of differentiating junior teachers from their seniors, and of having senior teachers evaluate new teachers, tenured teachers are less willing to evaluate each other. One teacher's comment, "I wouldn't want to rat on a fellow teacher," captures this reluctance well. Teachers also worry that peer evaluation might have a negative impact on teachers' collegiality. There may also be a gendered aspect to this response. Peer evaluation means rejecting the norm of "being nice," which the researchers Lyn Mikel Brown and Carol Gilligan maintain that women learn at an early age.[32] For teacher peer evaluation to make a difference in teaching quality, teachers must be willing to engage in honest dialogue with each other about the strengths and weaknesses of their teaching and be open to their colleagues' recommendations on how to improve. This would require a dramatic change in the culture of teaching.

Change is also required in teachers' relationships with administrators. There are two sides to this coin. On one side, evaluation has been the principal's responsibility. Addressing the problem of poor teaching has been the administrators' job, and many teachers still believe it is. Teachers have been in the protected position of not having to deal with the issue, but have felt free to complain if administrators failed to act. Given the difficulty of adequately documenting ineffective teaching and the high cost of removing incompetent teachers, the problem of poor teaching has often not been addressed. If peer review is to be viewed as legitimate by both teachers and administrators, there must be real consequences for teachers who put forth little effort or who show no willingness to improve. With peer review, teachers must be willing to join administrators in dealing with poor teaching, creating procedures that will assure due process but not be so cumbersome as to prevent action. More than half of the teachers surveyed by the American Federation of Teachers believed that effective procedures could be formulated.[33]

On the other side of the coin, the hierarchical, bureaucratic structure of schools and the traditional authority relationships between teacher and adminstrators have proven far more intractable than reformers imagined. Evaluation is a control mechanism that some administrators are reluctant to give up. Despite the rhetoric of shared decision-making, leaders in many school districts cling to the belief that quality education can be achieved through control and standardization.

Changes in the unionist labor-versus-management stance, in teachers' relationships with each other, and in teachers' relationships with administrators all require changes in well-entrenched beliefs about the nature of authority in schools. Other issues, such as creating the mechanisms to implement a peer review process and obtaining the resources to assure its success, are more concrete. Finally, a strong link must be forged between the evaluation process and professional development resources. The assumption of teacher peer review is that teachers will set and achieve their own professional goals. Without reframing how and for what purpose professional development monies will be used, reaching those goals could be difficult or even impossible.

Support for teachers' involvement in mentoring new teachers was particularly strong in all of our schools and has been one of the more popular reforms nationally. In Rochester, intern teachers are evaluated by both their principal and their mentor teacher; reappointment depends on positive reviews from both. Ten to fifteen percent of intern teachers are not rehired after their first year. As a result of the mentoring program the retention rate for first-year teachers has increased from 60 percent to 90 percent.

Teachers are, however, ambivalent about taking collective responsibility for evaluating and addressing poor performance by tenured teachers. Other studies besides ours reflect teachers' mixed feelings about assuming this responsibility.[34] In many respects the tension between judgment and nurturance in teachers' relationships with students carries over to their peers, with the scale tipping toward nurturance. "Part of the problem with our profession," commented one teacher, "is that just like we like to give kids another chance, we do the same thing with our colleagues." By a large majority, teachers surveyed by the AFT believed that most poor teachers could improve with assistance and that the best solution was to provide adequate support for them.[35]

Given the lack of agreement about peer evaluation of tenured teachers, what can be said about the efforts to create more meaningful teacher evaluation processes and to address poor performance? Teachers in two districts, Rochester and Pleasant Valley, were involved in creating new teacher evaluation procedures, Performance Appraisal

Review for Teachers (PART) in Rochester and Supportive Supervision in Pleasant Valley. Both were designed to enable tenured teachers to set professional goals for themselves. Peer involvement was intended to be a significant aspect of both plans, through peer coaching or collaborative work. In both cases the administrator's role was to shift from evaluator to facilitator of teacher-directed efforts.

When Performance Appraisal Review for Teachers was taken seriously—about half of Rochester's teachers expressed commitment to the process—it transformed teacher evaluation in the Rochester schools. For teachers who made the effort, PART supported reflection about their practice. It also created new connections with fellow teachers, which had positive consequences for students in terms of interdisciplinary teaching, improved instruction, and new opportunities. One lead teacher observed: "PART made me sit down and think of concrete ways to improve as a teacher. It also makes you do it. When you need to put goals down in writing, it makes you find the time to do them and change them. So for me PART has changed my teaching greatly and it's reinforced my belief in having my program student-driven." Another teacher summarized the responsibility for her own professional assessment this way: "I'm in control of my destiny. It's up to me, and at the end of three years what do I want to have speaking for what I've done as a teacher? You are in charge, and you are responsible, and you can't blame it on anyone else." This may seem a minimal advance to those who think public schools need a major house cleaning. Under the traditional evaluation process, however, it was rare for any Rochester teacher to be rated "improvement needed" or "unsatisfactory."[36]

Many Rochester teachers, though, did not take the process seriously, seeing it as an exercise that was more time-consuming than a once-a-year classroom visit by the principal. Teachers were candid in acknowledging that many of their colleagues were filling out the required forms without engaging in any real examination of their practice. In addition, administrators often scoffed at the idea that self-assessment with a committee of one's "friends" could be genuine, and complained that they had no authority to evaluate teachers.

Teachers who were dissatisfied with the PART process had multiple complaints about it. Many said that the paperwork required was burdensome and offered no real evidence of the quality of their teaching. Others felt that they did not receive enough feedback, since the only formal review was conducted just once in every three years. Perhaps most serious, teachers perceived that there were no consequences for minimal effort. As one teacher commented, "PART started out as a way for teachers to improve, but no one ever did anything with it. It lowered morale when there were no consequences for those who did nothing." In fact, there were a handful of teachers who did not receive salary increases because they failed to complete the PART process, but this was not widely known by teachers.

Given all the complaints, the 1997 teachers' contract provided the option for teachers to return to an annual evaluation by an administrator in place of peer review. About 50 percent of the tenured teachers made this choice. For teachers who continued with the Performance Appraisal Review process, administrators served as a third reviewer for the triannual assessment. This change was not welcomed by teachers who saw peer review as an important professional step, but it was a clear indication that many teachers did not view this version of peer review as an improvement in the teacher evaluation process.

The Pleasant Valley teacher evaluation system, Supportive Supervision, was created by a joint committee of teachers and administrators formed at the request of the superintendent, who hoped to engage experienced teachers in their own professional development. "Doing nothing is not an option," became the superintendent's slogan. During the first year teachers recognized that a more professional teacher evaluation process was at odds with the hierarchical administrative model of schooling. Some teachers were optimistic that Supportive Supervision would lead to broader changes. One teacher said, "I think that once teachers start taking charge of their professional growth, they will take charge of other things too." A department chair declared that Supportive Supervision had changed the focus from simply seeing teachers as "good" and "bad" to having a conversation about how individual teachers could improve.

Despite the implementation of Supportive Supervision, though, little else changed. Pleasant Valley teachers became increasingly frustrated because although Supportive Supervision required more effort, it had no larger impact on how their schools were run. After the initial training in cognitive coaching to support the initiative, there were few resources to support teachers in this new work. The schedule made it nearly impossible for teachers to have shared time to meet or observe each other's teaching. Many teachers who had initially been enthusiastic came to view Supportive Supervision as "extra" work rather than as a new way of thinking about their teaching. It was often the "first thing to be pushed to the back burner" in the face of more pressing demands from students and others. The most skeptical teachers suspected that it was simply a way for the district to squeeze more work out of them.

Despite these difficulties, Supportive Supervision offered teachers the first opportunity to rethink their relationships with administrators and with each other. Even though there have been administrative changes at both the building and district levels, Supportive Supervision has been retained and formally included in the teachers' contract. A majority of teachers have invested in the process and believe that they are responsible for their own professional growth. Support for professional development as envisioned by the developers of Supportive Supervision continues to be weak, however. There is little peer coaching or collaborative work among teachers, and teachers indicate that they have lost some of the eagerness to change their practice that they initially had.[37]

There are several reasons the new teacher evaluation systems had partial success in both Rochester and Pleasant Valley. In Rochester, there was little training available for teachers or administrators. In Pleasant Valley, there was no follow-up after initial training in cognitive coaching. Neither district provided adequate resources to support teachers' professional growth or included teacher evaluation in a broader district-wide improvement effort. A change in superintendents in both districts weakened the initial commitment made at the district level. Little was done to address personal issues, such as lack of awareness, distrust, stress, fear of failure, or poor time management, all of which can prevent teachers from achieving professional growth.[38]

Although creating effective peer evaluation systems is difficult, involving teachers in dealing with poor performance is far more challenging. Teachers' unions have traditionally focused almost exclusively on assuring due process, often with the result that they appear to be protecting teachers at all cost. Some teachers do not see addressing poor performance as their responsibility, preferring to leave it to administrators, but also complaining about administrative failure to act. "Everybody knows who the poor teachers are, but no one can do anything," was a common response. Several teachers correctly observed that there simply was no structured way for teachers to be involved in this issue.

Rochester is one of only a handful of districts nationwide that has created a program to involve teachers in addressing ineffective teaching. The Intervention Program, which began in 1986, before the reform contract, involves mentors in helping teachers who have been targeted by their administrators or by the teachers on a school-based planning team for intervention to improve their practice. Teachers who are recommended for intervention but refuse to participate, or fail to comply, can have their salary increases withheld.[39]

Since the program's inception, sixty-four teachers have been involved in intervention. Thirty-nine teachers have left the district as a result. In most cases, teachers left voluntarily, but in three cases teachers were terminated after intervention efforts proved unsuccessful. Another twenty-five teachers have successfully completed the intervention process. This may not seem to be a large number, but it is certainly greater than the number of disciplinary actions taken under section 3020-a of New York State's Education Law. A survey completed by the New York State School Boards Association concluded that only 21 percent of New York state school districts had any involvement with disciplinary charges between 1990 and 1993, and of these 80 percent were involved with just one disciplinary case. No district, except for New York City, reported involvement in more than four cases.[40]

Guarantees of due process have been incorporated into both the teacher evaluation process and the Intervention Program, and several teachers have filed grievances involving the actions of other teachers. In one case a teacher whose teaching did not improve through intervention and who was subsequently dismissed filed a grievance with the union grievance committee and requested arbitration to challenge the decision. Teacher members of the Career in Teaching Panel, which oversees the Intervention Program, served as the primary witnesses for the district. They found themselves on the opposite side of the table from the New York State United Teachers Association's attorney and two of the Rochester Teachers Association grievance committee members, who were there to defend the dismissed teacher. The dismissal decision was upheld, the arbiter concluding that the dismissed teacher had been given ample time and assistance to improve. Under the traditional union procedures such an outcome would be unthinkable.

Although the unions' focus on protecting teachers' rights remains strong, concern for assuring teaching quality is growing. Teachers are less willing to ignore poor teaching. Having the union promote the goal of high teaching standards ranked first among AFT members in the AFT survey, well above protecting job security and helping with grievances.[41] Teachers are eager to share their knowledge and skills with each other, but remain highly ambivalent about their role in evaluating their tenured colleagues. Support is stronger for mentoring and more effective evaluation of untenured teachers, in emulation of the extended apprenticeships and opportunities for early screening of poor performers in other professions.

Collaboration among teachers and shared responsibility for teaching quality is developing. Long-held norms of teachers' isolation and noninvolvement in their colleagues' teaching have been challenged. With organizational support, teachers' collaboration can be genuine and widespread.

Taking Responsibility for the Quality of Schools

In the late 1980s and early 1990s, numerous reform reports proposed that more democratic governance, including teachers, parents, and administrators in decision-making, was needed to improve schools. Teachers' unions, particularly the American Federation of Teachers, called for shared governance as a way to professionalize teaching and to improve schools. When both Rochester and Dade County, Florida, successfully included shared decision-making in their collective bargaining agreements in 1987, press coverage was extensive and exuberant about the potential for school improvement. That same year, Chicago adopted even more sweeping changes, turning each school's governance over to Local School Councils made of up six parents, two community members, and two teachers and the principal. Local School Councils had control of a portion of the school budget and the authority to hire and fire the principal. The notion of shared governance so captured policy-makers that it was mandated for all Kentucky schools under the Kentucky Education Reform Act of 1990 and adopted for New York state school districts in 1994. Many other states and school districts have adopted this approach as well. But despite this enthusiastic embrace of shared decision-making, little substantive research existed to support the claims that restructuring school governance would enhance the status of teaching or improve students' learning.[42]

Our nine schools offered a mixed picture about how much progress teachers have made in assuming responsibility for the quality of schools. All of the schools showed some shift toward shared governance, though with uneven results. In their attempt to achieve that governance, they encountered many of the stumbling blocks that can impede and even derail shared decision-making. Three schools, Hilltop Elementary School in Syracuse, Genesee School in Rochester, and Crestview Elementary School, demonstrated that shared governance can work when teachers and administrators are committed to fundamental changes in the traditional relationships within schools.

It is clear from our research that shared decision-making can be merely symbolic in one school and result in real power-sharing in another. The first question to be asked about shared governance in any school is which decisions are to be made collectively. Crestview, a suburban middle-class school, was the only one where we observed a clearly defined, commonly shared answer to this question. The autonomy of the teachers in their classrooms was respected, but decisions with a schoolwide impact were first reviewed by the appropriate committee, and then the staff and interested parents decided by consensus how to proceed. Of course, many decisions continued to be made on the spot. For the principal, as well as the teachers, the day was filled with requests for one decision after another. The Crestview principal was able to act when required because she had the "empowered trust" of the staff.

However, when the parameters of shared governance are not well defined, and are not understood and accepted by the staff, shared decision-making can create more confusion than clarity. In some schools, notably Rochester's Susan B. Anthony High School, conflict bordered on chaos. In others, problems arose at the most basic level. Even setting the agenda for the shared decision-making committee was often problematic. Meeting agendas often were either dictated by district office requirements—creating a strategic plan, for example—or set by team members who proposed topics, such as how to recognize AIDS Awareness Week or how to improve student behavior, in response to whatever problems cropped up. Few decision-making teams developed a vision of school change focused on improving the students' learning.

An inordinate amount of time was spent talking about the governance process.[43] Meeting procedures, the decision-making process, and the question of equal representation for teachers, parents, and the administration were raised continually. With no prior experience in shared governance, team members struggled to arrive at decisions, but then were uncertain about who had the responsibility to follow through. In many cases, teams just went through the motions, accomplishing nothing much except to agree when to hold the next meeting. Leadership from both the principal and key teachers was critical in a school's ability to move from talk to action, and loss of leadership was often detrimental to the process. When the well-regarded principal of Hilltop School left after only three years on the job, a teacher commented, "It is frustrating. You want a decision made, and there is no one to make it. You need to go through all these procedures. Or, you don't want them to make a decision for you, and they do it without our input." In some schools, as we saw in the Rochester story, it became increasingly difficult to get teachers to serve on the teams.

Without carefully defined agreements about the responsibilities of shared governance teams, the topics addressed were frequently safe and rather superficial. Little that would significantly change students' learning was tackled. How were plans coming on the Homework Hotline? How should the money for student clubs be allocated? In a study comparing the kind of decisions being made at schools with shared decision-making and schools without it, Carol Weiss found that there was virtually no difference between the two types of schools. Shared governance, at least in its developmental phase, provides no assurance that better, more meaningful decisions will be made and implemented to improve students' learning.[44]

Even in Chicago, which had given schools the strongest form of local decision-making in school councils that had control of part of the budget, there was little progress in sharing governance. After four years had passed, a careful study found that only a third of the schools had undertaken major reforms, that another third were still struggling to move toward reform, and that the last third showed "few signs of any meaningful changes."[45]

In spite of the difficulty of establishing clear guidelines for shared governance, we did see the beginnings of change in most of our nine schools. The process of hiring teachers has been broadened to include teachers' input; responsibility for professional development is shifting from the administration to the teachers; teachers have been included in strategic planning to improve schools and departments; schoolwide discipline policies have been instituted; and in some schools instructional issues were becoming a collective concern.

As with responsibility for raising the quality of teaching, taking professional responsibility for school improvement raises the question of teachers' relationships with each other. Shared governance can work only if the norm of collegiality is stronger than the norm of professional

Similar to time in the school day.

privacy.[46] Teachers must view shared governance as legitimate and agree to accept a decision-making committee's decisions. We watched teams confront difficult issues only to have their decisions undermined by faculties that were no more willing to follow the direction of peers than they were the direction of administrators. As one Raintree Middle School teacher complained, "That's what happens with committee work, and teachers having the power to be involved in decisions. It only takes one teacher to say, 'I'm not going to do it,' and you have no power to make them do it." The power of shared governance rests in its legitimacy in the eyes of the entire school community. Without that, it is simply ignored.[47]

Shared decision-making worked most effectively when a well-designed committee structure, involving teachers, parents, and support staff, supported the process.[48] After several frustrating years Genesee Elementary School finally created an organizational structure that involved nearly all of the staff and enabled them to become more effective in their shared governance process.

Widespread involvement also requires dispersed or shared leadership, another characteristic of schools that have successfully implemented shared decision-making. At Crestview Elementary School, leadership can best be characterized as shared leadership. Various staff members served as leaders, depending on the issue. A simple measure of shared leadership is the number of different facilitators for school-wide meetings. More often than not at Crestview, the principal stepped aside and a teacher, an aide, or a parent led the meeting. Crestview moved beyond a small core of leaders to share leadership activities broadly.[49]

Crestview's principal was described by the staff and parents as someone who really "gets it" when it comes to shared decision-making. She defined her job as helping to facilitate their collective work, supporting the relationships within the school community, and consulting with the faculty about how best to help students learn. Teachers regularly asked her to come in and observe or work with specific children. Because of her background in special education, they viewed her as another professional resource to help them in their teaching. The principal's authority was rooted in her insistence that the shared decision-making process be supported. After several years, the principal observed, "We are breaking down some barriers and you don't even know you are doing it until you stop and think about it." A picture of a different kind of principal emerged, one which other studies of schools with effective shared governance also described.[50] Like the Hilltop principal who promoted collaboration, Crestview's principal redefined her relationship with the faculty.

Although shared leadership is a key component for successful shared decision-making, authority relationships between the principal and the teachers rarely shift from the traditional, principal-dominated, hierarchical model of schools.[51] A Rochester teacher put it this way, "It is just really hard to break the mold. You have to have leadership that is willing to share authority. You get the talk, 'Let's all be a big family,' but in reality it is, 'I'm running the show.'" Teachers' willingness to participate in shared decision-making depends on the opportunity to redesign their relationship with their principal. Collaborative leadership is critical.[52] Where principals were willing to share their power, they were seen more as colleagues than as adversaries. Teachers wanted strong principals who could help establish the framework for shared governance and facilitate their schoolwide efforts. As a result of shared governance, teachers felt that they were more aware of the complex role of administrators and had a better appreciation of schoolwide issues.

Reshaping the principalship to fulfill these new expectations calls for administrators to be inspiring leaders as well as skillful negotiators and managers. We saw few administrators who had both kinds of skills in our nine schools despite substantial administrative turnover. All were well intentioned, even though some were uneasy in more collaborative roles. But many of them lacked the capacity to create an effective shared governance process.

Of course, high administrative turnover is crippling. Shared governance depends on a collaborative culture based on mutual trust and respect, and that takes time to develop. Yet seven of our nine schools had more than one principal during the course of the study. The tendency for district offices to regularly reassign principals does not support the conditions needed for shared decision-making to work.

The legitimacy teachers grant to the shared governance process is also related to the degree to which teachers perceive that power relationships in schools have truly changed. In most instances, authority for the most important decisions, such as setting the school budget, making administrative assignments, making the final decision on which teachers to hire, or permitting variances in district policy, was retained by the central administration.

Teachers were repeatedly frustrated by having decisions they had reached with difficulty overruled downtown. The Anthony High School School team, for example, ruled that students who had failed a course could not simultaneously take the next level of the subject and repeat the course they had failed. After a few phone calls from parents to the assistant superintendent, the policy was quickly reversed. There was a pervasive sense in all of the nine schools that despite a mandate for decentralized decision-making, the district office was still firmly in control. Peter McWalters, the Rochester superintendent who negotiated the 1987 reform contract, believed that schools and teachers should have more autonomy but also acknowledged that it was a "daily battle" to try to change Rochester's central administration. Not much had changed by 1997. There was much confusion about which decisions could be made at the school level and which could not. A Raintree Middle School teacher suggested that teachers' support for shared decision-making had diminished as a result. "We'll be excited about something and then, 'Whoa! you can't do that!'" As a result, the Raintree teachers thought any concession from the central office was a major victory. Getting the central office to agree to a date for a career day which differed from the dates in the rest of the district was seen as a major achievement. This is a far cry from the reformers' vision of autonomously operating schools.

More often than not, the principal was caught in the middle between teachers and the district office. Principals were still held accountable for what happened in their schools by school boards and superintendents. Those who were successful were strong advocates for their school's governance process, were capable of garnering additional resources for their schools, and often served as the buffer between the shared governance work in their schools and the standardizing tendencies of district offices. Often this required a degree of "creative noncompliance," finding a way to fulfill district office requirements while at the same time protecting and fostering the shared governance process in their schools.[53]

The Crestview case is illustrative here as well. When the school was created, the district had embraced shared governance at all levels under the leadership of a visionary superintendent. Upon his departure in 1992, his successor gave lip service to shared-decision making, but it quickly became clear that he had little real commitment to it. One of the Crestview teachers said, "Our former superintendent took the dream with him and the new one doesn't have a dream. Had our previous superintendent stayed, we might have ended up with wonderful stuff." Feeling pressure from a citizen's action group that had succeeded in defeating the school budget five years in a row, the new superintendent turned to district directives and standardization to raise test scores and prove he was accountable. By 1997 schools were being told to use shared decision-making only when time permitted, and principals were given wide latitude to decide whether it did. The Crestview staff found that they had to continually defend the slower pace of their governance process. Although their commitment to the school remained stronger than ever, they were discouraged by the negative environment at the district level.

The challenge for school districts will be to find the balance between reasonable district standards and individual school autonomy in devising means to reach those standards. Teachers have generally welcomed the call for higher standards, and most do not view new curricular guidelines as a constraint.[54] At the same time, the gains from adopting shared governance are worth preserving. When shared governance gains legitimacy, teachers' morale, satisfaction, and commitment to their work is improved. And although not all teachers aspire to be directly involved in governance, shared decision-making offers another important opportunity for professional engagement.[55]

Although it is clear that shared governance is far more difficult to achieve than first thought, teachers at our schools were not willing to give up. Even at Anthony High School, which was torn apart in the power struggle about the membership of the shared decision-making team, a teacher declared, "Maybe we are finally figuring out how to make this work." A Hilltop teacher commented, "It has always been the case that someone from on high hands down a decision that we are expected to carry out. Just having a voice makes a big difference. Having been listened to makes us feel like we can make a difference." At Raintree Middle School a teacher observed, "Teachers can see what can happen in a building. That is why if this were taken away, you could never get anybody to do anything again." A Crestview teacher agreed, "It is very hard but I don't think people would ever give up. We have seen the benefit." Despite the challenge, our research suggests that shared governance is here to stay; teachers will have it no other way.

Perhaps the most important set of relationships involved in teachers' responsibility for school quality is the relationship with students' families. For most professionals, the relationship they have with their clients is clearly defined. Physicians are concerned with their patients' health. Accountants expect that their business will be with their clients' finances. Even psychologists are careful to focus their involvement on the specific mental health issues individuals raise in their therapy sessions. Teaching is not so easily circumscribed.

It raises the perplexing question: What kind of relationship between teachers and their students' families is desired? Early in this century, as Florence Thayer's story shows, teachers had little say in determining the boundaries of their relationships with the community. They could be called on for whatever social service was needed, from teaching Sunday School to organizing social events. As teachers gained more say over their work, these expectations diminished, yet families still expect teachers to be willing chaperons at evening dances and on school trips. Parents, and even the general public, usually regard failure to fulfill these roles during contract disputes as teachers' selfishness, rather than a reasonable response to an employment conflict. The public, and vocal parents in particular, have also retained their voice in curricular matters at both the district and the classroom level. Students and their families have fought, sometimes successfully, to get creationism taught along with evolution in high school biology classes. At the classroom level, parents do not hesitate to complain if their children are being taught something that they find objectionable.

Despite such parental interference, teachers in our study, and throughout the country, view lack of parental involvement in their children's education as a major problem.[56] Increased pressures on families from all fronts have often left teachers feeling that they are expected to be surrogate parents, a role they know they cannot possibly fill. Increasingly, though, it has become the teachers' responsibility to try to engage students' families as well as students themselves. The evidence is convincing that when families are involved in their children's education, students are much more likely to succeed.[57]

So teachers are confronted, on the one hand, with laypersons who claim an equal voice in educational matters and, on the other hand, with a significant gap in the support they need to be more effective. From one day to the next, teachers are never sure what demands will come from students' families. It is understandable that teachers feel ambivalent about how to frame their relationship with students' families.

The control of public education by local citizens creates a tension regarding whose authority should prevail in educational decisions. Will strengthening teachers' authority because of their professional expertise conflict with the tradition of democratic, community-based authority over public education?[58]

All of the schools we studied wrestled with how to involve students' families. Although shared governance is intended to strengthen the role of parents as well as teachers, parents tended to become most involved in specific issues—African American students' performance in mathematics at Hamilton High, for example. Even at Crestview School, which was more successful than the others we observed in involving parents, the staff had to recruit parents for shared decision-making committees. Generally there were two or three parents on each of the school's committees. In our other schools there was even less parental involvement in shared governance committees. Parent representatives were usually not elected by a constituency, and therefore did not represent parents as a group. Some parents became involved solely to advance their own agendas, including the hope of eventually getting a school job. The number of parents willing to be involved in governance issues was small except when there were issues of personal concern to them. At all our schools, most teachers wished there was greater input from parents.

Some reformers have even envisioned teachers as extended family members, with schools more like a successful home than a successful business. Framing the relationship between teachers and families this way values the role of teachers as nurturers, acknowledging they are far more than educational clinicians, with the circumscribed relationships of other professions.[59]

Crestview School's teachers kept the image of the family in mind when organizing their school. Although there were few parents involved in governance at Crestview, parents were very much in evidence. It was unusual to spend any time in a Crestview classroom and not see a parent involved in some way, either tutoring, working with a small group, or helping with administrative tasks. In a district-wide parent survey nearly a third of the parents who responded indicated that they volunteered in school on a regular basis. Other research has shown that parents are most likely to become involved in school activities, such as classroom volunteering, that are closely tied to their children.[60] Crestview teachers knew their children's families and thought that parents were an important part of the school community. Parents and family members were welcome to come to school without an appointment anytime and were viewed as partners in addressing the learning problems of their children.

There are, however, limits to teachers' desire to act as extended family members. Teachers understandably resist when they feel they are being asked to be surrogate parents. There is great uncertainty among teachers about what the boundaries of their role as nurturers should be.[61] Particularly when children's needs are the greatest, teachers often feel overwhelmed and frustrated with the challenge of helping students learn. The philosopher Jane Roland Martin has argued that the need has grown so great that a new educational setting, the school-home, must be created. She describes an organization that can offer the individualized attention and nurturance once assumed to be the exclusive domain of children's families.[62] Teachers are ambivalent about this idea; many are raising their own children and feel they can't be expected to raise other parents' children too.

With their 1987 contract, Rochester's teachers agreed to strengthen the relationship between the school and the students' families. The plan called for middle and high school students to be assigned to a homebase guidance teacher, who would have the students for an extended homeroom period each day, and keep the same students while they attended the school. Teachers were to be advisors for their homebase students, keeping track of how they were doing in all their classes, and to serve as the primary communication link between the school and students' homes, in addition to their regular teaching assignments. The hope was that this program would make students feel more at home and less lost in the crowd.

In most schools this program did not succeed. Despite the contractual agreement, many teachers put little energy into this new role. Being an effective advisor meant really knowing how students were doing in all of their classes as well as what was happening at home. More often than not, teachers did not have the same students from one year to the next. Scheduling problems and a high student mobility rate made it difficult for teachers and students to develop the long-term relationships that had been intended. Teachers admitted feeling inadequate about how to help students with nonacademic problems, often commenting, "We aren't trained as counselors."

Teachers also struggled in their efforts to communicate with students' families. Frequent moves by students' families often made it difficult for teachers to locate them. Some families did not have phones, and there was no guarantee that a written message would be received. Some teachers admitted that they were not at ease with low-income, minority families, particularly if there were many family problems. An African American teacher who recognized this difficulty for some of her white middle-class colleagues observed, "I have an advantage because I can speak the dialect when I need to." With all these impediments, and little support for teachers in this role, homebase guidance quickly dwindled into an extended homeroom, except in a few schools. Where the homebase concept has worked, at schools such as Central Park East in East Harlem, New York, teachers have responsibility for fewer students overall and parents have made a commitment to help their children succeed in school. Although homebase guidance failed at most schools, the one lasting outcome in Rochester was an expectation that teachers would improve communication with students' families. Family outreach became part of the expectations for teachers in subsequent contracts, and parents now evaluate teachers on how well they communicate with them.

Although family contact has been more talked about than achieved by some, more teachers at all of our schools now take this role seriously, viewing families as potential allies and making the effort to involve them in their children's education. One Hilltop teacher reported that she now called families of new students to get a better understanding of her students and to begin her relationship with the family on a positive note. "I get butterflies in my stomach because you never know how they're going to react, but I have had a lot of positive comments back." When families and teachers are mutually supportive, students benefit. Teachers are often frustrated, though, by the lack of response from parents.

Assessing how well teachers have assumed responsibility for the quality of their school, and ultimately their students' success, is complex. The connection between teachers' professionalization and students' learning is indirect. The assumption is that professionalization leads to more qualified, skillful, and engaged teachers, which in turn improves teaching and the learning environment. Improved teaching should improve students' learning. Although there is growing evidence that the first part of this chain of reasoning is true—professionalization does lead to more qualified, skillful, and engaged teachers—evidence for the second part is sketchier. Some studies have validated this connection; others have not.[63] Two conclusions that are well documented, and that we also support from our research, are that the connection is more evident when teachers are directly involved in a new role and when reform efforts are substantively focused on curricular and instructional issues.[64] This finding suggests that when new roles for teachers have been carefully developed and supported with sufficient resources to broadly engage teachers, there is more strength to the claim that teachers' professionalization will improve students' learning.

Our research demonstrates that the process of creating and successfully implementing long-lasting changes in the teaching profession is proceeding slowly. The obstacles are many and pervasive. Repeatedly, though, teachers told us that they could see the possibilities these changes offered, and insisted that they would never agree to return to a more passive role in their schools. One Hamilton High teacher spoke for many, "I see it happening. Not overnight, but I think it's going to. When I first started teaching in the early sixties, I would never have envisioned things changing as much as they have."

9

Teaching in 2020

In Chapter 3, we portrayed the essential acts of teaching as the same from kindergarten to graduate school—as though all teachers belonged to the same profession.

In the public eye, they do not. Polls of the status of schoolteachers in the United States place them just above the average of all workers—above police officers but below engineers—whereas professors in urban research universities are ranked much higher, near medical doctors. But that was not always the case. In the late nineteenth century the status of high school teachers was not much different from that of college professors.

By the time of the Second World War, however, the change in the status of college and university professors was so great as to be called an academic revolution.[1] This first academic revolution was the revolt of the professoriate against the entrenched power of a largely clerical nineteenth-century college presidency. Before that revolution occurred, the presidents hired and fired the faculty; afterward the faculty took control of hiring, granting tenure, and much else, including determination of the curriculum.

What we have here called the slow revolution is a less clear-cut struggle to overturn a patriarchal system of elementary and secondary education that has its roots in the same era. That system, aptly named the "One Best System" by David Tyack, has proved to be both remarkably stable and highly resilient.[2] The age-graded, centrally controlled, and highly bureaucratized system of public schools has survived largely

slow Revolution [handwritten margin note]

in the form in which it was invented in the late nineteenth century. Virtually all the successful changes in the system could be classified as those that helped the system to expand, to extend its services, or to become more efficient. It gradually expanded to provide universal schooling through thirteen levels; it extended services to the disabled, to the disenfranchised, and to those of all ability levels. It elaborated the curriculum to serve children who would work in farms, factories, shops, and hospitals. It added a wide array of other courses of instruction to serve every interest group and to satisfy a wide range of utilitarian and recreational needs. The reforms that succeeded were often those, like the invention in 1906 of the Carnegie unit, that helped to improve the efficiency of the system by providing a standard measure of what counts as a year's academic credit in any subject. Even the teachers' and unions' militancy of the 1960s and 1970s did not fundamentally alter the system so much as it expanded the rights of one set of participants.

Contemporary reformers and educational change agents tend to underestimate the reasons for this stability and resilience. They often fail to appreciate how extraordinarily well the system has functioned to accomplish what its designers wanted it to achieve. And they are likely to forget the religious and revolutionary zeal of its founders, who wanted to create a system that would serve all children of a country that was seen as the world's greatest democratic experiment. It was a system that was founded on the core values of a highly individualistic, democratic nation. It resolved the tension between liberty and equality on the side of freedom, or opportunity for all to achieve, rather than on the side of more equal outcomes. It sought to realize that goal through a system that allowed for wide expression of individual beliefs, although the schools were deeply Protestant in their origins. Finally, with the aid of the psychological and cognitive tests refined in the early twentieth century, the system gained legitimacy as the central sorting and selecting agency of the society.

The reformers tend to be grudging about the success of the system. But in fact the system served as the foundation of the long-term success of both the economic and the democratic development of the country, while also preserving and enhancing the religious freedom that its founders had cherished. Defenders of the system are not dissuaded by data showing poor average outcomes for the system when compared, for example, with math and science achievement in other nations, because they believe that the system has served to provide opportunity for all and has allowed a sufficient number to achieve the highest academic levels. They are likely to point to the undisputed worldwide preeminence of the American college and university system as evidence of this. The kindergarten through grade 12 system, they would argue, was never intended or expected to provide equal group outcomes or even necessarily high average outcomes. It was meant to provide opportunity and the incentive for those who so chose to reach the highest levels of academic achievement, but it was not meant to command it.

Yet our own work during the last decade of careful observation of teachers in nine schools in four school districts has convinced us that a slow revolution is under way. We came to see the central metaphor of our study as the teachers' struggle to take charge of their practice and to break out of the constraints of the "One Best System," and we conceptualized our research as a study of teachers in new roles. It may be too early to call it a second academic revolution: It is proceeding incrementally and unevenly in fits and starts and with frequent slippage. But our data also show that it probably cannot be stopped because teachers will not give up the gains they have won.

It is not too far-fetched to conceive of the late-nineteenth-century construction of the modern public school system as an aggregation of one-room schoolhouses into a newly centralized system of education in which a mostly male administrative class established top-down direction of teachers. Teachers themselves had almost no say in the shaping of the system. They were isolated in classroom cells that were strung together down long school halls. No genuine communication among the teachers was established about the nature of their own practice; quite the contrary—it was sometimes forbidden.

As we have shown, that conversation has now begun, and has been expanding and raising the consciousness of teachers over the past decade. It will continue. It has been infused by feminism: Teachers are no longer willing to let a patriarchy write the rules and control the checkbook. It is partly the result of increased levels of education and training. As we noted in Chapter 2, most teachers now have a master's degree, whereas before the Second World War most did not have even a bachelor's degree. But more important, a new concept of the teaching profession is emerging. The conviction is growing among teachers that the kinds of outcomes that are being demanded for children—that all of them become competent problem-solvers and critical thinkers—can't be achieved if the teachers themselves are not similarly empowered to inquire into the nature of their own practice, and to have the ability to change its course. This conviction lies at the heart of the incipient second academic revolution.

Contrasts between the Two Revolutions

Comparisons with the first academic revolution—that of the academic professoriate—are instructive and sobering. The differences between the two revolutions and how they will be resolved by teachers in the early twenty-first century will affect generations of schoolchildren to come. We see seven frameworks of comparison as critically determining the outcome of the second academic revolution. These include comparisons between the nature of peer control among schoolteachers and professors, allocations of time and money, how each credibly serves a public good, contrasts between a revolution by "sons" and one by "daughters," pressures for more egalitarian outcomes in pre-college education, the differential effects of markets on demands for faculty skills in the two realms, and variance in the exercise of academic freedom.

The Nature of Peer Control

For most of the nineteenth century, college professors operated under the thumb of often autocratic presidents, most of them trained in the ministry. In the twentieth century they overthrew that administrative authority and established the rights of academic freedom and control over the tenure process. Although formal authority continued to rest with presidents and boards of trustees, the recommendations of faculty committees were rarely overturned, and top managers in universities saw themselves primarily as representatives of the faculty. Essentially the professors argued this way: Only our peers are fit to judge who is qualified to be a physicist or a philosopher, and to decide what physics and philosophy are. Only we have the knowledge to decide what the curriculum should be and how to teach it and how to prepare future philosophers and physicists. Moreover, the progress and prosperity of the society depends upon our developing new knowledge. We have the exclusive right to carry out research and conduct inquiries into the nature of that knowledge. And so the professoriate took charge of the curriculum and of the recruitment, training, induction, and assessment of new members of their profession. They assumed the exclusive right to define the objects of their research, although some also began to neglect the quality of their teaching.

At the same time as the professoriate was redefining the academic profession, school administrators were establishing themselves as the certified experts on the educational system by virtue of their use of emerging forms of scientific management. And as progressive school administrators with newly earned doctorates carried out massive school surveys early in the twentieth century, they also succeeded in establishing themselves in the public eye as the professional experts. They laid down elaborate curriculum guides and wrote the rules and regulations that govern modern school bureaucracies.

In the last decade, elementary and secondary school teachers have moved beyond traditional union demands for improving the conditions of work to assert similar claims. They cannot convincingly claim to be the discoverers of basic knowledge in the way that is true of university professors. But like the majority of college teachers, many schoolteachers can assert that they have genuine expertise in their subject matter (though more broadly defined than are college-level specialties) and that there is a body of pedagogical content knowledge that is specific to their work. Most important, they are no longer willing to let the administrators define themselves as the exclusive class of experts controlling either the content of the curriculum or decisions about who is fit to teach it.

In the previous chapter we assessed the uneven results of teachers' attempts to assert peer control and to define the knowledge base necessary to improve the practice of teaching. The jury is still out. The piece of evidence that is missing is a test of the knowledge base for teaching that is seen as valid by both the public and the teachers themselves. Tests of teachers' competence required for certification in most states have assessed only rudimentary knowledge of teaching and basic mathematics and verbal skill. That may soon change. For more than a decade, the National Board for Professional Teaching Standards has been developing national "boards" to assess teachers' competence. This group, composed of expert teachers, scholars, and policy-makers, set the goal of developing assessments of teaching that would be as rigorous as tests taken by lawyers, doctors, or architects. Like medical boards, the tests would be taken in specific areas in which teachers wanted to be certified. The assessment process requires several days to complete; it involves written tests as well as demonstration of the candidate's ability to assess and diagnose complex matters of teaching practice. Like the examinations given by doctors or professors, the test was developed by experts in the profession, not by a state bureaucracy. The professoriate relied on the doctoral examination—significantly known as a public defense—by scholars in the appropriate field of knowledge to assess a candidate's fitness for the Ph.D, which is the common "license" of college and university teachers, although it is an examination of research knowledge, not teaching expertise. Other processes of peer review of a college instructor's teaching and scholarship also govern promotions, the granting of tenure, and the assumption of expanded responsibilities. Although the National Board for Professional Teaching Standards had given only a few examinations by the late 1990s, we found that teachers who knew of its work were favorably impressed by the rigor and appropriateness of the test. Those who had been skeptical of the kinds of differentiation of teachers' roles tried in Rochester felt that selection of mentors and lead teachers based on the National Board examination would be fair. Teachers are reluctant to accept discrimination in pay or status if those judgments are made by administrators or teachers' unions, but those we interviewed felt that establishment of levels of expertise governed by a valid assessment process would be worth a try. Moreover, they will admit in private that teachers can no longer pretend that all of them should be paid on the same pay scale differentiated only by time on the job. They can point to a fourth-grade teacher who has a dozen years of experience but is only minimally competent compared with another of the same age who mentors teachers in training, helps write curriculum guides for a new social studies program, and is frequently consulted by colleagues about problems of practice. To regard them as teachers on the same level is patently unjust.

Allocation of Time and Money

The second salient difference between the first and second academic revolutions is that the first was accompanied by the professoriate's demand that it have more time for research and the responsibilities of running the university. Not only were teaching loads dramatically reduced in research-oriented institutions, but all college faculty largely shed the custodial and *in loco parentis* functions characteristic of the earlier era. They had time both to pursue their own scholarly agendas and to take on the work of evaluating their colleagues and deciding their fates in promotion and tenure committees.

Allow release time - over- whelming

The schoolteachers, even those who have most eagerly embraced new policy-making and mentoring responsibilities, seldom have been granted any major relief from either teaching or custodial responsibilities. Although the moral authority of teachers has been and is being contested in many public schools, teachers there are still held accountable for the amorphous responsibility of character development, and they are expected to exercise oversight of students in cafeterias and hallways. The earlier retreat from—if not wholesale abandonment of—reponsiblities for moral education at the college level has been rightly called into question in the last decade, and we would not urge that the same mistake be made in the name of professionalism in the elementary or secondary schools. But development of better teaching does require allotment of time for instructional planning with colleagues, time to mentor intern teachers, and time for research. In Rochester and Syracuse we found that teachers who had spent a year or two on school-based planning committees were often more than ready to relinquish such "privileges." Asking teachers to serve on such committees in addition to performing all other duties is like asking General Motors workers to invent the Saturn plant while they are still working a forty-hour week producing Pontiacs. It should come as no surprise that teachers themselves remain skeptical about the ability of their peers to assume responsibility for evaluating the competence of their colleagues. To deny tenure or counter malpractice requires a teacher to spend many hours observing and evaluating the work of her colleagues, to say nothing of the time required to change the teacher's own practice and to bring new knowledge to bear on the quality of her teaching.

Time and budgetary authority are closely related. Faculty costs at all levels of education are the single largest item in the budget. If faculty are allocated more time for planning, evaluation, or research, the budget must be increased to hire others to teach the students, or the classes must be enlarged, or different patterns of instruction must be developed that require students to do independent work. All these strategies were employed in the first academic revolution. Tuitions or tax monies were increased, lower-paid instructors or graduate assistants took over many instructional duties, classroom hours were reduced, class sizes often rose to more than a hundred students in introductory courses, and students spent many hours working on their own in libraries, studios, and laboratories.

Faculty committees, especially in the research universities, took significant control of the budgets, made decisions about hiring, course loads, sabbaticals, and aid to graduate students and research assistants. The period of unprecedented expansion of American higher education after the Second World War was also one of ever increasing budgets. Administrators considered it their job to raise the monies that faculty requested to build new laboratories, hire new and highly paid research stars, and stock the libraries with books and journals. This attitude was so deeply ingrained that when enrollment declines forced major cutbacks at most universities by the 1990s it came as a shock to a generation of faculty accustomed to gravy trains that had always arrived on time. At Columbia, twenty-six department chairpersons signed a petition protesting the cuts and threatening to resign unless they were rescinded, as if there was something inherently unfair about them.[3]

Except in Chicago, where Local School Councils composed of teachers and parents gained significant control of school budgets, the purse strings are still held tightly by central office administrators. It's a rare school, for example, where teachers could make a decision to reallocate salaries for two vacant senior teacher positions to hire four teachers' aides in order to implement a new pattern of instruction.

Credibly Serving a Public Good

As petulant as the Columbia faculty may have seemed in the midst of the financial crisis of the 1990s, it should be remembered that their generous budgets and increased autonomy had been won over decades in which the American university system produced an unparalleled record of accomplishment. Any form of work laying claim to the privileges of a profession must deliver on its promises. Essentially, professional authority and privileges are granted in exchange for serving a public good because the society is persuaded that its aims could not be achieved as well without those dispensations. The results achieved by the professoriate were remarkable. A higher education system that in the nineteenth century was not sharply distinguished from good secondary schools (or academies, as they were then more commonly known) moved to worldwide preeminence by the middle of the twentieth century. The fruits of academic freedom (the right of professors to pursue their research and teach as they saw fit) and tenure (protection from dismissal should their research upset the conventional wisdom) had produced a higher level of expertise that was obvious to all, whether measured in Nobel prizes or advances against disease or great feats of engineering. Federal funding for university research soared, first in the physical sciences and then in the biological sciences. By the 1960s, major funds were flowing to the social sciences, then enlisted in President Johnson's War on Poverty. Not only in research, but also in teaching and training, the American college and university system was the envy of the world. Saudis sent their young to the United States to learn engineering, and in the 1990s China entered into contracts with American universities to train its civil servants in public administration.

The profession that took credit for designing American elementary and secondary schools was mostly composed of white Protestant males who had advanced degrees in educational administration. They were the scientific managers of the Progressive era who laid out the structure of education and mandated the curriculum that a mostly female and temporary workforce taught—temporary, since in the formative decades of the system women had to resign once they married. That system, too, was seen as successful, having established the highest rates of literacy in the world in the early 1900s. The male superintendents won high pay and were granted significant professional authority, in contrast to the teaching force, who were seen as the blue-collar workers in an efficient mass educational system. We will return to this gendered pattern of professional authority in a moment. But now let us note that during its phase of leapfrog expansion in the first half of the twentieth century, the kindergarten through grade 12 system was largely a success story. Every decade the system expanded, providing credentials to more and more of each age cohort—credentials that were seen as economically valuable until nearly everybody had them. As the system approached that point in the 1950s and 1960s, criticism escalated. Superintendents who had justified their success in quantitative terms—more is always better—were being challenged to justify the quality of what was being taught. Not only did people think that the Russians were outdoing the Americans when they beat the United States in launching the first space satellite, but new social research produced withering indictments of the schools, beginning in the 1960s and continuing to the present. That research convincingly portrayed the inequalites and failures of the kindergarten through grade 12 system. It laid bare the racial and gender inequalities in the schools, and uncovered the huge gaps in outcomes between schools for children in affluent suburbs and those in the inner cities. It also highlighted international comparisons, demonstrating that the Japanese were graduating a higher proportion of the population from high school than the Americans and that those students were outperforming their peers in the United States. Leaders of the system could no longer claim that American schools were either the most democratic or the best. Demonstration of success in this context by a newly empowered profession of teaching is no small challenge.

A Revolution by Women

The first academic revolution was a traditional struggle among men. The sons, armed with new intellectual tools and advanced scientific degrees from European universities, overthrew a generalist patriarchy trained mostly in the ministry. They demanded that their fathers set them free intellectually and grant them new authority to run the household. The fathers turned their energies to funding the enterprise and to defending the values of the new university against attack from the philistines.

The second academic revolution pits mostly female workers, who have often been demeaned as high-paid babysitters, against entrenched male leaders that established themselves as the professional experts at a time when it was widely believed that women were not capable of professional self-regulation. They needed to be supervised by men. The men—and female school superintendents are rare even at the approach of the twenty-first century—were seen as having the special knowledge, certified by advanced degrees in educational administration, to run the system. They knew the finance, the relevant law, a smattering of social science survey research technique, some curriculum theory, and the political skills of policy-making.[4]

As we noted in Chapter 5, when female teachers stood up to speak at the early meetings of the National Education Association, they were told to sit down and be quiet. The women were thwarted and silenced by men with traditional views of female virtues. Although some male teachers—usually men in transit to "real" careers—might be needed to establish order among overgrown farm boys, the female virtues of caring and patience and moral education were seen as most appropriate for teaching children. It was "women's work." As the system grew and salaries rose with unionization, more men were drawn to teaching careers, most of them clustered in the high schools, where more weight is placed on specialized subject-matter knowledge than in elementary schools. Until recent decades, female teachers received significantly lower wages than males at the same level. And a male who enters elementary teaching is usually assumed to be headed for an administrative post, as if the work of educating nine-year-olds required no serious application of intellect and was not a worthy vocation for a man.

The roots of gender inequality lie deep in the formation of the kindergarten through grade 12 system. The tracking system laid down early in the rapid expansion of high schools shunted girls disproportionately into tracks for home economics and commercial-secretarial courses of study. Advanced classes in math and science and other college preparatory courses were taken mostly by boys. Girls who did not marry got little encouragement to pursue occupations other than the traditionally feminine careers of nursing, teaching, and social work.

Those who founded the new kind of normal schools that Florence Thayer attended had aimed to establish higher standards for entrance to what they hoped would be a true profession of teaching. In their first decades, shortly after the Civil War, places like the Brockport State Normal School offered a fairly rigorous curriculum in professional preparation for teaching in addition to liberal studies. Ironically, as more males were attracted to these schools by low tuition charges, they pushed for a reduction of the requirements in teacher preparation and an expansion of liberal studies that would allow them wider career choices. In the competitive market for students, the normal schools complied. And as the demands for teachers rose in the world's fastest expanding school system, male superintendents waived even the minimal training requirements then in place to hire any warm body who was willing to work for a low wage.[5]

The elite training for educators occurred in departments or schools of education that were formed in colleges and universities. These catered heavily to males oriented to either administration or high school teaching. If a young man wanted to aim for the top administrative positions in education, he applied to the doctoral program in educational administration at Harvard or Wisconsin or Syracuse. Women who entered master's programs in teaching at these universities might sit in the same lecture hall with men but were often shunted into separate sections for discussion, as was the case at Harvard.[6] Thus female tracks laid down in high school stretched to the graduate schools for at least the first half of the twentieth century.

To achieve a second academic revolution, then, we see that a profession composed mostly of women must meet two challenges the male professoriate did not face. First, schoolteachers must dislodge entrenched male administrators who have secured nearly exclusive rights to make the major educational decisions and whose powers are buttressed by the law and the bureaucracy. Second—the other side of the coin—they must show that they are not just generalized caring agents but have special knowledge unique to teaching that the administrators do not possess in the same measure. The male professoriate did not have to overturn a cultural stereotype that women were incapable of establishing a self-regulating profession.

Pressures for More Egalitarian Outcomes

The first academic revolution was congruent with the dominant societal values of individualism and an emphasis on equality of opportunity that presumed radical inequality of outcomes based on individual effort and talent. The first revolution produced a new tracking system in higher education that complemented and partly drove what was evolving in the American secondary schools. It established more rigorous qualifications and meritocratic grounds for appointment of faculty to leading institutions. As Christopher Jencks and David Riesman pointed out in *The Academic Revolution*, one of the first things these faculty did in leading colleges and universities was to eliminate both unscholarly students and unscholarly faculty. The formula for success was to hire the most distinguished Ph.D scholars, who would then attract the best students. Lesser institutions tried to emulate them. Thus the most ambitious systems of public higher education imitated the California master plan that assigned students to one of three levels of the state university and college system on the basis of their high school grades and scores on standardized tests.

The push that accompanies the second academic revolution is to do just the opposite: to untrack the schools and to educate all students to higher levels in more inclusive settings. An enormous change in values and beliefs is required to accept the new set of principles that underlies contemporary educational reform. It involves nothing less than a shift from sorting, selecting, and tracking to an emphasis on egalitarianism. No one argues for equality of outcomes across the board, although reducing the gap in achievement between racial and ethnic groups is strongly desired. The aim is more inclusive classrooms and cooperative learning that raises the average achievement of all children and assures that none fall below an acceptable minimum. It is to make the distribution of tests scores look more like that of the Japanese, who are said to have the "strongest bottom quarter" in the world—their low end is close to the U.S. median in mathematics, for example. This does not require the invention of new values, but it does require an important shift in the relative weights placed on individualism and cooperation on the one hand, and liberty and equality on the other. These have always existed in uneasy tension in American society, although until recent decades schools have placed greater emphasis on individual achievement and the opportunity to be unequal than on cooperative endeavors that create more equal outcomes for all. Now we are asking schools to create greater equality of outcomes while continuing to carry out sorting functions for the larger society. Teachers, who were themselves educated in a tracked system, are far from unanimous in their opinions on these questions. They mirror the broader societal struggles about the wisest course to follow in balancing the demands of equality and liberty. For teachers to agree on such a basic reorientation of values would itself be a revolution of major proportions. The professoriate had no such problems, since it was largely united on these questions at the time of the first academic revolution. Professors had no ambivalence about telling new students that half of them would flunk out before the year ended, and faculty beliefs were congruent with those of the larger society.

The Nature of Markets for Professional Skills

The reorganization of higher education, with institutions tracked by student admissions policies (now carefully indexed in college guides that give detailed information on Scholastic Aptitude Tests—the notorious SATs), began at a time when more than half of all students attended private colleges. The higher education market continues to have a more robust mix of private and public institutions than the kindergarten through grade 12 system, which has never been much more than 10 percent private in terms of student enrollment. It continues to be a highly competitive market for the best students and the best faculty. Institutions of higher education spend enormous amounts of money on both slick promotion materials and scholarships (now routinely referred to as "discounted tuition") to attract student customers. American parents and students are keen shoppers, and national weekly magazines that rate colleges and universities, and the departments within them, are big sellers on newstands worldwide. After investing for retirement, the single largest piece of financial planning for most middle-class families is saving for the children's college educations.

Because it is the faculty reputations that attract the students and research grants and other support, the market for faculty talent has usually been highly competitive. Even in the second-tier universities, salaries for full professors range from $50,000 to $120,000 or more. Salary offers are driven largely by scholarly reputations, but evaluations of teaching increasingly play a role; no longer can young faculty members be assured of tenure simply by attracting large research grants if they scant their teaching.

Even more important than salary in the first academic revolution were faculty demands for establishing the conditions professors thought necessary to doing their best work. These demands resulted in the peer control and forms of faculty governance that now characterize higher education, although administrative controls have been reasserted, often quite vigorously, in the last decade. Nevertheless, keen competition for faculty in a mixed public-private market continues to limit managerial authority in the realm of higher education in a way that has never been the case in the world of kindergarten through grade 12. Even though the differential markets between the two systems are not the only reason why schoolteachers are relatively disempowered, the effects of markets are significant. However, not all market effects necessarily improve professional services. The effects of market-driven managed medical care may pit better care against the profit margins of health maintenance organizations.

Sharing Authority with Parents

Three parties have a legitimate interest in shaping educational outcomes: the student, the parents, and the state. The interests, talents, and motivations of the student, even at a young age, should be given primary consideration. A democratic society has an interest in assuring that its citizens will be educated to participate actively in the tasks of self-governance and that the young become adults who are capable of earning a livelihood and do not become burdens on the state. The interests of the parents have special weight in the moral formation of the child up to the point that the child is capable of making and sustaining his or her own choices. The courts have disagreed about the exact age at which children can exercise the prerogatives of adults, but there has been a strong judicial tradition of giving primacy to the rights of parents until children reach the age when education is no longer compulsory, most often the age of sixteen.

In Pierce v. the Society of Sisters the Supreme Court in 1925 struck down an Oregon law mandating that children attend only public schools, on the grounds that the rights of parents to choose religous schools or other forms of moral education for their children could not be abridged.[7]

Fifty years later, in Yoder v. Wisconsin, the High Court upheld the rights of Amish parents to withhold their high school age children from public secondary schools even though their forms of home schooling did not meet the standards offered in the public secondary schools.[8] Similarly the courts have held that parents' interests must be taken into account in shaping the curriculum and policies of public elementary and secondary schools.

Hence the tradition in the United States of having local citizen school boards, often elected, act as the arbiters of such matters in the public schools. School board members often argue vigorously about the selection of library books and textbooks, whether to teach birth control or theories of evolution, and other morally laden issues. The courts have ruled that the autonomy and academic freedom of teachers is justifiably limited in the compulsory public schools in ways that are not necessary in institutions of higher education, where attendance is voluntary. Moreover, the broader academic freedom of researchers at the frontiers of knowledge is justified on the grounds that discovery of even unpopular new knowledge will in the long run benefit society, though it may initially be unappreciated or even opposed.

Thus teachers in the elementary and secondary schools have less academic freedom and more limits on their ability to take charge of their practice than do professors. This makes it difficult to draw the boundary around the sphere of expertise that schoolteachers should exercise. They will continue to share their authority with parents in ways that college and university faculty do not. But that does not mean that the present balance of authority between teachers and administrators should be retained.

parent input vs. administrator input

Three Scenarios for 2020

If we look ahead one generation to ask how these factors might interact to reshape the teaching profession, we see three possible scenarios. The first predicts that there will be no big change; a teacher's career will not look much different in 2020 than it does today. The second foresees a reassertion of top-down direction of the educational system and a repeal of the first academic revolution; both teachers and professors lose ground. The most optimistic scenario would be the hastening of the slow revolution.

No Radical Change

The odds are at least even that there will be no radical change in the short run. The resilence and staying power of the current system will ensure that in 2020 it will look much as it does today. Teacher empowerment will turn out to be one more passing fad. Most teachers will continue to work in a top-down system that is heavily stratified by race and class, and the best-paid teachers will be concentrated in the affluent suburbs. There may be some modest aggregate improvement in students' achievement levels, but there will be no significant improvement for poor children in large urban school systems.

Although a few leaders of the teachers' unions may pay lip service to the "new professionalism," traditional blue-collar unionism with its emphasis on pay, benefits, and work rules will govern the life of most teachers. Teachers will resist assuming genuine accountability for their practice; and the school day will not be structured to provide time for the rigorous peer review that roots out incompetence and rewards excellence. Traditional unionists will also undercut the development of tests by the National Board for Professional Teaching Standards as a means of assessing different levels of skill and knowledge among teachers. New forms of mentoring may spread in leading school districts, but induction into the profession will be mostly a haphazard process, with only a brief orientation period for new teachers. Poorly trained teachers with temporary licenses will continue to find employment in urban school districts. These teachers—and many others—will seek comfort and security in following the manuals and plodding chapter by chapter through assigned textbooks. Their students will complete thousands of worksheets, memorize many lists, and watch films every Friday.

Teachers will have some voice in school-based management teams, but it will be mostly advisory. Real devolution of budgetary authority and school-level decision-making will be rare. Teachers will not have a major role in the appointment or tenuring of new teachers. Structural change that permits more collegial planning, team-teaching, reorganization of the curriculum, and new forms of assessment will be limited. Teachers who have enthusiastically embraced schoolwide change and membership on school managment teams will withdraw, dissatisfied with merely advisory roles that are added on to existing duties.

Increased competition for students and new forms of school choice will develop in a way that increases teachers' fears and further strengthens the hand of protectivist blue-collar unionism. Vouchers will be structured to encourage the operation of profit-making chain schools where teacher-technicians follow company directives and rely heavily on programmed curriculums that emphasize drills to achieve quick gains in test scores.

Perhaps the most distressing trend will be that the unstable cycles of funding in urban schools continue to wipe out gains and to disable teacher reforms. In Syracuse, the original proposed budget of $194 million for the 1998–99 school year was cut to $175.8 million when city aid and state aid were both reduced. These cuts came as Alan Greenspan, chairman of the Federal Reserve Board, announced that the United States was enjoying the best economy in fifty years. More than 10 percent of all professional positions were eliminated by the summer of 1998, including the positions of twenty-seven of the thirty-four teachers who had been promoted to mentoring and staff development roles. Andrena's position was one of those sacrificed. She left to take a better-paying job in a suburban school district. And this happened at the end of a year when the work that Andrena and others had been doing had begun to pay off—Syracuse children achieved the highest scores in thirty years on statewide reading and mathematics tests. In Rochester, loss of state funding cut the Career in Teaching Program by 40 percent, severely reducing the number of interns who could be assigned a mentor in their first years of teaching.

Repeal of the First Academic Revolution

If the first academic revolution is repealed, there would of course be no downward spread to schoolteachers of the kind of empowerment professors won in that revolution. On the contrary, there would be—and to some extent already is—an upward spread of the tightly engineered "One Best System" and a resurgence of top-down direction of colleges and universities. Tenure has already been effectively repealed in all but the elite colleges and major research universities with the spread of part-time faculty and the contract system of academic appointments. The proportion of part-time faculty in higher education has doubled in the past two decades, and part-timers now account for 40 percent of all faculty.[9] The chairman of the Board of Higher Education in Massachusetts, James F. Carlin, a multimillionaire who previously ran insurance and real estate companies, personifies this trend. He has put the faculty on notice that a counter-revolution has begun and that if he has his way colleges and universities will be run more like General Motors. Boston newspaper editorialists cheered when he announced that he wouldn't accept the faculty rights written into current contracts. Carlin views tenure as "an absolute scam" that has turned faculty jobs into sinecures and made tuition excessive. Carlin complains: "Clause after clause says the faculty run the academic side of the institutions. That's like telling General Motors that the president can't be involved with making cars." Winning applause as he appealed to popular anti-intellectual sentiments, Carlin set himself up as an arbiter of "meaningless research" and asserted that 50 percent of research outside the hard sciences was "a lot of foolishness." These attacks, fanned by politicians such as Senator Alphonse D'Amato of New York, have affected the public's view of tenure. In a 1997 poll, 58 percent of New York voters said they were opposed to giving teachers tenure; 36 percent favored it.[10]

Academic freedom is eroded in the twenty-first century as curriculum controls are imposed in the name of greater efficiency to drive tuition costs down in a buyers' market. The corporate structure of the new University of Phoenix with its forty-odd campuses strung across the nation becomes the norm. At Phoenix, prepackaged courses are developed at the corporate headquarters, and then faculty are hired to teach them in shopping malls and rented classroom quarters. More college and university presidents are unabashed about referring to themselves as CEOs who must attend to the bottom line. A few of them, such as Donald Kennedy, the former president of Stanford, are writing persuasive replies to the "Profscam" accusations, but more are embracing the new corporate line: "We are a business, not a cloistered intellectual monastery . . . a corporation with an extremely diversified client base of over 20,000, each student seeking an intellectual (non-material) customized product from over 600 employees."[11]

Although the language may be more aggressively corporate, it is hardly new. The commercial strain has been interwoven with the history of American higher education. What may be new is the attempt by some universities to assert new intellectual property rights over courses developed by faculty—what one analyst has called the new "Digital Diploma Mills." The University of California at Los Angeles initiated an "Instructional Enhancement Initiative" that would require computer web sites for all its arts and sciences courses. Faculty at York University in Toronto went on strike against the university's establishment of its own subsidiary (Cultech) dedicated to the commercial development and exploitation of online education, transforming courses into courseware that would be the property of the corporatized university, not the professors who created them. Nearly half of all colleges and universities in the United States now enable students to take courses at home via computers.[12]

With weakened job security and the progressive loss of academic freedom, talented individuals turn away from academic careers. The most profitable research shifts to privately run corporations situated in a Silicon Valley world. But in the long term, the United States loses its leadership position in scientific research, which depends for its sustenance on the basic research that once flourished in the universities but now languishes for lack of talent or is strangled in newly bureaucratized settings. Russian émigré scholars joke that the new American university feels more and more like the old Moscow State University. The loss of tenure protection spreads downward to schoolteachers, and culture wars increase as teachers who want to keep their jobs adopt the party line of the school board in power.[13]

The Hastening of the Slow Revolution

Some "leveling" of professions in America will occur. More of the work of the traditional high-status professions, particularly medicine, will occur in bureaucratic or large organizational settings under the watchful eye of managers, whether these be administrators of health maintenance organizations in the case of doctors or bureaucrats who supervise the work of lawyers employed in government agencies. While doctors are accepting more and more regulation, the schoolteachers and nurses will slowly break out of long-established bureaucratic hierarchies and share more of the autonomy previously enjoyed by members of the high-status professions. The increasing political strength of the womens movements will create upward pressure to elevate the status and pay of the traditionally female "helping professions" of teaching, nursing, and social work. The gender gaps in professional work will also close as more men enter traditionally female fields and more women are employed as lawyers, doctors, and architects. Nearly half the students at leading law and medical schools were women by the late 1990s; at Harvard, slightly more than half the first-year medical class was female in 1997.

However, although the status gap between various professions will decline, the professions will become more stratified internally. Elites within each of the professions will emerge as bureaucratic and managerial supervision of most professional workers increases. The independent, fee-setting professional will be rare. As Eliot Friedson and other students of the professions have pointed out, the new internal elites will have a critical role in setting standards and shaping professional values.[14] This could turn out to be a bad thing. In medicine, for example, it could mean that the elites are predominantly male, high-paid specialists, while the mass of practitioners who do primary care function more as "barefoot doctors" under heavy supervision in what are seen as dead-end positions. Medical care could degenerate in a bureaucratically regulated system, though still be adequate for most needs. It might not be so different from the structure of the precollege education system we have criticized.

It is not clear whether most public schools have reached the point where they see no alternative to change. But we can foresee—and would support—a revolution in teaching that would create some internal stratification of the Rochester type and that would also both empower teachers and benefit children. The public will not support across-the-board pay increases for a profession that refuses to make distinctions about levels of expertise, but it will grant major increases to teachers who demonstrate that they are qualified to assume roles as mentors and lead teachers. This kind of revolution would have the following characteristics:

- *Few layers:* Although some hierarchical distinctions would be made—as between interns, teachers, and lead teachers or mentors—the profession would not be highly stratified in the manner of the military. Roles would be differentiated at the upper levels according to teachers' preferences. For example, some lead teachers might be engaged in curriculum design, others in mentoring or development of new uses of computers in the classroom.

- *Fair and rigorous assessment:* Teachers would gain promotion and the right to take on different roles through demonstrations of competence, skills, and depth of experience. These assessments would need to be seen as fair by the teachers themselves and as rigorous by the wider public.
- *Enhanced peer control:* A successful slow revolution would enable teachers to take charge of their practice in ways that would improve the conditions of work and strengthen the essential acts of teaching discussed in Chapter 3. School management teams at the school level would control most of the school budget, and possess the authority to reorganize the school day to provide for more teamwork among teachers. Teachers would have a significant voice in the hiring, promotion, and demotion of their peers.
- *New links between research and practice:* A stronger sense of a common professional community would emerge among professors and schoolteachers, who are, after all, engaged in the same essential acts of teaching. Professional development schools would become commonplace. Like teaching hospitals, these would be real schools serving real children with strong teaching and research connections with universities. Some classroom teachers would have university appointments, and university scholars and teacher trainers would be actively involved in the school, doing research and training teacher interns. These collaborations would produce widespread change in teaching practice.
- *Better results:* This revolution would result in improved quality of education and reduction in disparities between children of different social classes, genders, and ethnic backgrounds.

Whether or not this second academic revolution will occur depends primarily on three of the factors discussed earlier. One of these—the effect of markets—is largely outside the control of teachers. The two others they only partially control: the kind of assessments of professional competence that are used, and the quality of the results achieved by granting teachers more control over their practice.

These three factors are interrelated. The most critical will be the further development of the sophisticated assessments of teachers' competence initiated by the National Board for Professional Teaching Standards more than a decade ago. The NBPTS recently turned over further refinement of these "teacher boards" to the Educational Testing Service, which has successfully developed professional tests for architects as well as the Scholastic Aptitude Test widely used as part of the college application process. When further expanded and refined, the teacher boards promise to be the first truly rigorous tests that capture the complexities of the theory and practice of teaching. They will require teachers to reflect on the actual situations of practice, drawing on the learning and experience that candidates acquire in internships and the early years of teaching, as well as demonstrate more abstract knowledge of child development, subject-matter preparation, and pedagogical theory. Such assessments would discriminate between teachers like Andrena—who have continued to develop professionally through advanced graduate work, mentoring, and summer institutes—and those who have stagnated or treated teaching as a second job while they put more of their efforts into running a real estate business after school hours. They will be tests that incompetent teachers and many educational administrators who have spent only a few years in the classroom will be unable to pass. They will also be specific to different subject-matter domains and levels of teaching.

Leaders of the two major teachers' unions—the American Federation of Teachers and the National Education Association—have been represented on the NBPTS board since its inception. If they drop the false egalitarianism that holds that all teachers are equally skilled and competent and cannot be differentiated except by seniority, and begin to bargain with school boards to require National Board certification as part of the requirement for advanced status as lead teachers or mentors, it will be a major turning point. Adoption of this rigorous form of assessing teachers' competence would establish high standards for teachers in the same way that the bar exam for lawyers or the licensing exam for architects has established high standards in those professions. If it is as successful as those exams, it will also have a marked effect on the kind of training provided in professional schools of education, too many of which today are willing to certify any student who can pay the tuition. The quality of the professional schools would come to be judged in part by the success their graduates achieve in taking the national teacher boards. Although the board exams are still in their infancy, first reports indicate that teachers regard them as both fair and rigorous. Of the first 2,000 candidates to undergo the two-day assessment process, 594 achieved board certification. By 1998 thirteen states and twenty-eight school districts were paying the assessment fees for their teacher candidates, and eight states were tying major salary benefits to board certification. In North Carolina, for example, board certified teachers now receive a 12 percent increase in their base pay. Board exams will be offered in twelve different specializations by 1999 and will soon cover nearly all teachers. James Kelly, the president of the National Board, predicts that more than 100,000 teachers will be board certified by 2005.[15]

The market value of board certification is also likely to rise. Both major national political parties now favor expanded school choice. Though they differ in their enthusiasm for vouchers—which would provide parents with a tuition payment they could cash at any public or private school of their choice—both the Democrats and the Republicans now endorse the expansion of charter schools (public schools given a charter that frees them from most regulations) and other measures that would enable more students to choose schools outside their neighborhood or public school zone. Although vouchers are still rare, Gallup Poll data show remarkable shifts in the last decade, with 51 percent of the public supporting a voucher plan in 1998 that would allow students and parents to choose a private school to attend at public expense. Support is strongest among African American voters, especially those of child-bearing age, 86 percent of whom, in an earlier poll, supported the use of vouchers. More than half the states have passed legislation enabling the formation of public charter schools exempt from most state regulation. The last decade has also seen a great expansion in public magnet schools, which may be chosen by any child within a particular school district. Twenty states now allow some form of interdistrict transfer.[16] It is conceivable that by 2020 as many as a quarter of all students could be enrolled in some "school of choice," whether private or public. The percentage of students enrolled in private schools might increase by 50 percent, giving them 16 percent of the total kindergarten through grade 12 enrollment.

One way that schools could seek to attract students in a more competitive market would be to advertise that a significant percentage of their teachers were board certified. Then, not only would a new form of rigorous teacher assessment become more fully established, but board certified teachers would also have more leverage in setting the conditions of their work in their schools. The parallels between such increased leverage and the increased bargaining power of the professoriate during the first academic revolution are not exact, but the effects of each could be similar.

It is the third factor—producing results for children—that is the most important and will be the most difficult to achieve. Although teachers deserve better conditions of work regardless of whether test scores improve or more students graduate from high school, improving the quality of education for children—not enhancing the power or status of teachers—should be our primary aim. In the end, the value of board certification, increased autonomy for teachers, and better working conditions must be judged by their contribution to improving the quality of life and learning for children. The success of the second academic revolution will depend on achieving results no less than did the first.

However, any fair assessment of what teachers achieve must take into account causes of school failure over which teachers have little control. Today, more children than ever before come to school with addictions, diseases, and disorders such as fetal alcohol syndrome, and without having had sufficient sleep, food, or supervision at home. Teacher bashing often fails to take account of the appalling inequalities that continue to characterize American society. The medical profession now faces some of the criticism that teachers have long encountered. The easy victories have been won. The miracle drugs of penicillin and insulin had wondrous results for millions of patients, just as the expansion of the schools and mass production of new skills and diplomas had for millions of students in the first half of this century. Now medicine faces tighter controls and more exacting measures of its success. A patient contemplating heart surgery in New York state can now consult success rates published for each hospital performing heart bypass surgery. Doctors complain that it is not fair to measure their success by some rates, such as infant mortality, since they have little control over many relevant factors, such as poverty, poor nutrition, and inadequate motivation on the part of patients who fail to show up for appointments in the prenatal clinic.

But doctors, like teachers, do have some responsibility here. Although they should not be held totally accountable for societal inequalities, they can do a better job of teaching and motivating their clients.

They are learning that it is not sufficient just to put pamphlets on the waiting room table. Good medical practice now demands that doctors develop videos to help diabetics understand new technology involved in using insulin pumps, make clinical help more accessible to the indigent, and form networks of "peer tutoring" in which young mothers who have quit smoking and stopped using drugs work in group therapy sessions with pregnant teenagers in the inner city.

Like doctors, professors and teachers are facing demands for changes in their practice. They must develop new techniques to teach and motivate those in the bottom half—students who were formerly expected to drop out or were sometimes pushed out by schools and colleges that expended most of their efforts on students in the top quartile. As we have said, this requires an immense shift in teaching practice from a concentration on stratifying and classifying to an emphasis on teaching all students. This reorientation will be helped by the growing movement toward new forms of assessment that require students to develop portfolios, engage in live debates, and arrange exhibits and demonstrations of their work, just as the new teacher boards will require teachers to do. Rather than just seeing where students rank, parents and children will see what students can do, and get more feedback about what they are competent to do and what they need to improve. It will be a more visible and useful form of demonstrating "results" than traditional report cards or percentile rankings on standardized tests.

But new forms of assessment alone will not produce better results in education any more than they will in medicine. Better results cannot be achieved unless teachers embrace forms of teaching that are more inclusive and inviting, that emphasize problem-solving and peer tutoring, and that affect motivation to learn by engaging the genuine interests of all students.

If the second revolution triumphs, it will also help raise the status and quality of teaching in higher education. Except for professors in a few leading research universities, the real work of the professoriate is teaching, and although some sneer at those who hold teaching too dear, most faculty care about it. Recent surveys of full-time faculty show that they spend most of their time teaching, devoting only 18 percent of the workweek to research, although the proportion devoted to research rises to 35 percent at private research universities. Since the advent of the first academic revolution, however, the most prestige and the largest economic rewards have gone to those who have the highest scholarly and research reputations. Insofar as there has been an academic market, it has been primarily a market for research talent, not for teaching quality. But this is changing. Signs of a major transformation have been under way for more than a decade. Harvard and Stanford and many other universities have appointed major committees to assess and improve the quality of teaching. Some, like Syracuse University, have initiated faculty-supervised mentoring programs for teaching assistants who will later become college teachers, and have rewritten promotion and tenure guidlelines to give equal weight to teaching and research. Symposia and workshops designed to improve teaching and advising are well attended. The culture of teaching at Syracuse has changed. Good teaching is honored and rewarded by appointment to named professorships with major stipends attached. Student and peer evaluations of teaching have become mandatory, as they have at most institutions; low marks for teaching can put both tenure and raises in jeopardy. Although most professors are still far from regarding schoolteachers as their colleagues, some common interests in the improvement of teaching are developing.[17]

Just as radically improving the training of teaching assistants is the key to long-term improvement of college teaching, so the training of new schoolteachers in the colleges of education is central to the success of the second revolution. Because of delayed retirements in the 1990s, and an increase of half a million in the number of teachers by the year 2006 (for a total of 3.4 million teachers in public and private elementary and secondary schools), there will be a virtual replacement of the nation's teaching corps in the first decades of the twenty-first century.[18] Training these new teachers will be the most difficult challenge of the second revolution, requiring deemphasis of the deep-rooted norms of selection and stratification and an insistence on devising forms of education that are more inclusive and reduce invidious forms of tracking. But if successful, this effort will produce great benefits for children and for society.

Research Methods

This book draws on years of research in grade schools, high schools, colleges, and universities. It includes information gathered in observations of more than five hundred teachers from all sections of the United States as well as visits to schools and universities in England, Japan, and the former Soviet Union. In two earlier books and in other research on higher education, Grant reported on his visits to more than a hundred colleges and universities.[1] His work took him into many classrooms where faculty members were attempting to change the curriculum to become more effective teachers. His research on the National Institute of Education project *What Makes a Good School?* involved visits to thirty-three public and private schools.[2] He taught for two years in an urban public high school in the mid-1980s. His teaching experience at Harvard, Syracuse, and Colgate universities and Murray's teaching and administrative experience at the Johns Hopkins School of Advanced International Studies, Keuka College, Eisenhower College, and the State University of New York College at Brockport also provided a form of "data" for this book. In 1988, Grant conducted the first evaluation of Theodore Sizer's Coalition of Essential Schools, perhaps the most ambitious and sustained American effort in recent decades to change teaching practice from the bottom up. With Murray he visited a national sample of Coalition schools again in 1995 when the Coalition had grown to include nearly a thousand schools.[3]

Although most of our work falls into the "qualitative" tradition of interview and and observation, we have also analyzed a wide range of national and international quantitative data. Insights gained in observation of small samples of teachers should be tested against large data sets, and the meanings of surveys can best be interpreted by understanding the full context of teachers' work.

Although we followed standard research protocols in our observations and interviews, we departed from convention in writing two chapters. Andrena's story in Chapter 6 is based on interviews, observations, and events in a real school, but she is a composite of several teachers we observed over two decades at that school. Similarly, our case study of the Rochester experiment in Chapter 7 is based on actual events but is conveyed through the thoughts and actions of several composite characters. In order to establish trusting relationships with the teachers whose lives we invaded, we assured them that their privacy would be protected. We also disguised the names of the schools in which they taught. But with the exception of Pleasant Valley, we used the actual names of the school districts and the school and union leaders within them. These are public figures acting in public. It would be impossible to disguise the unique and widely publicized educational experiment that took place in Rochester. Syracuse negotiated a breakthrough contract at the same time as Rochester did, placing teachers in a wide variety of new curriculum and policy-making roles. Syracuse's experiment was not as widely known as Rochester's, but it would not be hard to guess the city's identity.

Our research roots go deep in both cities. Murray has done research in Rochester since the mid-1980s, and wrote her dissertation on the history of the teaching profession using Rochester teachers as a case study.[4] Grant has done research in Syracuse schools since 1979. Accounts of educational change are often short-sighted. Change in any large human system is usually slow and complex, even though particular dramatic episodes of downsizing or strategic planning or new curricular emphases may seem determinative at the time they occur. Educational enterprises are usually freighted with many reform efforts, often simultaneous, and nearly every school superintendent believes his (still rarely "her") reform or reorganization will outlast all the others. The same reform plan will produce great variance in outcomes in different schools and school districts. In order to capture this variance, we observed changes in nine schools in four school districts—Rochester, Syracuse, a small rural district, and a suburban school system. Each of these districts had placed teachers in new roles as mentors, curriculum planners, developers of peer review systems, or school site managers. With the aid of four research assistants, we observed teachers in these new roles in all nine schools, beginning that phase of the research in 1990 and completing it in 1998. We spent hundreds of hours in teachers' classrooms, sat through meetings with them on nights and weekends, and conducted periodic reviews with a core sample of nearly ninety teachers to obtain their understandings of the changes they were engaged in. We also attended to developments at the district level by interviewing school adminstrators, school board members, and union officials. The struggle by teachers to take charge of their practice occurred not in isolation but in a complex relationship with other parts of the educational system; an initiative at one level produces a reaction at another.

The data gathered in what we called the New Roles Study was vital to our conceptualization of the book but it represents only part of the research on which it rests.

Since 1990 we have applied for grants as co-principal investigators and published separately and jointly findings from this research, with first authorship shifting according to the responsibilities undertaken. For this book, Murray wrote Chapters 5, 7, and 8, and Grant wrote all the others, although every chapter was subjected to criticism by both. There would have been no book at all, however, without the help at every stage of our gifted research assistants, John Covaleskie, Wendy Poole, and Rajeswari Swaminathan. They wrote thousand of pages of field notes on the work of teachers in new roles; their fidelity to their task was extraordinary and their thoughtful challenges to our interpretations of the data have saved us from embarassment. Our debt to them is incalculable. John Manly, who joined the project at a later date, also gave us valuable assistance as a researcher in two schools. Lorraine Bédy and Karen Stearns were high school teachers who became research assistants when we asked them to keep journals and analyze problems of teaching they encountered in the classroom. Their accounts, on which we draw in Chapters 3 and 4, have an immediacy and power not attainable through conventional research techniques.

Notes

1. Two Professions?

1. Christopher Jencks and David Riesman explain the rise of the professoriate in *The Academic Revolution* (New York: Doubleday, 1968); Gerald Grant and David Riesman describe a counter-revolution waged against the newly dominant research universities in *The Perpetual Dream: Reform and Experiment in the American College* (Chicago: University of Chicago Press, 1978); Laurence Veysey wrote the best single-volume history of the American university, *The Emergence of the American University* (Chicago: University of Chicago Press, 1965). For an account of the systematization of American public schools, see David Tyack, *The One Best System: A History of American Urban Education* (Cambridge, Mass.: Harvard University Press, 1974).

2. Talcott Parsons's major work is *The Social System* (New York: Free Press, 1951); see also Parsons, "The Professions and Social Structure," *Social Forces*, 17 (1939), 457–67, and "Professions," *International Encyclopedia of the Social Sciences*, vol. 12 (1968), pp. 536–547, and Robert Merton, *Social Theory and Social Structure* (New York: Free Press, 1968). A broad review of theories about the professions can be found in Eliot Freidson, *Professionalism Reborn: Theory, Prophecy, and Policy* (Chicago: University of Chicago Press, 1994). For historical perspectives, see Burton J. Bledstein, *The Culture of Professionalism: The Middle Class and the Development of Higher Education in America* (New York: W. W. Norton, 1976), and Nathan O. Hatch, ed., *The Professions in America History* (Notre Dame, Ind.: University of Notre Dame Press, 1988).

3. Randall Collins, "Market Closure and the Conflict Theory of the Professions" in Michael Burrage and Rolf Torstendahl, eds., *Professions in Theory*

and History: Rethinking the Study of the Professions (London: Sage, 1990). Elliott A. Krause, in *Death of the Guilds: Professions, States, and the Advance of Capitalism, 1930 to the Present* (New Haven: Yale University Press, 1996), analyzes the subordination of professions to corporate and state control. See also Margali S. Larson, *The Rise of Professionalism: A Sociological Analysis* (Berkeley: University of California Press, 1977).

4. Paul Starr, *The Social Transfomation of American Medicine: The Rise of a Sovereign Profession and the Making of a Vast Industry* (New York: Basic Books, 1982).

5. Sari Knopp Biklen, *School Work: Gender and the Cultural Construction of Teaching* (New York: Teachers College Press, 1995), especialy chaps. 2 and 8, and Biklen, "Teachers, Professionalism, and Gender," *Teacher Education Quarterly*, 14 (Spring 1987), 17–24. See also Madeline Grumet, *Bitter Milk: Women and Teaching* (Amherst, Mass.: University of Massachusetts Press, 1988).

6. Andrew Abbott, *The System of the Professions: An Essay on the Division of Expert Labor* (Chicago: University of Chicago Press, 1988).

7. Mary M. Kennedy, "Inexact Sciences: Professional Education and the Development of Expertise," in E. Z. Rothkopf, ed., *Review of Research in Education*, vol. 13 (Washington, D.C.: American Education Research Association, 1987), pp. 133–168.

2. Assessing America's Teachers and Schools

1. For recent portraits of teachers in the heroic mode, see Samuel Freedman, *Small Victories: The Real World of a Teacher, Her Students, and Their High School* (New York: Harper and Row, 1990); Jay Mathews, *Escalante: The Best Teacher in America* (New York: Henry Holt, 1988); Tracy Kidder, *Among Schoolchildren* (Boston: Houghton Mifflin, 1989), and Gloria Ladson-Billings, *The Dreamkeepers: Successful Teachers of African American Children* (San Francisco: Jossey-Bass, 1994). For more anguished views, see Theodore R. Sizer, *Horace's Compromise: The Dilemma of the American High School* (Boston: Houghton Mifflin, 1984); Emily Sachar, *Shut Up and Let the Lady Teach: A Teacher's Year in a Public School* (New York: Poseidon Press, 1991), and Arthur G. Powell, Eleanor Farrar, and David K. Cohen, *The Shopping Mall High School* (Boston: Houghton Mifflin, 1985).

2. National Education Association (hereafter cited as NEA), *Status of the American Public School Teacher, 1995–96* (Washington, D.C.: NEA, 1997), pp. 74–77.

3. National Center for Educational Statistics (hereafter cited as NCES), *America's Teachers: Profile of a Profession* (Washington, D.C.: U.S. Department of Education, 1993), pp. 10–11.

4. NEA, *Status of the American Public School Teacher, 1990–91* (Washington, D.C.: NEA, 1992), p. 62; Robert B. Kottkamp, Eugene F. Provenzo, Jr., and Marilyn M. Cohn, "Stability and Change in a Profession: Two Decades of Teacher Attitudes, 1964–1984," *Phi Delta Kappan*, 67, no. 8 (April 1986), 559–567.

5. Robin R. Henke, Sonya Geis, and Jennifer Giambattista, *Out of the Lecture Hall and into the Classroom: 1992–93 College Graduates and Elementary/Secondary School Teaching* (Washington, D.C.: U.S. Department of Education, 1996), p. 10.

6. NEA, *Status, 1995–96*, p. 72.

7. Organization for Economic Co-operation and Development (hereafter cited as OECD), *Education at a Glance: OECD Indicators* (Paris: OECD, 1995), pp. 187–191; Stanley Elam, Lowell Rose, and Alec M. Gallup, "Poll of the Public's Attitudes toward the Public Schools," *Phi Delta Kappan*, 78, no. 1 (September 1996), 54.

8. Henke, Geis, and Giambattista, *Out of the Lecture Hall*, p. 16.

9. Ibid., p. 24. See also "The Recent College Graduates Study," cited in NCES, *America's Teachers*, p. 62.

10. NEA, *Status, 1995–96* p. 19; NCES, *Schools and Staffing Survey* (Washington, D.C.: U.S. Department of Education, 1993), p. 46.

11. NCES, *America's Teachers*, pp. 29–30; Richard Ingersoll, "Putting Qualified teachers in Every Classroom," *Education Week*, June 11, 1997, p. 60; and Linda Darling-Hammond, *Doing What Matters Most: Investing in Quality Teaching* (New York: National Commission on Teaching, 1997), p. 26.

12. National Board for Professional Teaching Standards, *State and Local Action Supporting National Board Certification* (Detroit, 1998).

13. Ronald Ferguson, "Paying for Public Education: New Evidence on How and Why Money Matters," *Harvard Journal of Legislation*, 28 (Summer 1991), 465–498, cited in Darling-Hammond, *Doing What Matters Most*, p. 8. See also Carl Bereiter and Marlene Scardamalia, *Surpassing Ourselves: An Inquiry into the Nature and Implications of Expertise* (Chicago: Open Court Press, 1993); P. P. Grimmett et al., "Reflective Practice in Teacher Education" in R. T. Clift, W. R. Houston, and M. C. Pugach, eds., *Encouraging Reflective Practice in Education* (New York: Teachers College Press, 1990), pp. 20–38; Lee S. Shulman, "Knowledge and Teaching: Foundations of the New Reform," *Harvard Educational Review*, 19, no. 4 (1987), 4–14; Robert J. Sternberg and Joseph A. Horvath, "A Prototype View of Expert Teaching," *Educational Researcher*, 24, no. 6 (1995), 9–17.

14. NCES, *America's Teachers*, p. 70.

15. NEA, *Status, 1995–96*, pp. 65–66; NCES, *School and Staffing Survey*, p. 120.

16. NCES, *America's Teachers*, pp. 105–121.

17. Louis Harris and Robert F. Wagner, Jr., *Testing Assumptions: A Survey of*

Teachers' Attitudes Toward the Nation's School Reform Agenda (New York: The Ford Foundation, 1993), p. 22.

18. National Commission on Excellence in Education, *A Nation at Risk: The Imperative for Educational Reform* (Washington, D.C.: U.S. Department of Education, 1983); National Educational Goals Panel, *The National Education Goals Report: Building a Nation of Learners* (Washington, D.C.: U.S. Department of Education, 1995).

19. Barbara Kantrowitz and Pat Wingert, "An 'F' in World Competition," *Newsweek*, February 17, 1992, p. 57; David Berliner and Bruce Biddle, *The Manufactured Crisis: Myths, Fraud and the Attack on America's Public Schools* (Reading, Mass.: Addison-Wesley, 1995).

20. Robert Sternberg, *Successful Intelligence* (New York: Simon and Schuster, 1996), quoted in Kathleen Cushman, "Failure by Design: Why Tests Don't Show What Students Can Do," *Horace* (a publication of the Coalition of Essential Schools, Brown University), 14, no. 2 (November 1997), 3.

21. OECD, *Education at a Glance: OECD Indicators* (Paris: OECD, 1993), p. 153, and OECD, *Education at a Glance*, 1995, p. 208.

22. Lawrence C. Stedman, "International Achievement Differences: An Assessment of a New Perspective," *Educational Researcher*, 26, no. 3 (April 1997), 4–15; Gerald W. Bracey, "International Comparisons and the Condition of American Education," *Educational Researcher*, 25, no. 1 (January–February 1996), 5–11.

23. NCES, *Pursuing Excellence: A Study of U.S. Fourth-Grade Mathematics and Science Achievement in International Context: Initial Findings from the Third International Mathematics and Science Study* (Washington, D.C.: U.S. Department of Education, 1997); U.S. National Research Center, *TIMSS High School Results Released* (East Lansing, Mich.: Michigan State University, 1998).

24. Stedman, "International Achievement Differences," and OECD, *Education at a Glance*, 1995. Alexandra Beatty et al., *NAEP 1994 U.S. History Report Card: Findings from the National Assessment of Educational Progress* (Washington, D.C: U.S. Department of Education, 1996).

25. Chester E. Finn, Jr., and Diane Ravitch, *Education Reform, 1995–96* (Indianapolis: Hudson Institute, 1996), p. 11.

26. Educational Testing Service, *Reaching Standards: A Progress Report on Mathematics* (Princeton, N.J.: ETS, 1995), p. 2.

27. Ibid., pp. 5–9.

28. Dale Whittington, "What Have 17-year-olds Known in the Past?" *American Educational Research Journal*, 28, no. 4 (Winter 1991), 759–780; George W. Bohrnstedt, "U.S. Mathematics and Science Achievement: How Are We Doing?" *Teachers College Record*, 99, no. 1 (Fall 1997), 19–22.

29. Bracey, "International Comparisons," pp. 5–10; Stedman, "International

Achievement Differences," pp. 4–15; David P. Baker "Response: Good News, Bad News, and International Comparisons," pp. 16–18, and Bracey, "Rejoinder: On Comparing the Incomparable," pp. 19–26, and Stedman, "Response: Deep Achievement Problems: The Case for Reform Still Stands," pp. 27–29, in *Educational Researcher*, 26, no. 3 (April 1997).

30. NCES, *Education in States and Nations* (Washington, D.C.: U.S. Department of Education, 1996), pp. 115–116.

31. Bruce J. Biddle, "Foolishness, Dangerous Nonsense, and Real Correlates of State Differences in Achievement," *Phi Delta Kappan*, 79, no. 1 (September 1997), 12. See also Suet-Ling Pong, "Trends in Achievement Gains: What Do We Know?" *Teachers College Record*, 99, no. 1 (Fall 1997), 23–28.

32. Richard J. Coley, *What Americans Study Revisited* (Princeton: Educational Testing Service, 1994)).

33. NEA, *Status, 1995–96*, pp. 39–40; OECD, *Education at a Glance*, 1995, p. 182.

34. Linda McNeil, *Contradictions of Control* (New York: Routledge and Kegan Paul, 1986).

35. P. Jakwerth, *U.S. Curriculum Analysis Report*, TIMSS Report no. 6 (East Lansing, Mich.: U.S. National Research Center, Michigan State University 1996), cited in Stedman, "International Achievement Differences," p. 10; and William Schmidt et al., *A Splintered Vision: An Investigation of U.S. Science and Mathematics Education* (East Lansing, Mich.: U.S. National Research Center, Michigan State University, 1996), cited in Stedman, "International Achievement Differences," p. 10.

36. James W. Stigler and Harold W. Stevenson, "How Asian Teachers Polish Each Lesson to Perfection," *American Educator*, 12, no. 20 (Spring 1991), 12–20, 43–47; James W. Stigler and James Hiebert, "Understanding and Improving Classroom Mathematics Instruction: An Overview of the TIMSS Video Study," *Phi Delta Kappan*, 79, no. 1 (September 1997), 14–21; William Schmidt, "Are There Surprises in the TIMSS Twelfth Grade Results?" in U.S. National Research Center, *TIMSS High School Results Released*, pp. 3–8.

37. Mathematics teachers themselves have undertaken ambitious and promising reforms. Most recent surveys show considerable changes in teachers' beliefs: 70 percent of elementary teachers and nearly 60 percent of high school teachers now believe science and math instruction should focus on deeper coverage of fewer concepts, for example. See Iris S. Weiss, "The Status of Science and Mathematics Teaching in the United States: Comparing Teacher Views and Classroom Practice to National Standards," *NISE Brief* (University of Wisconsin), 1, no. 3 (June 1997), 6. A slim majority of teachers also endorse cross-age peer tutoring, with older students tutoring younger ones, cooperative learning, and more use of com-

puters in the classroom, practices which research shows correlate with higher achievement, as noted in Louis Harris and Robert F. Wagner Jr., *Testing Assumptions: A Survey of Teachers' Attitudes Toward the Nation's School Reform Agenda*, a report by The Ford Foundation, September 1993, p. 29.

38. Educational Testing Service, *Reaching Standards*.

39. Stanley Elam, *How America Views Its Schools: The PDK/Gallup Polls, 1969–1994* (Bloomington, Ind.: Phi Delta Kappa Educational Foundation, 1995), pp. 39–50.

40. Jean Johnson and John Immerwahr, *First Things First: What Americans Expect from the Public Schools* (New York: The Public Agenda, 1994), p. 10.

41. Elam, *How America Views Its Schools*, p. 44.

42. Albert Shanker, "Privileging Violence: Too Much Focus on the Needs and 'Rights' of Disruptive Students," *American Educator*, 18, no. 4 (Winter 1994–95), 10.

43. Elam, *How America Views Its Schools*, pp. 44–45; Johnson and Immerwahr, *First Things First*, p. 24.

44. NCES, *Report in Brief: NAEP 1996 Trends in Academic Progress*, (Washington, D.C.: U.S. Department of Education, 1997), pp. 5–6, 13–16. For an account of the impact of these social revolutions in one urban high school, see Gerald Grant, *The World We Created at Hamilton High* (Cambridge, Mass.: Harvard University Press, 1988).

3. The Essential Acts of Teaching

1. One of the best philosophical discussion of these issues can be found in Thomas F. Green, *The Activities of Teaching* (New York: McGraw-Hill, 1971). Israel Scheffler's essay "Philosophical Models of Teaching" in his *Reason and Teaching* (Indianapolis: Bobbs Merrill, 1973) is also instructive. Mike Rose's *Lives on the Boundary* (New York: Penguin, 1989) is a passionate memoir of learning how to teach. Other notable essays in a more discursive tradition include Jacques Barzun, *Teacher in America* (New York: Doubleday, 1954); Wayne Booth, *The Vocation of a Teacher: Rhetorical Occasions, 1967–1988* (Chicago: University of Chicago Press, 1988); Herbert Kohl, *The Discipline of Hope: Learning from a Lifetime of Teaching* (New York: Simon and Schuster, 1998); and James M. Banner, Jr., and Harold C. Cannon, *The Elements of Teaching* (New Haven: Yale University Press, 1997).

2. Ethel Newcomb, "A Typical Lesson," in Houston Peterson, ed., *Great Teachers Portrayed by Those Who Studied Under Them* (New York: Random House, 1946), p. 295.

3. Private correspondence with David Turner, November 1997.

4. Madeleine Simon, "Teaching by Silence," in *Monastic Studies*, no. 15 (Pine

City, N.Y.: The Mount Saviour Monastery and the Benedictine Priory of Montreal, 1984), pp. 42–45.

5. Vivian Gussin Paley, *You Can't Say You Can't Play* (Cambridge, Mass.: Harvard University Press, 1992), pp. 4, 14, 18.

6. William Ayers, *To Teach: The Journey of a Teacher* (New York: Teachers College Press, 1993), p. 33.

7. David Carroll and Pat Carini, "Assessment Rooted in Classroom Practice," *Insights*, 6, no. 1, pp. 3–8, quoted in Ayers, *To Teach*.

8. For a splendid portrait of Jessica Siegel, partially paraphrased here, see Samuel G. Freedman, *Small Victories: The Real Word of a Teacher, Her Students, and Their High School* (New York: Harper and Row, 1990). Shirley Brice Heath explains in *Ways with Words* (Cambridge, Eng.: Cambridge University Press, 1983) how she taught teachers to hear the speech patterns of culturally different children in order to help them phrase questions in ways that children could "hear."

9. See Michelle Fine, *Framing Dropouts: Notes on the Politics of an Urban Public High School* (Albany: State University of New York Press, 1991).

10. Private correspondence with David Turner, November 1997.

11. Eleanor Duckworth says that teachers grow as excited as fourth-graders when they are asked to become naive moon watchers, and that it is necessary for teachers to rediscover a sense of genuine puzzlement if they are to teach well. See "Teaching as Research," chap. 10 of her *"The Having of Wonderful Ideas" and Other Essays on Teaching and Learning* (New York: Teachers College Press, 1987), pp. 122–140.

12. Harold W. Stevenson, "The Asian Advantage: The Case of Mathematics," in James J. Shields Jr., ed., *Japanese Schooling: Patterns of Socialization, Equality, and Political Control* (University Park: Pennsylvania State University Press, 1989), pp. 85–95.

13. For an account of what transpired, see Kathleen Cushman, "The Arts and Other Languages," in *Horace* (a publication of the Coalition of Essential Schools at Brown University), 12, no. 5 (May 1996), 2.

14. For a detailed account of the research method employed by the team, see "New Methods for the Study of a Reform Movement" in Gerald Grant et al., *On Competence: A Critical Analysis of Competence-Based Reforms in Higher Education* (San Francisco: Jossey-Bass, 1979), pp. 439–490.

15. Thomas Rohlen, "Seishin Kyoiku in a Japanese Bank," in George D. Spindler, ed., *Education and Cultural Process: Anthropological Approaches* (Prospect Heights, Ill.: Waveland Press, 1987), p. 456.

16. Girl Scouts of the United States of America, *Girl Scouts Survey on the Beliefs and Moral Values of America's Children* (New York, 1989).

17. Nell Noddings, *The Challenge to Care in Schools: An Alternative Approach to Eduction* (New York: Teachers College Press, 1992), p. 8.

18. Don Haviland and John Randall, "Mentoring and Support for Youth in the

Syracuse Metropolitan Community," in Gerald Grant, ed., *The Educational Life of the Community: Outcomes of a Metroplitan Study* (Syracuse, N.Y.: Edloc Press, 1996), pp. 185–222.

19. Adapted from E. T. Donaldson, ed., *Chaucer's Poetry: An Anthology for the Modern Reader* (New York: The Ronald Press, 1958), p. 15.

20. Sarah Lawrence Lightfoot, *The Good High School: Portraits of Character and Culture* (New York: Basic Books, 1983), p. 231.

21. Grant et al., *On Competence*, p. 157.

22. Judith Haymore Sandholtz, Cathy Ringstaff, and David C. Dwyer, *Teaching with Technology: Creating Student-Centered Classrooms* (New York: Teachers College Press, 1997), pp. 180–181.

23. From "Mathematical Development, Secondary Survey Report #1, Assessment of Performance Unit (APU), Department of Education and Science, Great Britain (1980)," quoted in Kathleen Cushman, ed., "Performances and Exhibitions: The Demonstration of Mastery," *Horace*, 6, 3 (March 1990), 7.

24. This discussion is indebted to our reading of D. Bob Gowin, *Educating* (Ithaca: Cornell University Press, 1981).

4. Three Questions Every Teacher Must Answer

1. Much has been written on the differences between novice and expert teachers. A good place to start is Pamela L. Grossman, Suzanne M. Wilson, and Lee S. Shulman, "Teachers of Substance: Subject Matter Knowledge for Teaching," and Marlene Scardamalia and Carl Bereiter, "Conceptions of Teaching and Approaches to Core Problems" in Maynard C. Reynolds, ed., *Knowledge Base for the Beginning Teacher* (New York: Pergamon Press, 1989).

2. Nel Noddings, *Philosophy of Education* (Boulder, Colorado: Westview Press, 1995), p. 171. See also Noddings, *The Challenge to Care in Schools: An Alternative Approach to Education* (New York: Teachers College Press, 1992).

3. Martin Buber, *Between Man and Man* (New York: MacMillan, 1965), p. 88, quoted in Noddings, *Philosophy of Education*, p. 172.

4. Noddings, *Philosophy of Education*, pp. 172–173.

5. Mortimer Adler, *The Paidaiea Proposal: An Educational Manifesto* (New York: Macmillan, 1982), and E. D. Hirsch, Jr., ed., *What Your Fourth Grader Needs to Know: Fundamentals of a Good Fourth Grade Education* (New York: Dell Publishing, 1994).

6. Noddings, *Philosophy of Education*, p. 176.

7. Georgia Heard, *For the Good of Earth and Sun* (Portsmouth, N.H.: Heinemann, 1989), pp. 38, 42.

8. David T. Hansen, *The Call to Teach* (New York: Teachers College Press, 1965), p. 36, and Lisa Delpit, "Skills and Other Dilemmas of a Black Educator," *Harvard Educational Review*, 56, no. 4 (1986), 379–385.

9. Jane Tompkins, *A Life in School: What the Teacher Learned* (Reading, Mass.: Addison-Wesley, 1996), pp. xvi–xviii.

10. Celia Oyler, *Making Room for Students: Sharing Teacher Authority in Room 104* (New York: Teachers College Press, 1996), p. 47.

11. Lorraine Bédy, personal communication with Grant, February 1997.

12. Dan C. Lortie, *Schoolteacher: A Sociological Study* (Chicago: University of Chicago Press, 1975), p. 169.

13. Ibid., pp. 184–186.

14. See Judith Warren Little, "Norms of Collegiality and Experimentation: Workplace Conditions of School Success," *American Educational Research Journal*, 19 (1982), 325–340, and Jane Close Conoley, "Professional Communication and Collaboration among Educators," in Reynolds, ed., *Knowledge Base*, pp. 245–254. Sharon Kruse and Karen Seashore Louis discuss the dilemmas teachers often face when some members of a team would prefer to comfort their colleagues rather than critically confront difficult problems of practice. See their "Teacher Teaming—Opportunities and Dilemmas" in *Brief to Principals*, 11 (Spring 1995), a publication of the Center on Organization and Restructuring of Schools, University of Wisconsin Center for Education Research.

15. This discussion is adapted from Gerald Grant, *The World We Created at Hamilton High* (Cambridge, Mass.: Harvard University Press, 1988), p. 251.

16. OECD, *Education at a Glance: OECD Indicators* (Paris: OECD, 1993), pp. 133–43.

17. OECD, *Education at a Glance: OECD Indicators* (Paris: OECD, 1995), pp. 64–65, 56–57.

18. Jean Johnson and John Immerwahr, *First Things First: What Americans Expect from the Public Schools* (New York: The Public Agenda, 1994), pp. 41–53, and Stanley Elam, *How America Views Its Schools: The PDK/Gallup Polls, 1969–1994* (Bloomington, Ind.: Phi Delta Kappa Educational Foundation, 1995), p. 31.

19. George S. Counts, *Dare the School Build a New Social Order?* (New York: John Day, 1932).

20. Lorraine Bédy, private communication with Grant, January 25, 1997.

21. Mary Mercer Krogness, "Censorship and Imagination," *English Journal*, 8, no. 7 (November 1996), 127–129.

22. Michel Foucault, *Power/Knowledge* (New York: Pantheon, 1980), and Henry Giroux, *Teachers as Intellectuals: A Critical Pedagogy for Practical Learning* (South Hadley, Mass.: Bergin and Garvey, 1988).

23. Karen Stearns, personal communication with Grant, February 28, 1997.

24. Deborah Meier, *The Power of Their Ideas: Lessons for America from a Small School in Harlem* (Boston: Beacon Press, 1995), pp. 3–4.

25. Counts, *Dare the School.*

26. In a 1974 poll, 30 percent of British teachers said they voted for the leftist Labour Party; in Grace's sample of seventy London teachers nominated by their headmasters as outstanding, thirty described themselves as conservatives, thirty-four as "liberal-reformist," and six as "radical or Marxist." Gerald Grace, *Teachers, Ideology, and Control: A Study in Urban Education* (Boston: Routledge and Kegan Paul, 1978), pp. 238–240. Data on American teachers' affiliations are for public teachers only (if private schools, which are mostly religious, were included, there would probably be a higher proportion of conservatives), and are drawn from the NEA, *Status of the American Public School Teacher, 1995–96* (Washington, D.C.: NEA, 1997), pp. 83–87.

27. Paolo Friere, *Pedagogy of the Oppressed* (New York: Seabury Press, 1974), bell hooks, *Teaching to Transgress: Education as the Practice of Freedom* (New York: Routledge, 1994), and Kathleen Weiler, *Women Teaching for Change: Gender, Class, and Power* (New York: Bergin and Garvey, 1988). Two other significant studies on the relationship between gender and radical pedagogy are Sari Knopp Biklen, *School Work: Gender and the Cultural Construction of Teaching* (New York: Teachers College Press, 1995), and Deborah Britzman, *Practice Makes Practice* (Albany: State University of New York Press, 1991). Conservative critics include Dinesh D'Souza, *Illiberal Education: The Politics of Race and Sex on Campus* (New York: Free Press, 1991), Thomas Sowell, *Inside American Education: The Decline, the Deception, the Dogmas* (New York: Free Press, 1993), and Nathan Glazer, *We Are All Multiculturalists Now* (Cambridge, Mass.: Harvard University Press, 1997), a more balanced book.

28. Lionel S. Lewis and Philip G. Altbach, "The Dilemma of Higher Education," *Academe*, 83, no. 4 (July 1997), 28–29.

29. Gerald Graff, *Beyond the Culture Wars* (New York: W. W. Norton, 1992), quoted in Robert N. Bellah, "Class and Cultural Wars in the University Today: Why We Can't Defend Ourselves," *Academe*, 83, no. 4 (July 1997), 25.

30. William Bigelow, "Inside the Classroom: Social Vision and Critical Pedagogy," *Teachers College Record*, 91, no. 3 (Spring 1990), 437–448. See also Henry Giroux, *Theory and Resistance in Education: A Pedagogy for the Opposition* (South Hadley, Mass.: Bergin and Garvey, 1983).

31. Amy Gutmann, *Democratic Education* (Princeton: Princeton University Press, 1987), pp. 75–82.

32. See Joseph W. Newman, *America's Teachers* (New York: Longman, 1998), pp. 137–159, and Martha McCarthy, "Legal Rights and Responsibilities

of Public School Teachers," in Reynolds, ed., *Knowledge Base*, pp. 255–266.

5. The Modern Origins of the Profession

1. The account of Florence Thayer is based on her diary and Rochester City School District school records.
2. *Brockport Normal and Training School Bulletin,* 1890, pp. 3–4.
3. Christopher J. Lucas, *Teacher Education in America* (New York: St. Martin's Press, 1997).
4. Kate Rousmaniere, "Good Teachers Are Born, Not Made: Self-Regulation in the Work of Nineteenth Century American Women Teachers," in Kate Rousmaniere, Kari Dehli, and Ning de Coninch-Smith, eds., *Discipline, Moral Regulation, and Schooling: A Social History* (New York: Garland Publishing), pp. 117–134; Harry Smaller, "Regulating the Regulators: The Disciplining of Teachers in Nineteenth Century Ontario," in *Discipline, Moral Regulation, and Schooling*, pp. 97–116.
5. *Tenth Annual Report of the Local Board of the State Normal and Training School, Brockport,* for the year ending December 31, 1876, *Methods of Instruction* report.
6. Smaller, "Regulating the Regulators."
7. *Tenth Annual Report of the Local Board of the State Normal and Training School, Brockport,* for the year ending December 31, 1876, *Training School, Intermediate Department* report.
8. John L. Rury, "Who Became Teachers? The Social Characteristics of Teachers in American History," in Donald Warren, ed., *American Teachers: Histories of a Profession at Work* (New York: MacMillan, 1989), pp. 23–25.
9. Geraldine Joncich Clifford, "Man/Woman/Teacher: Gender, Family, and Career in American Educational History," in Warren, ed., *American Teachers*, pp. 293–343; Kathryn Kish Sklar, *Catherine Beecher: A Study in American Domesticity* (New York: W. W. Norton, 1973).
10. Rury, "Who Became Teachers?" pp. 28–29.
11. David B. Tyack and Elisabeth Hansot, *Managers of Virtue: Public School Leadership in America, 1820–1980* (New York: Basic Books, 1982); Clifford, "Man/Woman/Teacher," p. 304.
12. Clifford, "Man/Woman/Teacher," p. 316.
13. Linda M. Perkins, "The History of Blacks in Teaching," in Warren, ed., *American Teachers*, p. 358.
14. Lester F. Ward, *Dynamic Sociology or Applied Social Science,* 2 vols. (New York: D. Appleton and Co., 1910), vol. 2, pp. 617–618.
15. Stephen Jay Gould, *The Mismeasure of Man* (New York: W. W. Norton, 1981), pp. 103–107, 113–119.

16. Henry A. Armstrong, excerpt from "The Mosely Commission Report," *Report of the Commissioner of Education for the Year ending June 30, 1905*, vol. 1. (Washington, D.C.: Government Printing Office, 1907), p. 7; Clifford, "Man/Woman/Teacher," p. 326, and Sheila M. Rothman, *Woman's Proper Place: A History of Changing Ideas and Practices, 1870 to the Present* (New York: Basic Books, 1978).

17. Nancy A. Hewitt, *Women's Activism and Social Change: Rochester, New York, 1822–1972* (Ithaca: Cornell University Press, 1984); Ida Husted Harper, *Life and Work of Susan B. Anthony* (Salem, N.H.: Ayer Publishing Co., 1983; reprint ed.), vol. 1, p. 98.

18. Ibid., pp. 98–99.

19. Ibid., p. 1117.

20. Carolyn Shipman, "Teaching as a Profession: A Protest," *Educational Review*, 20 (November 1900), 415; and Sari Knopp Biklen, *School Work: Gender and the Cultural Construction of Teaching* (New York: Teachers College Press, 1995).

21. Daniel Fulcomber, "A Sociological Ideal View of Normal Schools," *Addresses and Proceedings of the International Congress of Education* (New York: NEA, 1894), p. 423; Charles R. Skinner, *Fiftieth Annual Report of the Board of Public Instruction* (Albany, N.Y.: Oliver A. Quayle, 1904), p. xxiv; William B. Aspenwall, "The Necessity of Professional Training for Teachers," *Education*, 23 (1902), 27–31; and Jurgen Herbst, "Teacher Preparation in the Nineteenth Century," in Warren, ed., *American Teachers*, pp. 213–236.

22. Clifford, "Man/Woman/Teacher," p. 309.

23. Marjorie Murphy, *Blackboard Unions: The AFT and the NEA, 1900–1980* (Ithaca: Cornell University Press, 1990), p. 36.

24. Harlan H. Horner, *Education in the State of New York, 1784–1954* (Albany: University of the State of New York, 1954), pp. 137–138.

25. State of New York, Department of Public Instruction, *Forty-Eighth Annual Report of the State Superintendent* (Albany: J. B. Lyon, 1902), pp. 254–255.

26. Charles R. Skinner, *Fiftieth Annual Report of the Board of Public Instruction* (Albany: Oliver A. Quayle, 1904), p. xv.

27. Rochester Board of Education, *The Fifty-Third Annual Report of the Board of Education of the City of Rochester* (Rochester: Board of Education, 1904), p. 29.

28. State of New York, *Forty-Eighth Annual Report of the State Superintendent*, pp. 12–13.; State of New York, Education Department, *New York State Board of Education Report for 1911* (Albany: New York State Education Department, 1911), p. 578.

29. Horner, *Education in the State of New York*, p. 32.

30. *Fairport Classical Union School Catalog*, 1893–94; Wayne E. Fuller, "The Teacher in the Country School," in Warren, ed., *American Teachers*, pp. 102–103; and Clifford, "Man/Woman/Teacher."

31. *Fairport Classical Union School Catalog*, 1893–94.

32. Larry Cuban, *How Teachers Taught: Constancy and Change in American Classrooms, 1890–1990*, 2nd ed. (New York: Teachers College Press, 1993).

33. Willard Waller, *The Sociology of Teaching* (New York: John Wiley, 1932), p. 43; Richard J. Altenbaugh, *The Teacher's Voice: A Social History of Teaching in Twentieth-Century America* (New York: The Falmer Press, 1992), pp. 61–62; Tyack and Hansot, *Managers of Virtue*, p. 191.

34. Fuller, "The Teacher in the Country School," pp. 112, 114.

35. Margaret K. Nelson, "The Intersection of Home and Work: Rural Vermont Schoolteachers, 1915–1950." in Richard J. Altenbaugh, ed., *The Teacher's Voice: A Social History of Teaching in Twentieth Century America* (New York: Falmer Press, 1992), pp. 29–30. For further discussion of the concept of virtuous womanhood, see Rothman, *Woman's Proper Place*.

36. Clifford, "Man/Woman/Teacher," p. 315; Nelson, "The Intersection of Home and Work, p. 35; Rousmaniere, "Good Teachers Are Born, Not Made, pp. 117–134; Courtney Vaughn-Roberson, "Having a Purpose in Life: Western Women Teachers in the Twentieth Century," in Richard J. Altenbaugh, ed. *The Teacher's Voice: A Social History of Teaching in Twentieth Century America* (New York: Falmer Press, 1992), p. 21.

37. William J. Reese, *Power and the Promise of School Reform: Grassroots Movements during the Progressive Era* (Boston: Routledge and Kegan Paul, 1986), p. 43.

38. Kathleen Weiler, "Reflections on Writing a History of Women Teachers," *Harvard Educational Review*, 67 (Winter 1997), 643.

39. Ward, *Dynamic Sociology*, vol. 2, p. 627.

40. William H. Maxwell, "The American Teacher," *Educational Review*, 25 (February 1903), 155; J. M. Greenwood, "The Professional Culture of Teachers after They Have Been Regularly Employed in School Work," *Education*, 26 (January 1906), 280–284; Walter E. Ranger, "Higher Recognition for the Teacher," *Education*, 31 (1911), 616–617; F. W. Atkinson, "The Teacher's Social and Intellectual Position," *Atlantic Monthly*, 77 (April 1896), reprinted in David Tyack, ed., *Turning Points in American Educational History* (Waltham, Mass.: Blaisdell Publishing Co., 1967), pp. 446–448.

41. Horatio M. Pollack, untitled editorial, *American Education*, 12 (June 1909), 440.

42. Rousmaniere, "Good Teachers Are Born, Not Made."

43. William H. Maxwell, "The Teacher's Compensation," *Educational Review*, 27 (May 1904), 477.

44. David B. Tyack, *The One Best System: A History of American Urban Education* (Cambridge, Mass.: Harvard University Press, 1974).

45. Blake McKelvey, *Rochester: The Quest for Quality, 1890–1925* (Cambridge,

Mass.: Harvard University Press, 1956); and Reese, *Power and the Promise of School Reform.*

46. Tyack, *The One Best System;* and Herbert S. Weet, *The Development of Public Education in Rochester, 1900–1910,* Rochester Historical Society Publications, vol. 17 (Rochester: Rochester Historical Society, 1939), p. 185.

47. Raymond E. Callahan, *Education and the Cult of Efficiency* (Chicago: University of Chicago Press, 1962); Tyack, *The One Best System;* and Tyack and Hansot, *Managers of Virtue.*

48. Rochester Board of Education, *The Fifty-Fourth Annual Report of the Board of Education of the City of Rochester, 1905–1907* (Rochester: Board of Education, 1907), pp. 31–32.

49. Florence M. Thayer, promotion lists file, Rochester Science Museum Library; and Rochester Board of Education, *Fifty-Fourth Annual Report,* p. 51.

50. Rochester Board of Education, *Fifty-Fourth Annual Report,* pp. 36, 41–42; see also, pp. 186–187.

51. Ibid., p. 66.

52. State of New York, Education Department, *Annual Report for 1910,* vols. 2 and 3 (Albany: State of New York Education Department, 1910).

53. W. C. Bagley, "How to Promote Efficiency of the Teaching Force," *American Education,* 11 (January 1908), 260.

54. Rochester Board of Education, *Fifty-Fourth Annual Report,* and NEA, *Report of the Committee on Salaries, Tenure, and Pensions of Public School Teachers in the United States* (Washington D.C.: NEA, 1905), p. 52.

55. Charles Gilbert, "Freedom of the Teacher," in *Journal of the Proceedings and Addresses of the NEA, 42nd Annual Meeting* (Chicago: University of Chicago Press, 1903).

56. State of New York, Education Department, *Annual Report for 1910,* p. 133; Rochester Board of Education, *Fifty-Third Annual Report,* p. 205, and *Fifty-Fourth Annual Report,* pp. 189–190, 194.

57. Edwin C. Broome, "The Attitude of the Teacher Towards His Profession," *Education,* 31 (May 1911), 606.

58. McKelvey, *Rochester: The Quest for Quality,* p. 74, and NEA, *Report of the Committee on Salaries, Tenure, and Pensions.*

59. Patricia Carter, "Becoming the 'New Women': The Equal Rights Campaigns of New York City Schoolteachers, 1900–1920," in Altenbaugh, ed., *The Teacher's Voice;* Tyack and Hansot, *Managers of Virtue,* p. 114; Tyack, *The One Best System,* pp. 255–268; and Wayne J. Urban, *Why Teachers Organized* (Detroit: Wayne State University Press, 1982).

60. Ella Flagg Young, *Isolation in the School* (Chicago: University of Chicago Press, 1901), p. 93.

61. Carolyn Terry Bashaw, "Ella Flagg Young and Her Relationship to the Cult of Efficiency," *Educational Theory,* 36 (Fall 1986), 363–373; Kate

Rousmaniere, "Re-inventing an Old Wheel: School-Based Management Reforms in the History of American Teachers," paper delivered at the 1993 American Education Research Association annual meeting.

62. Wayne Urban, "Teacher Activism," in Warren, ed., *American Teachers*, p. 193; and Rousmaniere, "Re-inventing an Old Wheel," pp. 6–9.
63. Murphy, *Blackboard Unions*, pp. 25–31.
64. Ibid., p. 52.
65. Ibid., p. 73; Harper, *Life and Work of Susan B. Anthony*, vol. 3, p. 1292.
66. Murphy, *Blackboard Unions*, pp. 57–60.
67. Ibid., p. 92.
68. Ibid., pp. 83–85.

6. Reforming Teaching in the Midst of Social Crisis

1. This chapter reflects research conducted over a period of nearly twenty years at the school called "Hamilton High." It draws in part on work previously published in Gerald Grant, *The World We Created at Hamilton High* (Cambridge, Mass.: Harvard University Press, 1988). All the incidents described and the quotations used are derived from actual observations and interviews in a real high school (though renamed here) in Syracuse, New York. But the person named Andrena is a composite of teachers at Hamilton High and not an actual person. This disguise is required by the agreements under which the research was conducted.
2. Andrena's complete course of study would have included three education courses: speech methods in English, psychology of reading improvement, and a seminar analyzing her experience as a practice teacher. She also would have had 12 hours studying the history of England and America; 12 hours of speech, including courses in theater for secondary schools and the oral interpretation of literature; 12 hours of communication arts (mostly writing courses); 12 hours of speech; and a year in foreign language if she had taken two years of that language in high school, otherwise two years. The total of 132 hours was filled out with one-semester courses in biology, economics, math, sociology, physical science, music and art, and physical education. This information is from the State University College at Brockport catalogs for the relevant years.
3. "Hamilton Students Talk out Grievances," *Syracuse Herald-Journal*, May 17, 1968.
4. American Civil Liberties Union, *Academic Freedom in the Secondary Schools* (New York: ACLU, 1968), pp. 9–20; reprinted in Robert H. Bremmer, ed., *Children and Youth in America: A Documentary History*, vol. 3 (Cambridge, Mass.: Harvard University Press, 1975) pp. 244–245.
5. Syracuse Board of Education regulations, adopted in spring 1972.

6. Elizabeth G. Cohen, *Designing Groupwork: Strategies for the Heterogeneous Classroom* (New York: Teachers College Press, 1986), and Peter Elbow, *Writing without Teachers* (New York: Oxford University Press, 1973).

7. Greta Morine Dershimer, *Talking, Listening, and Learning in the Elementary Classroom* (New York: Longman, 1985).

8. Howard Gardner, *Frames of Mind: The Theory of Multiple Intelligences* (New York: Basic Books, 1983).

9. Philip Cusick, *Inside High School: The Student's World* (New York: Holt, Rinehart and Winston, 1973), and *The Egalitarian Ideal and the American High School* (New York: Longman, 1983); and Sara Lawrence Lightfoot, *Worlds Apart: Relationships between Families and Schools* (New York: Basic Books, 1978).

10. Carnegie Forum on Education and the Economy, *A Nation Prepared: Teachers for the Twenty-First Century* (New York: Carnegie Forum, 1986).

11. National Commission on Excellence in Education, *A Nation at Risk: The Imperative for Education Reform* (Washington, D.C.: U.S. Department of Education, 1983).

12. Samuel Bowles and Herbert Gintis, *Schooling in Capitalist America: Educational Reform and the Contradictions of Economic Life* (New York: Basic Books, 1976). p. 102.

13. Linda M. McNeil, *Contradictions of Control: School Structure and School Knowledge* (New York: Routledge and Kegan Paul, 1986).

14. Quotation from Mike Rose, *Lives on the Boundary: A Moving Account of the Struggles and Achievements of America's Underclass* (New York: Penguin, 1990), p. 190.

15. "Hamilton High School Strategic Plan, 1994–97," published in the summer of 1995 by the Syracuse City School District.

7. Teachers' Struggle to Take Charge of Their Practice

1. This chapter reflects research conducted over a ten-year period in the Rochester City School District. It draws on interviews and observations completed at three Rochester schools, and interviews with key individuals in the district and the Rochester Teachers Association. The individual teachers' stories are composites drawn from this research.

2. James N. Baker, "Raises, Reform, and Respect," *Newsweek*, October 5, 1987; Barbara Vobejda, "Changing Children's Fate by Changing Teaching: In Rochester Experiment, Educators Pay and Responsibilities Grow," *Washington Post*, May 31, 1988; Jerry Buckley, "A Blueprint for Better Schools," *U.S. News & World Report*, January 18, 1988, 60–65; and "Why Al Shanker Wants a Revolution in the Classroom," *Rochester Democrat and Chronicle*, January 17, 1988.

3. Carnegie Foundation for the Advancement of Teaching, *The Condition of Teaching: A State by State Analysis, 1988* (Princeton: Carnegie Foundation, 1988).

4. CED/Urban League Community Task Force on Education, *A Call to Action* (Rochester: CED/Urban League, 1986).

5. Arthur E. Wise, Linda Darling-Hammond, Emil Haller, et al., *Effective Teacher Selection: From Recruitment to Retention—Case Studies* (Santa Monica: The Rand Corporation, 1987), p. 160.

6. Rochester City School District, *Guidelines for School Based Planning, 1988–89* (Rochester: Rochester City School District, 1988), p. 10.

7. "Spotlight on Schools Finds Flaws," *Rochester Democrat and Chronicle*, April 14, 1989, pp. 1A, 9A; Lisa W. Foderaro, "Teachers as Social Workers: Experiment Finds Resistance," *New York Times*, April 14, 1989, pp. 1, B2; and Will Astor, "Rochester's School Reform Lurches Along," *City Newspaper* May 18, 1989.

8. Adam Urbanski, "Taking the Next Step," *Rochester Teacher*, 14 (November–December 1989).

9. Patricia Albjerg Graham, "Schools: Cacophony about Practice, Silence about Purpose," *Daedalus* 113 (Fall 1984), 29–57.

10. Vincent Taylor, "School Based Planning Is City's Newest Reform," *Rochester Democrat and Chronicle*, March 5, 1989.

11. Linda Darling-Hammond, "Accountability for Professional Practice," *Teachers College Record*, 91 (Fall 1989), 59–80; Christine E. Murray, "In Search of Accountability: Lessons Learned from Rochester," paper delivered at the 1992 meeting of the American Education Research Association; Manuel Rivera, "Accountability and Educational Reform in Rochester, New York," analytical paper, Harvard University, 1994.

12. RTA/RCSD Task Force on Shared Accountability for Improved Student Learning, *Report to the Negotiations Committees of the Rochester City School District and the Rochester Teachers Association* (Rochester: Rochester City School District and Rochester Teachers Association, 1990).

13. Linda Wertheimer, "School Funding Makes Others Envy Rochester," *Rochester Democrat and Chronicle*, May 20, 1991, p. 1A, 10A.

14. *Rochester Democrat and Chronicle*, January 12, 1992, p. 7B.

15. Linda Wertheimer, "Parent Council Urges Teacher Concessions," *Rochester Democrat and Chronicle*, February 6, 1992, p. 1B.

16. Jessica Portner, "School Violence Up over Past Five Years, 82 Percent in Survey Say," *Education Week*, January 12, 1994, p. 9.

17. Linda Wertheimer, "Proposed Pay Hike Decried," *Rochester Democrat and Chronicle*, March 10, 1993, p. 1B; and *Rochester Democrat and Chronicle*, March 26, 1993, p. 14A.

18. Kyle Hughes, "Regan Lashes Cost to Run City Schools," *Rochester Demo-*

crat and Chronicle, April 1, 1993, p. 1A; *Rochester Democrat and Chronicle*, May 26, 1993, p. 8A; and John Wolfe, "Bound by Bureaucracy," *Rochester Business Profiles*, May 1993, pp. 8–14.

19. Ann Bradley, "A.F.T. Shifts Emphasis to Focus on Improving Traditional Schools," *Education Week*, December 16, 1992, pp. 14–15.

20. *Rochester Democrat and Chronicle*, September 9, 1993, p. 16A, October 10, 1993, p. 4B.

21. *Rochester Democrat and Chronicle*, June 8, 1994, p. 10A.

22. *For All Our Children . . . No More Excuses*, report commissioned by William A. Johnson, Jr., mayor of Rochester, and Robert L. King, Monroe County executive, December 1994, quotation from p. 5.

23. Marc Tucker, "Still Hopes for A+ City Schools," *Rochester Democrat and Chronicle*, July 14, 1995, p. 11A.

24. Clifford B. Janey, "A New School Day," *Rochester Democrat and Chronicle*, May 21, 1995, p. 11A.

25. Clifford B. Janey, "Figuring Teacher Pay," *Rochester Democrat and Chronicle*, September 23, 1996, p. 7A; "First Report Card: Janey Gets a B+," *Rochester Democrat and Chronicle*, July 15, 1996, p. 4A; and Erika Rosenberg, "City School Teachers Give Janey Below-Average Grade," *Rochester Democrat and Chronicle*, November 23, 1996, p. 5B.

26. Erika Rosenberg, "City Schools Ranked Second-Neediest," *Rochester Democrat and Chronicle*, December 31, 1997, p. 1A.

27. Erika Rosenberg, "Kids' Reading Scores Show Significant Gain," *Rochester Democrat and Chronicle*, March 6, 1998, pp. 1A, 8A.

28. Jean Anyon, "Teacher Development and Reform in an Inner-City School," *Teachers College Record* 96 (Fall 1994), 14–31.

8. The Progress of the Slow Revolution throughout the Nation

1. Albert Shanker, "Our Profession, Our Schools: The Case for Fundamental Reform," *American Educator*, 10 (Fall 1986), 10–17, 44–45.

2. J. Myron Atkin, "Teacher Research to Change Policy: An Illustration," in Sandra Hollingsworth and Hugh Sockett, eds., *Teacher Research and Educational Reform: Ninety-Third Yearbook of the National Society for the Study of Education, Part 1* (Chicago: University of Chicago Press, 1994), pp. 103–120; Howard Ebmeier and Ann Weaver Hart, "The Effects of a Career-Ladder Program on School Organizational Process," *Educational Evaluation and Policy Analysis*, 14 (Fall 1992), 261–281.

3. Our "New Roles for Teachers" project involved research in nine schools between 1990 and 1997. Eighty-nine teachers and twenty-one administrators were interviewed, many three or four times over the years of the

research. Field work was completed on a regular, often weekly, basis between 1991 and 1994. Archival data, such as standardized tests scores, was obtained for each school. The final set of interviews included thirty-seven teachers, three to six from each school.

4. NEA, *Status of the American Public School Teacher, 1995–96* (Washington, D.C.: NEA, 1997), p. 89.

5. Michael G. Fullan with Suzanne Stiegelbauer, *The New Meaning of Educational Change* (New York: Teachers College Press, 1991); David Tyack and Larry Cuban, *Tinkering toward Utopia: A Century of Public School Reform* (Cambridge, Mass.: Harvard University Press, 1995).

6. Marilyn M. Cohn and Robert B. Kottkamp, *Teachers: The Missing Voice in Education* (Albany: State University of New York Press, 1993); Tom Donahoe, "Finding the Way: Structure, Time, and Culture in School Improvement," *Phi Delta Kappan,* 75 (December 1993), 298–305; Susan Moore Johnson, *Teachers at Work: Achieving Success in Our Schools* (New York: Basic Books, 1990); and Susan J. Rosenholtz, *Teachers' Workplace: The Social Organization of Schools* (New York: Longman, 1989).

7. Seymour B. Sarason, *Revisiting the Culture of the School and the Problem of Change* (New York: Teachers College Press, 1996), p. 335.

8. Andy Hargreaves, *Changing Teachers, Changing Times* (New York: Teachers College Press, 1994).

9. Judith Warren Little, "Norms of Collegiality and Experimentation: Workplace Conditions of School Success," *American Educational Research Journal,* 19 (Fall 1982), 325–340; Dan C. Lortie, *Schoolteacher: A Sociological Study* (Chicago: University of Chicago Press, 1975); Karen Seashore Louis, Helen M. Marks, and Sharon Kruse, "Teachers' Professional Community in Restructuring Schools," *American Educational Research Journal,* 33 (Winter 1996), 757–798; and Rosenholtz, *Teachers' Workplace.*

10. L. M. Smith, P. F. Kleine, J. P. Prunty, and D. C. Dwyer, *Educational Innovations Then and Now* (New York: Falmer Press, 1986).

11. Judith Warren Little, "The Persistence of Privacy: Autonomy and Initiative in Teachers' Professional Relations," *Teachers College Record,* 91 (Summer 1990), 509–534.

12. Milbrey Wallin McLaughlin, "What Matters Most in Teachers' Workplace Context?" in Judith Warren Little and Milbrey Wallin McLaughlin, eds., *Teachers' Work: Individuals, Colleagues, and Contexts* (New York: Teachers College Press, 1993); and Brian Rowan, "The Shape of Professional Communities in Schools," paper delivered at the 1991 meeting of the American Education Research Association.

13. Rowan, "The Shape of Professional Communities in Schools."

14. Hargreaves, *Changing Teachers, Changing Times;* Little, "Persistence of Privacy"; and Judith Warren Little, "Teachers as Colleagues," in V.

Richardson-Koehler, ed., *Educator's Handbook: A Research Perspective* (New York: Longman, 1987), 491–518.

15. Michael Huberman, "The Model of the Independent Artisan in Teachers' Professional Relations," in Little and McLaughlin, ed., *Teachers' Work*, pp. 11–50.

16. Tyack and Cuban, *Tinkering toward Utopia*.

17. Carl F. Kaestle, "The Awful Reputation of Educational Research," *Educational Researcher*, 22 (January–February 1993), 23–31.

18. Millicent Lawton, "Ky. To Showcase Performance-Linked Curricula," *Education Week*, November 26, 1997, p. 5.

19. Paula A. White, "Teacher Empowerment under 'Ideal' School-Site Autonomy," *Educational Evaluation and Policy Analysis*, 14 (Spring 1992), 69–82.

20. Cynthia L. Book, "Professional Development Schools," in *Handbook of Research in Teacher Education* (New York: MacMillan/ATE, 1996), pp. 194–210; Linda Darling-Hammond, *Professional Development Schools: Schools for Developing a Profession* (New York: Teachers College Press, 1994); Nancy E. Hoffman, W. M. Reed, and G. S. Rosenbluth, *Lessons from Restructuring Experiences: Stories of Change in Professional Development Schools* (Albany: State University of New York Press, 1997); and Marsha Levine and Roberta Trachtman, *Making Professional Development Schools Work* (New York: Teachers College Press, 1997).

21. Judith Warren Little, "Teachers' Professional Development in a Climate of Educational Reform," *Educational Evaluation and Policy Analysis*, 15 (Summer 1993), 129–151; and Penelope L. Peterson, Sarah J. McCarthey, and Richard F. Elmore, "Learning from School Restructuring," *American Educational Research Journal*, 33 (Spring 1996), 119–153.

22. Kenneth M. Zeichner, "Personal Renewal and Social Construction through Teacher Research," in Hollingsworth and Sockett, eds., *Teacher Research and Educational Reform*, pp. 66–84.

23. Patricia A. Wasley, *Stirring the Chalkdust* (New York: Teachers College Press, 1994).

24. Fred Newmann et al., *Authentic Achievement: Restructuring Schools for Intellectual Quality* (San Francisco: Jossey-Bass, 1996). See also Valerie E. Lee and Julia B. Smith, "High School Restructuring and Student Achievement: A New Study Finds Strong Links. *Issues in Restructuring Education*, 7 (Fall 1994), pp. 1–5, 16.

25. Rowan, "The Shape of Professional Communities."

26. Little, "Norms of Collegiality and Experimentation"; Louis, Marks, and Cruse, "Teachers' Professional Community"; McLaughlin, "What Matters Most?"; Peterson, McCarthey, and Elmore, "Learning from School Restructuring."; Wasley, *Stirring the Chalkdust*; and M. F. Wideen, *The Struggle for Change* (London: Falmer Press, 1994).

27. Joseph Blase and Jo Roberts Blase, *Empowering Teachers: What Successful Principals Do* (Thousand Oaks, Calif.: Corwin Press, 1994); Fullan, *The New Meaning of Educational Change;* Ellen B. Goldring and Sharon F. Rallis, *Principals of Dynamic Schools: Taking Charge of Change* (Newbury Park, Calif.: Corwin Press, 1993); Joseph Murphy and Karen Seashore Louis, eds., *Reshaping the Principalship: Insights from Transformational Reform Efforts* (Thousand Oaks, Calif.: Corwin Press, 1994); and Wideen, *The Struggle for Change.*

28. Milbrey Mclaughlin, "Embracing Contraries: Implementing and Sustaining Teacher Evaluation," in Jason Millman and Linda Darling-Hammond, eds., *The New Handbook of Teacher Evaluation* (Newbury Park, Calif.: Sage Publications, 1990), pp. 403–415; and Johnson, *Teachers at Work.*

29. Brian Rowan, "Comparing Teachers' Work with Work in Other Occupations: Notes on the Professional Status of Teaching," *Educational Researcher*, 23 (August–September 1994), 4–17, 21; Robert J. Sternberg and Joseph A. Horvath, "A Prototype View of Expert Teaching," *Educational Researcher*, 24 (August–September 1995), 9–17.

30. National Board for Professional Teaching Standards, *What Teachers Should Know and Be Able to Do* (Detroit: National Board for Professional Teaching Standards, n.d.).

31. Peter D. Hart, "Teaching Quality and Tenure: AFT Teachers' Views," unpublished American Federation of Teachers member survey, 1997.

32. Lyn Mikel Brown and Carol Gilligan, *Meeting at the Crossroads: Women's Psychology and Girls' Development* (Cambridge, Mass.: Harvard University Press, 1992).

33. Hart, "Teaching Quality and Tenure: AFT Teachers' Views."

34. Mark A. Smylie, "Teacher Participation in School Decision Making: Assessing Willingness to Participate," *Educational Evaluation and Policy Analysis*, 14 (Spring 1992), 53–67; and White, "Teacher Empowerment under 'Ideal' School-Site Autonomy."

35. Hart, "Teaching Quality and Tenure: AFT Teachers' Views."

36. Rochester City School District and the Rochester Teachers Association, *Performance Appraisal Redesign for Teachers: A Report on Initial Efforts* (Rochester: Rochester City School District, 1989).

37. Wendy Poole, "The Management of Meaning: Innovation in Teacher Supervision and the Interpretive Process," Ph.D. diss., Syracuse University, 1993.

38. Daniel L. Duke, "Removing Barriers to Professional Growth," *Phi Delta Kappan*, 74 (May 1993), 702–704, 710–712; Milbrey McLaughlin, "Embracing Contraries."

39. Lisa Birk, "Intervention: A Few Teachers' Unions Take the Lead in Policing Their Own," *The Harvard Educational Letter*, 10 (November–Decem-

ber 1994), 1–4; and New York City Peer Intervention Program, *Teachers Not Making the Grade? How to Set Up a Peer Assistance Program* (New York: United Federation of Teachers and the New York City Board of Education, 1995).

40. New York State School Boards Association, *Disciplinary Proceedings* (Albany: New York State School Boards Association, 1994), section 3020-a.

41. Hart, "Teaching Quality and Tenure: AFT Teachers' Views."

42. William H. Clune and Paula A. White, *School Based Management: Institutional Variation, Implementation, and Issues for Further Research* (Madison, Wisc.: Center for Policy Research in Education, 1988); James A. Conway and Frank Calzi, "The Dark Side of Shared Decision Making," *Educational Leadership,* 53 (December–January 1996), 45–49; Betty Malen, Rodney T. Ogawa, and Jennifer Kranz, "What Do We Know about School-Based Management? A Case Study of the Literature," in *Choice and Control in American Education,* vol. 2: *The Practice of Choice, Decentralization, and School Restructuring,* ed. William H. Clune and John F. Witte (London: Falmer Press, 1990); and Rodney T. Ogawa, "The Institutional Sources of Educational Reform: The Case of School-based Management," *American Educational Research Journal,* 31 (Fall 1994), 519–548.

43. Daniel U. Levine and Eugene E. Eubanks, "Site-Based Management: Engine for Reform or Pipedream?" in John J. Lane and Edgar G. Epps, eds., *Restructuring the Schools: Problems and Prospects* (Berkley: McCutcheon Publishing, 1992), pp. 61–82; and Priscilla Wohlstetter, Susan Albers Mohrman, and Peter J. Robertson, "Successful School-Based Management: A Lesson for Restructuring Urban Schools," in Diane Ravitch and Joseph P. Viteritti, eds., *New Schools for a New Century: The Redesign of Urban Education* (New Haven: Yale University Press, 1997).

44. Carol H. Weiss, "Shared Decision Making about What? A Comparison of Schools with and without Teacher Participation" *Teachers College Record,* 95 (Fall 1993), 69–92; Levine and Eubanks, "Site-Based Management"; and Betty Malen and Rodney T. Ogawa, "Site-Based Management: Disconcerting Policy Issues, Critical Policy Choices," in Lane and Epps, eds., *Restructuring the Schools,* pp. 185–206.

45. Anthony S. Bryk, David Kerbow, and Sharon Rollow, "Chicago School Reform," in Ravitch and Viteritti, eds., *New Schools for a New Century,* p. 175.

46. Smylie, "Teacher Participation in School Decision Making."

47. Carol Weiss, Joseph Cambone, and Alexander Wyeth, "Trouble in Paradise: Teacher Conflicts and Shared Decision-Making," *Educational Administration Quarterly,* 28 (August 1992), 350–367.

48. Wohlstetter, Mohrman, and Robertson, "Successful School-Based Management."

49. Ann Lieberman and Lynne Miller, "Problems and Possibilities of Institutionalizing Teacher Research," in Hollingsworth and Sockett, eds., *Teacher Research and Educational Reform*, pp. 204–220; Sheila Rosenblum, Karen Seashore Louis, and Richard A. Rossmiller, "School Leadership and Teacher Quality of Work Life in Restructuring Schools," in Murphy and Lewis, eds., *Reshaping the Principalship*, pp. 99–122; and Joseph Rost, *Leadership for the Twenty-First Century* (New York: Praeger, 1991); Wasley, *Stirring the Chalkdust*.

50. Carl D. Glickman, Lewis R. Allen, and Barbara Lunsford, "Voices of Principals from Democratically Transformed Schools," in Murphy and Lewis, eds., *Reshaping the Principalship*, pp. 203–218; and Ulrich C. Reitzug, "A Case of Empowering Principal Behavior," *American Educational Research Journal*, 31 (Summer 1994), 283–307.

51. Malen and Ogawa, "Site-Based Management"; Levine and Eubanks, "Site-Based Management"; and White, "Teacher Empowerment under 'Ideal' School-Site Autonomy."

52. Smylie, "Teacher Participation in School Decision Making"; and White, "Teacher Empowerment under 'Ideal' School-Site Autonomy."

53. Seymour Fliegel, "Creative Non-Compliance," in *Choice and Control in American Education*, vol. 2: *The Practice of Choice, Decentralization, and School Restructuring*, ed. William H. Clune and John F. Witte (New York: Falmer Press, 1990), pp. 199–216.

54. Douglas A. Archbald and Andrew C. Porter, "Curriculum Control and Teachers' Perception of Autonomy and Satisfaction," *Educational Evaluation and Policy Analysis*, 16 (Spring 1994), 21–39.

55. William A. Firestone and Beth D. Bader, *Redesigning Teaching: Professionalism or Bureaucracy?* (Albany: State University of New York Press, 1992); Mark A. Smylie, "Redesigning Teachers' Work: Connections to the Classroom," in Linda Darling-Hammond, ed., *Review of Research in Education* (Washington, D.C.: American Education Research Association, 1994), pp. 129–177; and White, "Teacher Empowerment under 'Ideal' School Site Autonomy."

56. Cohn and Kottkamp, *Teachers: The Missing Voice in Education*.

57. James P. Comer, Norris M. Haynes, Edward T. Joyner, and Michael Ben-Avie, *Rallying the Whole Village: The Comer Process for Reforming Education* (New York: Teachers College Press, 1996); and U.S. Department of Education, *Strong Families, Strong Schools: Building Community Partnerships for Learning* (Washington D.C.: U.S. Department of Education, 1994).

58. Kenneth Strike, "Professionalism, Democracy, and Discursive Communities: Normative Reflections on Restructuring," *American Educational Research Journal*, 30 (Summer 1993), 255–275.

59. Terry A. Astuto, David L. Clark, Anne-Marie Read, Kathleen McGree,

and L. deKoven Pelton Fernandez, *Roots of Reform: Challenging the Assumptions That Control Change in Education* (Bloomington, Ind.: Phi Delta Kappa Educational Foundation, 1994); and Jane Roland Martin, *The Schoolhome: Rethinking Schools for Changing Families* (Cambridge, Mass.: Harvard University Press, 1992).

60. Fullan, *The New Meaning of Educational Change.*

61. Johnson, *Teachers at Work.*

62. Martin, *The Schoolhome.*

63. Ebmeier and Hart, "The Effects of a Career Ladder Program on School Organizational Process"; Malen, Ogawa, and Kranz, "What Do We Know about School-Based Management?"; Helen M. Marks and Karen Seashore Louis, "Does Teacher Empowerment Affect the Classroom? The Implications of Teacher Empowerment for Instructional Practice and Student Academic Performance," *Educational Evaluation and Policy Analysis*, 19 (Fall 1997), 245–275. Smylie, "Redesigning Teachers' Work"; and Zeichner, "Personal Renewal and Social Construction through Teacher Research."

64. Smylie, "Redesigning Teachers' Work"; Mark A. Smylie, Virginia Lazarus, and Jean Brownlee-Conyers, "Instructional Outcomes of School-Based Participative Decision Making," *Educational Evaluation and Policy Analysis*, 18 (Fall 1996), 181–198; Patricia Wolhstetter, Roxanne Smyer, and Susan Albers Mohrman, "New Boundaries for School-Based Management: The High Involvement Model," Educational Evaluation and Policy Analysis, 16 (Fall 1994), 268–286.

9. Teaching in 2020

1. Christopher Jencks and David Riesman, *The Academic Revolution* (New York: Doubleday, 1968); for a list of statuses of all occupations, see Otis Dudley Duncan, "Properties and Characteristics of the Socioeconomic Index," in Albert J. Reiss, ed., *Occupations and Social Status* (New York: Free Press, 1961).

2. David B. Tyack, *The One Best System: A History of American Urban Education* (Cambridge, Mass.: Harvard University Press, 1974).

3. Anthony DePalma, "As a Deficit Looms, Twenty-Six Threaten to Quit Key Columbia Posts," *New York Times*, November 27, 1991, p. A-1.

4. David Tyack and Elisabeth Hansot, *Managers of Virtue: Public School Leadership in America, 1820–1980* (New York: Basic Books, 1982).

5. Andrew Gitlin and David F. Labaree, "Historical Notes on the Barriers to the Professionalization of American Teachers," in Ivor F. Goodson and Andy Hargreaves, eds., *Teachers' Professional Lives* (London: Falmer Press, 1996), pp. 88–108; and Donald Warren, "Learning from Experience: History and Teacher Education," *Educational Researcher*, 14, no. 10 (1985), 5–12.

6. Arthur Powell, *The Uncertain Profession* (Cambridge, Mass.: Harvard University Press, 1980).

7. Pierce v. Society of Sisters, 268 U.S., 510 (1925).

8. Wisconsin v. Yoder, 406 U.S., 205 (1972).

9. Data are from the 1993 poll by the National Center for Educational Statistics, reported by Courtney Leatherman, in "Do Accreditors Look the Other Way When Colleges Rely on Part-Timers," in *The Chronicle of Higher Education,* November 7, 1997, p. A12.

10. Patrick Healy, "A Take-No-Prisoners Approach to Changing Public Higher Education in Massachusetts," *The Chronicle of Higher Education,* December 5, 1997, pp. A41–42; William H. Honan, "The Ivory Tower under Siege: Eveyone Else Downsized; Why Not the Academy?" *New York Times,* "Education Life" section, January 4, 1998, pp. 33–44. The poll was conducted by the Quinnipiac College Polling Institute, and reported in the *Syracuse Post Standard,* "Poll: Most Oppose Teacher Tenure," December 15, 1997, p. A2. See also George Dennis O'Brien, *All the Essential Half-Truths about Higher Education* (Chicago: University of Chicago Press, 1997).

11. Donald Kennedy, *Academic Duty* (Cambridge, Mass.: Harvard University Press, 1997). The quote is from Neal Raisman, president of Onondaga Community College, "OCC Refocuses Its Finances on Education and Training," *Syracuse Post Standard,* December 17, 1997, p. A19.

12. David F. Noble, "Digital Diploma Mills: The Automation of Higher Education," unpublished manuscript, October 1997. Nationally, 10,380 courses are offered over computer connections to students at home or at work; 49 percent of all higher education institutions offer some courses via computer, with the fastest growth (62 percent offering such courses) in the western United States. NCES *Distance Education in Higher Education Institutions* (Washington, D.C.: U.S. Department of Education, 1997), pp. 12–13.

13. For an earlier history of teacher firings, including the story of the Toledo school board that in the 1930s assigned students to spy and report on presumed "radical teachers," see Howard K. Beale, *Are American Teachers Free?* (New York, 1936), p. 117, quoted in Robert L. Church, *Education in the United States: An Interpretive History* (New York: Free Press, 1976), pp. 361–363.

14. Eliot Friedson, *Professionalism Reborn: Theory, Prophecy, and Policy* (Chicago: University of Chicago Press, 1994).

15. Data from *Education Week,* October 29, 1997, p. 4; National Board for Professional Teaching Standards, *State and Local Action Supporting National Board Certification* (Detroit: National Board, 1998), and interview with James Kelly, NBPTS president, February 2, 1998. Although the NBPTS

exam culminates in a two-day formal assessment, it is a months-long process in which candidates must first complete a portfolio documenting their teaching, including examples of their students' work and videotapes of their classroom teaching.

16. Chester E. Finn, Jr., and Rebecca L. Gau, "New Ways of Education," *The Public Interest*, 130 (Winter 1998), 79–92; and Tamara Henry, "Majority Backs Public Money for Private Schools," *USA Today*, August 26, 1998, p. D1.

17. NCES, *Instructional Faculty and Staff in Higher Education Institutions: Fall 1987 and Fall 1992* (Washington, D.C.: U.S. Department of Education, 1997), pp. 32–33; Lionel S. Lewis, *Marginal Worth: Teaching and the Academic Labor Market* (New Brunswick, N.J.: Transaction Publishers, 1996); and Richard J. Light, *The Harvard Assessment Seminars: Explorations with Students and Faculty about Teaching, Learning and Student Life* (Cambridge, Mass.: Harvard University, first report, 1990, second report, 1992). Research on changes in the teaching culture at Syracuse University is drawn from Donald J. Haviland, "Becoming a Student-Centered Research University: A Case of Organizational Change," Ph.D. diss. in progress, Syracuse University, 1998; Larry Cuban tells the story of repeated efforts to reform teaching at Stanford University without much success in *Scholars Trump Teachers* (New York: Teachers College Press, in press).

18. NCES, *Projections of Education Statistics to 2006* (Washington, D.C.: U.S. Department of Education, 1996), p. 2.

Research Methods

1. Gerald Grant and David Riesman, *The Perpetual Dream: Reform and Experiment in the American College* (Chicago: University of Chicago Press, 1978), and Grant et al., *On Competence: A Critical Analysis of Competence-Based Reforms in Higher Education* (San Francisco: Jossey-Bass, 1979).

2. Gerald Grant, ed., *What Makes a Good School? Five Case Studies* (Washington, D.C.: National Institute of Education, 1981); and Grant, *Education, Character, and American Schools: Are Effective Schools Good Enough?* (Washington, D.C.: National Institute of Education, 1982).

3. Gerald Grant, "An Evaluation of the Coalition of Essential Schools," a report to the CES Advisory Committee, Brown University, 1988; Gerald Grant and Christine Murray, "An Evaluation of the Centers Project of the Coalition of Essential Schools," a report to CES Chairman Theodore Sizer and the Dewitt Wallace Foundation, June 1995.

4. Christine E. Murray, "The Incremental Revolution: Transforming the Teaching Profession," Ph.D. diss., Syracuse University, 1990.

Acknowledgments

Any book of this kind has dozens of unacknowledged assistants and "co-authors," especially the teachers who admitted us to their classrooms and shared their reflections in interviews, correspondence, and reactions to our site reports on each school. We wish we could thank each of them by name for their time and generosity of spirit. Researchers are bound by agreements that protect the privacy of respondents, but we often wanted to find a way to give credit and praise to exceptional people we encountered in the course of the work. This was the case with one of the teachers on whom we drew for the Andrena composite in Chapter 6. In fact, we asked her permission to use her real name and to base the chapter solely on her life experience but she was firm in her desire to guard her privacy.

An invisible college of critical friends also stands behind any major work of scholarship. We owe special thanks to our colleagues and friends who read early drafts of our chapters with sympathy and a critical eye: Betsy Ann Balzano, Lorraine Bédy, Sari Knopp Biklen, Jerome Bisson, Robert Bogdan, Walter Brautigan, John Briggs, Joan Burstyn, David Cohen, John Covaleokie, Larry Cuban, Philip Cusick, Thomas Ewens, James S. Fleming, Thomas Gillett, Henrietta Gingold, Judith Dunn Grant, Robert Ashton Grant, Judy Gray, Thomas Green, Charles Howell, Christopher Jencks, John Manly, Diane McClain, Carl O'Connell, Dennis Pataniczek, Arthur G. Powell, Wendy Poole, Carl Puehn, David Riesman, Cheryl Riley, Emily Robertson, Katharine G.

Rooney, Kate Rousmaniere, Harry Smaller, Richard Stear, Karen Stearns, Kenneth Strike, Rajeswari Swaminathan, Pat Tinto, David Turner, David Tyack, Adam Urbanski, William Veenis, and Nancy Zarach. Special thanks is owed to our editors at Harvard Press, Michael Aronson and Nancy Clemente.

Much of what is good in our book is owed to all of them; what is faulty is due to the mote in our own eye. Our secretarial assistants also saved us from many errors in giving us extraordinary support through the many phases of this work. Thank you Tashera Jenkins, Susan Kelly, Barbara Pauley, Phyllis Romano-Eldred, and Karen Thompson.

Our historical research on Rochester was assisted by Charles Cowling, State University of New York College at Brockport archivist, and Susan C. Roberts, Town Historian of Perinton, New York. Andrew McGowan and the staff members of the Rochester City School District Department of Research, Evaluation, and Testing were unfailing in their willingness to provide statistical data.

In our search for relevant survey data, we benefited greatly from assistance by the American Federation of Teachers research department and the staff at the National Center for Educational Statistics of the U.S. Department of Education, especially Emerson Elliott and Sharon Bobbitt.

Work of this scope stretches over years and involves team research that cannot be accomplished without major financial support. We are grateful to the U.S. Department of Education for its early funding of this work, to Syracuse University for generous sabbatical and research support, to Colgate University for support that enabled Gerald Grant to spend the spring of 1997 there as the A. Lindsay O'Connor Professor of American Institutions, and to the State University of New York College at Brockport for academic leave and research support. We are most grateful to the Spencer Foundation, which provided three grants to fund this work and supplemented them at critical points in the evolution of our project. The staff at the Spencer Foundation is rare in the interest it takes in the work of grantees after sending the check, and the response it makes to early reports of the research. In this regard we express special affection for Patricia Albjerg Graham, John Barcroft, Rebecca Barr, and Elizabeth Lynn.

Index

Abbott, Andrew, 6, 7

ability grouping and tracking, 26; race, 109, 111, 117–118; gender, 223; revolution, 224–225, 238

academic freedom, 226–227

academic revolution: first, 2; slow (second), 2, 3, 4, 8, 15–16, 56, 67, 137, 182–212

Academic Revolution, The, 224

accountability of teachers, 96–97, 152–154, 156, 171, 193–201, 228

achievement test scores, 2–3, 4, 17–18, 144, 191; reading, 18; science, 18–19; geography and history, 19–20; mathematics, 20–24, 25, 181; social revolution, 29–30; Genesee Elementary School, 169; Raintree Middle School, 190. *See also* accountability of teachers; assessment; effectiveness of teaching

activism, 83–85, 93, 98–102, 143

Adler, Mortimer, 59

administration: gender, 1, 221, 222; teacher regulation, 2, 4; teacher licensure, 87–88; scientific management and centralization, 93–99, 206–207, 217, 221; Hamilton High, 106, 110, 111, 125–126, 129–130, 135–136; the Rochester reforms, 142, 145, 146, 147, 154, 159, 165, 169, 171, 178,

180; the status of reforms, 184; teacher collaboration, 191–193; peer review of teachers, 195–196, 197, 198, 199; Chicago Local School Councils, 201, 220; "empowered trust," 202; and traditional hierarchy, 205; turnover rate, 205; higher education budgets, 220; university programs, 221, 223. *See also* governance, shared

Alverno College, 47

American Association of University Professors, 1

American Civil Liberties Union (ACLU): *Academic Freedom in Secondary Schools*, 113–114

American Federation of Teachers, 100, 101–102, 166, 194–195, 196, 201, 234, 270

"An 'F' in World Competition" (*Newsweek*), 17

Anthony, Andrena, 9, 103–140, 240

Anthony, Susan B., 83–85, 93, 100

Apple Classrooms of Tomorrow, 49

Armstrong, Henry E., 83

assessment: of teachers, 2, 4–5, 7, 14, 56, 238; of students, 17–18. *See also* accountability of teachers; achievement test scores; effectiveness of teaching; judging and evaluating